Lying with Truth

Judith Cuffe

POOLBEG

This book is a work of fiction. The names, characters, places, businesses, organisations and incidents portrayed in it are either the product of the author's imagination or are used fictitiously. Any resemblance to actual persons, living or dead, events or locales is entirely coincidental.

Published 2020
by Poolbeg Press Ltd
123 Grange Hill, Baldoyle,
Dublin 13, Ireland
Email: poolbeg@poolbeg.com

A catalogue record for this book is available from the British Library.

ISBN 978178199-389-7

www.poolbeg.com

About the Author

Judith Cuffe lives in County Wicklow, Ireland with her husband, three children and faithful writing companion, Wilbur, the dog. A book lover and a fan of the written word, she finally got round to following her dream and writing that book. *Lying With Truth* is the third and final novel in the Evolve trilogy, following on from the first two, *Sing Me Home* and *When Destiny Sings*. Judith is now excited to be writing her next book, Unexpected Events.

When she isn't writing, she can be found in the gym, running, following the latest fashions or ferrying the children around as Mum's Taxi. To find out more about Judith, follow her on Facebook (Judy in The Middle) and Instagram (@judy_middle), or on her website www.judyinthemiddle.com

Acknowledgements

Much of this book was completed during very uncertain times. A pandemic has the power to pale everything else into insignificance, even a lifelong dream! Nonetheless, I ploughed through, taking refuge in the characters of *Lying With Truth,* the final book in the Evolve trilogy. The characters – some old, some new – buoyed me during the lockdown. As my hair turned fifty shades, I fired every ounce of colour I could muster into this final instalment.

This book, in particular, has a special place in my heart, perhaps because of the current times in which we find ourselves. Maybe even because I identify a little with Lucie Woods, often priding myself on my honesty, trying to make the most out of whatever life throws my way. Or perhaps it's because it's the end of one journey and the beginning of another. Finishing what I've come to refer to as my apprenticeship is a bittersweet moment. Three books in two years hasn't been easy, but it's filled me with a passion that I never knew existed. (I might even say I enjoyed it more than clothes shopping . . . wonders never cease!) Writing *When Destiny Sings, Sing Me Home* and *Lying With Truth* has been the most profound, whirlwind-y, fabulous, "straight out of the left-field" adventure.

For allowing me to do so, I'm forever indebted to Poolbeg Press Ltd, in particular Paula Campbell – hilarious, honest, encouraging, lovely . . . there aren't enough words. To the typesetters, cover designers, proofers, thank you. To my copy editor, Claire Dean, for teaching me far more than I ever learned studying at UCD! But then there's a huge difference when you're eager to learn. From tenses to italics, dialogue, formatting, ellipses . . . I could go on and on. For giving me the confidence that I so often lost in the process and for your patience, not to mention incredible speed! Thank you.

To my children, Martha, Bruce – my adventurous son, to whom this book is dedicated – and to Gertie. Yes, it's true, as Huey Lewis once sang, "I am happy to be stuck with you." Lockdown locked us together as a family. I adore you with everything I am. This book, in particular, couldn't have been completed without your help.

To Mal, who is, and always has been, "my person". Quite the mad few years! Happy to be dreaming big with you at my side. Lockdown date nights forever!

To Nicole and Lucie. My readers – for always pushing me for *more* to read. Nicole, for being the most encouraging person I know, in all of my ventures. For getting right in there with plot-storming, reading terrible drafts, encouraging. Texting far too late at night when a thought hits you! I couldn't do it without you. Please don't desert me after the trilogy. To my very own Lucie, for lending me your name in book one and for getting an entire "Lucie" book for the last one! Lucie Woods isn't based on you, but there are similarities. Both are loyal to a fault, kind, caring, funny. Thank you for reading draft after draft. You're now on a retainer for upcoming books. Someday we'll all walk a red carpet together. It's the goal!

To Jenn Drew, my legal adviser and bestie. Thank you for your input in this book – for sending me articles and similar cases. There are some crazy people out there! We're clearly part of that category, of which I'm glad.

To my dad – deep-sea diver-cum-pirate (or "technical" as he likes to refer to himself!). The diving element of the book is inspired by my father, the hero, and his true passion. My favourite image of you will always be standing on the pier in Kilmore Quay, Wexford, watching you arrive back from diving the wonders below – hair tousled, smile on your face, questionable sweater on. I have to admit, I always liked it when you filled the drysuit with air, too! Michelin Man Dad joke!

My son inherited your adventurous soul. It may have bypassed me, but your passion for doing something you adore didn't. Thank you for helping with the story of Rose. And I'm glad you always found your way back home to us. Perhaps one day we'll sit and write your stories of those days, which could undoubtedly fill a book. Just please, not the slide show, not again!

To Double Bay, Australia. Listen, I've never been! It's a real place, but I made the rest up, so if you happen to be reading this and are from Double Bay, having taken offence to anything – sorry. I *am* going to visit someday – and I can just imagine turning to my husband and saying "This is where I want to live when I grow up." And for the record, I think I'd fit right in. I wear activewear for lounging, too!

To Tanya, my friend in Oz. Thanks for the visuals you sent me. I will get to visit you someday.

To all the readers – I suppose, if you think about it, it's all for you! For all the messages, reviews, photos, from the bottom of my heart – thank you.

To my sister Sharon, who I didn't mention in the last acknowledgements! This is for you. We all get two lives. Only some of us are brave enough to embrace the second, to withstand judgement, to take the harder path. You, my much older sister, are brave.

To Wilbur, the boxer, for being my daily company. Imagine! we're heading for a fourth book . . . Puppy power!

And finally, to Felicity, Margot, Reverend Michael, Sammy, Tess, Paddy, Lucie, Ann, Nathan, Mark, Olive, Eugene, Jessica, Sophie, Hamish, Max, Bella, Declan, Nina, Rose, Doug . . . and all the other characters in the trilogy. I have no idea where you came from, but you'll be with me for the rest of my days. A story begins with an idea. An idea grows into a story. A story is its people. You guys were my people.

So, what now? Lucie Woods is about to begin a new chapter in her life, as am I. Thank you for coming along on my journey, from Knockmore to Australia and back. Just keep evolving! Next book, coming right up! It's about unexpected events . . . life is full of them.

Much love,
Judith
x

For my son, Bruce – my adventurous one – the one I fear I may someday lose to the draw of adventures in foreign lands. I sincerely hope it's surfing in Galway and not Australia! But if it is, I hope you'll always know where home is. (Or I'll be forced to follow you!) Always stay true to yourself, little dude. Stay cool forever.

"The truth is rarely pure and never simple."

Oscar Wilde

Prologue

Truth

The truth is, no one wants the truth, not entirely, in its sometimes raw and gruesome form. No one wants to hear that they've made mistakes, chosen the wrong path, wronged a loved one, become someone other than the honest person they set out to be. We don't want to hear that we're overweight, underweight, work too hard, not hard enough. We don't want to be told that we don't spend enough time with our children, neglect our partners, have a dependency, have wasted our lives, that we've become stale or bitter, that we've changed. Let alone that we've focused on the wrong thing all of our lives, that we've left it too late, that we've failed . . .

The truth can hurt, no matter if it comes from someone else's mouth, or by your own admission. And yet we're told from an early age that the truth will prevail. The truth and only the truth will eventually set us free. The truth will out. Seek the truth. Tell the truth or someone will tell it for you. The truth is the truth.

The truth is, the truth isn't always some huge life-altering revelation, nor some sordid uncovered secret – it can be as simple as an honest declaration. The truth is, life is a series of choices and it's often far more comfortable to cling to what you believe you are, what others see, even if deep down you know it's a lie. The truth is, very few of us tell the whole truth, nor abide by the integrity on which we often pride ourselves. The truth is, we're *all* liars, in some shape or form.

We are *all* liars.

We mislead, deceive, exaggerate, distort, contort, trick, manufacture, twist, bend, inflate, stretch. We all do it – learn what we can and can't say, what will make us stand out, what will make us fit in, what will make us appear *normal.* After all, to reveal all those secret inner criticisms and prejudices, all the little thoughts that pass through our minds when someone is speaking (or lying), would be risking social ostracisation. And so we compromise. We listen to other people's myths while we tell our own, but deep down we *all* know our inner truth – the real story.

"Lies are the one thing I won't stand for," Lucie's mother had once told her. "Always tell the truth unless it's to save someone's feelings. And even then . . ."

"Sorry, Mam, but that dress is pure terrible on you. Gross," she'd giggled from where she was sitting on the end of her mother's bed.

"The cheek of you! I'll tell you, that mouth of yours will get you into trouble someday."

"But you said . . ."

Tess Maguire had sat down beside her and put her hand on her daughter's. "I'm serious, love. I'm trying to tell you everything I know before you head off into the sunset, leaving me here." Mam paused to wipe the sudden tears from her eyes. "The truth can hurt, but I suppose it's better to take the pain quickly and then move on. Lies cause more trouble in the long run. Sure, haven't we seen that with our own eyes with Felicity?" Tess had always had a soft spot for her son's now wife and Lucie's best friend, who'd suffered a miserable childhood at the hands of a dishonest mother. She stood again to look in the mirror, smoothing her hands over her stomach. "It *is* terrible, isn't it?"

"Dreadful," Lucie grinned.

"Right. I'll change. See – a lesson learned. And another thing. Don't ever lie to yourself, love. That's the worst person you can lie to. Do you hear me? Always be honest with yourself. No matter if you're here or in Australia. Be true to yourself . . . I still can't believe you're going."

Lucie had ignored the last part, knowing it would cause another fit of heaving sobs. "Sure, aren't I the most honest person in the entire world? You said so yourself."

"Don't I know it!" Tess ruffled her daughter's hair. "Too honest. Too bloody honest."

Even then, when she'd yet to embark on her own life, Lucie *had* witnessed first-hand how shattering an illusion can come with a level of discomfort far more damaging than an unflattering dress. Way back then, she'd seen it with her best friend, Felicity, whose so-called perfect life had crumbled when she'd fallen pregnant as a teen with Lucie's older brother, Sammy.

In more recent years, Ann's life had unravelled before she'd found the strength to pick up the pieces and start again. Lucie had observed her niece from a distance, cheering Ann on, marvelling at her courage and wondering when her own turn would arrive – when the make-believe existence she'd created for herself would come undone. In a way, Lucie had become all the things she'd consistently tried to avoid: settled, serious, no longer striving for extraordinary, getting through life, existing.

It wasn't how she'd ever expected to be. It certainly wasn't how it all started when she first arrived in Australia all those years ago as the freckly Irish girl with red hair as fiery as her ambitions. She'd immediately embraced her new life with open arms, finding instant comfort among a nation of people known for their laid-back honesty, their "say it as it is" attitude, their zest for life.

As much as Lucie had felt as though she'd found an entire continent of like-minded individuals, she'd always planned to return home to Ireland someday. She had family there. She couldn't stay away forever – eventually, she'd go back. When each year became a new one, she promised herself once more – *next year, I'll go home.* Until next year became the year after and the year after that.

Back then, Lucie told herself her first official lie – that she'd left it too late.

After that, the lies came easier. It wasn't compulsive lying, nor ridiculous fabrications – it was more the silence. The silence had become the lie.

The truth is, it's only ever the good things we want to hear as we travel through life hungrily craving recognition, praise, good news, positivity.

Tell me I'm amazing.

Tell me I'm honest.

Tell me everything will be fine.

Tell me it always works out.

Tell me if it's for me, it won't pass me by.

Tell me I did my best with the choices I had.

But what if it *is* true what they say? That no matter

how silent you remain about the rest, the truth will eventually force its way out. And what if there is absolutely nothing you can do to stop it?

People had always liked Lucie. Lucie was honest. Lucie was real. But just as Lucie's mother had warned her never to do, as she'd sworn she never would, she'd been lying to herself for a very long time. It turns out it's easy to lie to yourself. The truth is, for much of her life, no one had wanted *her* truth – not from Lucie Woods, with the perfect husband, the two adorable children, the enviable figure, the enormous smile, the perfect house, the lovely job – until, that is, someone had. Until out of the blue, a total stranger began to poke at everything she'd kept carefully hidden. Once it was out, as soon as she'd heard herself say it aloud, she'd realised there was no other choice but to confront it.

And here it was – the moment of truth.

Sitting here now, staring at the faces before her, it was as if she were staring straight at the truth of her entire life – past truth, present truth, future truth. For a moment she felt giddy, wondering how she'd kept it in for so long, pondering how on earth she'd found herself in this absurd reality. She'd been gifted a long period of isolated reflection, a time to think back over her life, face what she'd always refused to face.

It hadn't been easy. At first, she'd had to force herself to stare at it all, but so far, through some of her earlier admissions, she'd found a piece of the old Lucie again. Perhaps by releasing these final burdens, she would find all of herself, regardless of the hardship that lay ahead – and it would be hard. The truth *was* going to hurt, and not just her – it was going to destroy everyone she held dear.

Maybe in time, she could revert to being the girl sitting on the end of her mother's bed, giggling over the horrible dress, frankness as her secret weapon. But first, she finally needed to relinquish the burden, and it *had* been a burden. Even in happier times, she'd felt it pressing down, weighing heavily on her soul. But in the same way she'd known that it's the truth that has the power to set you free, she'd also known that this day would come.

And here it was, her opportunity for freedom.

Taking a breath, she closed her eyes and exhaled before opening them and finally saying the words.

"My name is Lucie Woods. I swear to tell the truth, the whole truth and nothing but the truth, so help me God."

Part One

Present Truth

Chapter one

Seeing Bella sitting there motionless with her back to her instantly infuriated Lucie. Clenching her fists, she had to use all of her reserve to stop herself from reaching out and plunging her fingers into her daughter's freshly straightened mane of red hair and tossing it about. The outward calm of Bella's hair felt like a taunt, exaggerating the unruly mass that hung around Lucie's own face that morning.

She must have been up for hours already taming it, erasing any resemblance it bore to Lucie's hair – the same hair for which Bella so often criticised her mother for passing down to her. Lucie wondered if the technology had been available in her day, would she have spent as much time flattening her thick, wiry hair, smoothing it into something totally different to how it was supposed to be.

Then again, when Lucie had been a teen a thousand years ago, it had always been about the bigger, the better. Back then, she'd felt edgier than the pine desk jammed into the corner of her childhood bedroom, despite her voluminous peroxide blonde-and-red bouffant. She could still remember sitting in front of her red plastic mirror, using a thin comb to back-comb her hair to make it even fuller.

How different everything was nowadays to those innocent times when you had to make the best of what you were given. In Lucie's case: freckles, fuzzy hair and translucent skin. Bella was the same. Of course, you wouldn't know it any more, with her daughter's permanent layer of fake tan, carefully applied concealer and glossy poker-straight hair. It felt like a slight – as if the genetic hand her daughter had been gifted was below standard, not quite good enough. Then again, everything Lucie did lately wasn't to the standard her daughter expected.

"I'll pay for it myself," Bella had been pleading for months. "Let me get highlights, please. I want to be blonde."

"But your hair is beautiful. It's what makes you unique. Why would you want to be like everyone else?"

Even saying it, Lucie had known that it wasn't about Bella being like everyone else – it was about not being anything like Lucie.

"Why didn't Declan get this horrible bushy red leprechaun hair and see-through skin? *I'm* not Irish. It's not fair." Bella had pulled at her own hair and then pointed at her mother's accusingly.

Lucie hadn't bothered to answer.

"Did the revolutionary idea of waking me not enter your head?"

Lucie stomped past Bella now, grabbed a cup and stuck it under the coffee-maker. Then she grabbed two slices of bread, frantically buttered them and threw a slice of cheese between them.

"Declan, grab the rest of your lunch, quick," Lucie

gestured as her ten-year-old son entered the kitchen. "Bella, well?"

"I've never had to wake you before. It's not like you're . . . like busy or anything."

"Don't start, Bella. Not today."

"Whatever."

Bella didn't look up. Instead, she sat staring at her phone, tilting her chin ever so slightly in different directions and snapping photos of her unmoving duck face. Satisfied, she used her thin, elegant finger to swipe the screen shut and then tucked it in the crested breast pocket of her black school blazer before glancing up at her mother.

"Are you seriously wearing *that*? Shouldn't you . . . like, change?"

"Are you wearing *that*?" Lucie mimicked, turning her back and making a face.

Getting into an argument now with her thirteen-year-old daughter would do nothing to improve the type of morning she was already having. Besides, lately, she was sort of afraid of Bella. It was a strange thing when your child was suddenly taller than you. It took away some of your authority, especially now that Bella was able to look down on Lucie with contempt. Or was it disdain? Aversion? Defiance? Hatred? It was hard to tell any more. Perhaps she should try standing on a chair when talking to Bella, look down on her for a change.

Declan poured some cereal, then held the milk carton above his head and poured the liquid from a height. Lucie watched it splash out of the bowl, hit the worktop and edge its way towards Bella's check uniform skirt.

"You little shit!" Bella screamed with the intensity one might reserve for having a bucket of water tipped over them and not a few droplets of milk. "I'm a mess." She jumped off the stool, swiped at her brother's head and stormed out of the room.

"Hardly. Just give it a quick wipe and hurry up," Lucie called after her.

She picked up a sodden dishcloth, which had been left to stew in last night's dishwater. Declan's nose turned up as Lucie squeezed the cloth to rid it of the now brown water to wipe up the milk. Then she threw it back in the sink, looked around the kitchen in frustration and groaned. Now, that *was* a mess.

For someone who wasn't *like* "busy", as Bella kept telling her, the house had never been untidier and by the look of her drawn face in the mirror that morning, Lucie had never looked worse.

Initially, Lucie had had all sorts of plans. She'd even written them down somewhere – she couldn't remember where, but she definitely had, she was sure of it. First, she was going to conquer the mountain of washing in the utility room. Like a modern-day Edmund Hillary, she would place a flag on top of the Everest-like washing basket when she'd finished. She was finally going to uncover the location of the soul mates of all the lonely socks residing inside what had started off as a net bag within which to wash delicate items. *Delicates?!* The delicate items bag was now a dedicated "odd sock bag", which hung on the back of the laundry room door as a reminder that no one may ever know where those socks were. But Lucie would. She'd crack the case of the missing socks, eventually.

Obviously, she was going to take up yoga. She had huge aspirations to be one of those bendy yokes who casually sit with their leg flung around the back of their neck, filing their toenails. Toenails – yes, those, too. She was going to paint them at least once a week, maybe more. Skincare, tick. There would be moisturiser applied *everywhere*, after every shower. Cuticles would be cared for. Legs shaved. Eyebrows plucked. Hair in check.

She was going to get rid of those extra few pounds that had started to hang around like an unwanted stalker. Hell, she may even join a cycling group, cladding herself in unflattering Lycra and those shoes that turned up at the toes. And meditate. She'd meditate three times a day, allowing all of her muscles to sink into the floor and spread out. She'd be so calm that you'd have to use a shovel to scoop her up off the floor and pour her back into her activewear. Activewear! Yes, yes, yes! Every morning, Lucie was going to saunter into the kitchen, having been up since six stretching, hair ironed, wearing activewear, even if she had no plans to be active that day.

She was going to get all of their diets under control, ensuring they all got their daily requirements of vitamins and minerals through food, and not by cheating and taking all those out-of-date bullet-like multivitamins. And best of all, she was finally going to cook. One by one, she'd make her way through all those recipes she'd ripped out of magazines over the years and shoved in the spare drawer beside the cutlery one. The one that contained everything from light bulbs to old batteries, chalk, hair bobbles and keys with no lock that you'd better keep, just in case. As a matter of fact, Lucie was going to clean out that drawer, once and for all. Come to think of it, that was probably where her list was.

It took Lucie a few months to realise that having more time on her hands hadn't prompted her to become utterly fabulous and organised. Waking with Declan's nose pressed against hers, shouting that they were late, had become a regular occurrence. So, too, was the discovery that someone (*Bella*) kept taking her phone charger, despite covering it in bright blue tape to indicate ownership. As a result, her phone was constantly dying. Meaning Lucie rarely got to hear the morning alert of the mystical sounds of whales and dolphins as they swam peacefully towards her, to wake her from another disturbed slumber.

Mind you, that morning, even from the confines of the dead phone, those mammals had appeared to spray her with half the ocean. Another regular occurrence – waking up drenched in salty sweat. Lucie had stood up too quickly, the ground shifting beneath her. She'd steadied herself on the chest of drawers and peeled off her soaked nightdress before glancing back at the bedclothes, to see the all-too-familiar sign that she would spend another day doubled over in agony.

"Do you have the money for the school trip?"

Bella appeared once more, eyeing her mother with . . . yes, that was contempt. Lucie shivered – Bella really was terrifying.

"I told you to ask your father."

Lucie stared back, trying not to picture the girl from *The Exorcist*. No, Bella's hair was far too neat, but the eyes were similar at times.

"He's not here."

"Well, I can see that. Where the hell is he?"

"He's playing golf."

Of course Hamish was playing bloody golf.

"I'll get it for you later. Come on. We'll be late."

It wasn't until they were halfway down the road with no time to return that Bella dropped another bombshell.

"I need you to come in and sign the permission form for the swim meet."

"What?"

"I told you."

Had she? Oh, Jesus.

Lucie looked down at what she was wearing, wishing she'd taken more heed of Bella's earlier words. In a rush, she'd pulled on a pair of black "inactive" leggings and the same T-shirt she'd been wearing the night before. Lucie licked her finger and rubbed frantically at the sticky red stain on the front. It was either bolognese sauce or ketchup. It could have been either. She had in fact been wearing the T-shirt for two days in a row before putting it on a third time that morning. The splodge, which she'd now made worse, may have been from the actual dinner she'd made two days prior, or from last night's desperation dinner: frankfurters wrapped in slices of bread, since they'd run out of hotdog buns. At least it wasn't red wine. There was always a positive. *Not always. There isn't always a positive.*

She felt her stomach flip and her mind go suddenly hot as the thought of that blasted day suddenly hit her. No matter where she was, or what she was doing, the feeling of that day was always there in some form. It hadn't gone away over time, as she'd kept telling herself it would. *If only. If only. If only . . .*

There were far too many to go through each one every single time. Lately, Lucie had come to settle on what she believed was the most relevant *"if only"* – the reason she was driving towards her destination filled with dread to accompany the dragging in her abdomen. The quick lug from the bottle of children's paracetamol had done nothing to abate what the day had gifted her.

If only that day she'd employed the same mantra she'd tried to drill into her children, the one that so often she'd ignored over the years: stop, breathe, count to ten, and then to twenty for good measure. It will prevent you from doing something you may regret for the rest of your life.

If only.

Chapter two

It really was beautiful: serene, leafy, safe, sort of Lego-ish. "The perfect place to raise a family." The estate agent had taken one look at Lucie's rounded belly and gone in for the kill. Of course, Lucie already knew the area, had driven through years before, giggling at the enormous houses and the type of person she believed would choose to live in a place like Double Bay, Sydney.

"Never," she'd said, looking around her at the groups of yummy mummies, the Stepford-style wives, the bronzed retired men in their seventies strutting about in far less than they should have been. "Not for me."

It was Hamish who'd pushed it, well aware that they weren't only purchasing a home, but also buying into a "way of life". It was the type of plasticky life he adored, but she'd come to appreciate its fabricated prettiness over the years. People changed, priorities changed. Lucie still remembered the day they'd taken a drive to look at the house they could ill-afford at the time, glancing at the brochure:

Capturing ocean views from the master balcony, this first-class entertainer embraces outdoor living with a custom-designed kitchen featuring a stone-paved terrace that can be used as an outdoor room. Within striking distance of the village shopping hub, in close proximity of the harbour and surf beaches, and with plenty of top-notch schools, this location couldn't be better – a commuter's paradise.

"It's all a bit much, no?" She'd turned to Hamish in the car on the way there, her hand caressing her stomach as she spoke. She'd only gone along to placate him. There was no way they could afford a house like it.

"It's perfect. What does it say? First-class entertainer? Can you imagine the lads' faces if I invited them over for a few cold ones and they turned up here." He'd looked far too excited, his eyes round with theoretical possibility. "Surfing before work. Hey, and wouldn't you like the shopping hub?"

"There wouldn't be any money left for shopping – the price! Come on, can't we go and look at the other one? The starter one, with room to develop."

"I'm sure those schools will come in handy sooner rather than later," he'd smiled, ignoring her, reaching over and resting his hand protectively on her stomach. "Top-notch schools for a top-notch baby."

"It's totally out of our price range and still a big enough commute to the city, despite what the brochure says, especially in my condition."

"Let's just look." He'd patted her hand before doing some form of cringeworthy American accent. "Stick with me, schweetheart. Anything is possible."

Hamish *had* made it possible, somehow, and even she

had to admit there were parts of Double Bay that she adored. But this morning, driving past the buzzing coffee shops and the picturesque jetty already filled with people taking in the outstanding views of the harbour did nothing to lift her mood. No, this morning, she felt sick.

It hadn't always been this way. Up until *that day*, three months before, leaving the house for the day ahead had always filled Lucie with a sense of fulfilment. Driving past the early morning swimmers on the beach, people out walking their dogs – even the retired men in their too-tight swimming trunks – had given her a form of satisfaction. She, too, was going about her day as they made their way from their home on George Street, watching the road twist towards the gates of the school.

Back then, she'd pull into the staff car park, quickly kiss Bella and Declan goodbye, then watch them run round to the front of the enormous building to join all the other privileged children. Then she'd hurry to the staff room for a blast of caffeine with the other socially inferior staff members, as they called themselves, before the day started.

Lucie had known when she took the job as school nurse for the "Illustrious Australian Education System" that was Woodfield Grammar that she'd landed a cushy number. Despite the advantages, she'd had her reservations. It had seemed like a step down from her stressful but adored position at Sydney General Hospital. There, she'd forged a successful nursing career, ending up at the top of her game as Clinical Theatre Manager.

"You Irish love a bit of drama, that's why you like theatre," her oldest friend and hospital work colleague, Nina, had teased Lucie when she first took the managerial role at the hospital. "So, let me get this straight, you have a baby and then you take on more responsibility!"

Nina and Lucie had been pregnant at roughly the same time, both returning to work within weeks of each other.

"Crazy Irish! I'm heading to an easier life in out-patients, edging my way out of the door after them!"

It was Lucie, though, and not Nina, who three years later waved the understaffed hospital and irregular hours goodbye. Working full-time, with Bella as a toddler and pregnant with Declan, commuting in and out to the city, it was too much.

"Stop having babies!" Nina had told her. "I'm happy with one. I'll miss you, Lu. Never thought I'd see the day you'd wave this place goodbye. All those years . . ."

All those years was right. All those memories. But even Lucie had to admit that eventually, despite adoring her work at the hospital, she needed to adjust to a life more conducive to raising a family. Didn't she? So, *she'd* taken the step down.

The "step down" had come with a step up in salary, no need for childcare, school holidays off and the added bonus of her children receiving a superior education at a fraction of the extortionate fees. She'd almost choked when she heard how much the other parents were paying to have their children flourish, with "smaller class sizes, allowing them to reach academic excellence". Apparently, "a Woodfield education results in responsible and well-rounded citizens who are confident in their ability to succeed in their chosen path in life."

Well, you couldn't argue with that. Of course, she was wise enough to know that such well-rounded citizens would come with an air of superiority, backed by their sometimes less well-rounded parents. But she'd handled worse. Surely, it would be a breeze.

"It's a no-brainer, Lu. Do it for a few years," Hamish

had encouraged. "This new business I'm working on is about to take flight and sooner rather than later, you won't be working if you don't want to. Then you can be just like the other mothers . . . Also, don't forget the contacts I can make here. Woodfield is *the* school for anyone who's anyone around here."

"Mum, we're going to be late," Bella droned from the passenger seat as she took yet another selfie, pouting her little mouth and pulling free a strand of red hair either side of her face.

"Well, if it wasn't for you forgetting the bloody permission slip, I wouldn't have to go in this morning. Clearly, I hadn't planned to."

"Don't bother, then. I don't want to go on the stupid swim-team meet, anyway. I'm still on my . . . period." Bella turned towards her mother and mouthed the word with a dollop of attitude, then sucked in her cheeks and rolled her eyes.

"You have to go. And you can't still be on your . . . period," Lucie mouthed back. "It's been a week. I'm not stupid, Bella." Over her years working as the school nurse, Lucie had heard almost every implausible excuse in the book. "And I'm going as fast as I can," she added.

Bella looked out of the window as two students sauntered past the car.

"There's people walking faster than you're driving, Mum," Bella exhaled impatiently.

"I'm looking for somewhere to park, okay?"

Lucie glanced over at the group of activewear-clad women gathered in their usual position near the entrance of the car park, probably in full-fledged discussion over whatever piece of idle gossip they'd managed to glean over the weekend. Hamish had been right. The job was a no-brainer, but it hadn't taken her long to figure out that she wasn't like the other mothers, nor would she ever be – and therein lay the reason she was driving into Woodfield Grammar, trying to avoid them.

"How would you know, anyway?" Bella seemed intent on finishing their earlier conversation about her period. "Like, it's not like you even get yours any more."

Lucie jammed on the brakes and swivelled towards her teenage daughter. It wasn't as dramatic a move as she'd hoped for, since the car was barely moving to begin with.

"Bella. I'm warning you. One more word of cheek and so help me God, I'll turn this car round and you'll bloody walk to school." She was speaking with her teeth clenched, her lips moving in an exaggerated way as if doing a foreign language voice-over. "And for your information, I do still have mine. In fact, I have it right now. I just don't feel the need to tell everyone every five minutes and to use it as an excuse to get out of normal life. It's *not* an illness, Bella. It's life – and the sooner you get used to it, the better," Lucie finished with a crazed shake of her head.

"Sorry, Mum," Bella said, her eyes round from her mother's outburst.

Lucie's shoulders slumped and she exhaled. "It's okay. It gets easier, I promise. I know it's hard." She reached over and patted Bella's shoulder.

It wasn't Bella's fault that her transition into womanhood was coinciding with Lucie's own perimenopausal explosion. Bella had mood swings, and Lucie had lost all patience and clearly her sense of humour. Her daughter getting her period should have been a milestone, but it was one Lucie couldn't bear to think of, especially with what she was currently experiencing.

No one had warned Lucie that going through this phase in her life would take years, coupled with still having to endure what had now become a twice-, and sometimes more, monthly cycle. It was cruel, like having newborn twins and being pregnant with triplets. She'd never had any problems before with her cycles. Why was it bloody starting now?

Lucie glanced over to see the group of women staring at her from where she'd "abruptly" stopped the vehicle.

"Shit."

"Language, Mother." Declan lifted his head from his book.

She'd almost forgotten he was there.

"Declan, I'm an adult, I can fucking well swear if I want."

Lucie could see his shocked little face peering at her from the rear-view mirror. Now she'd gone and upset both of her children. What the hell was wrong with her?

"Shit," she muttered again. "Sorry, sweetie. You're right. Let's try the prayer."

"Hail Mary, full of grace, please find us a parking space," Lucie and Declan whispered together.

"It's worked. Look." Declan pointed out of the window. "Score. Now you don't need to be angry with us."

Lucie felt her heart tug. Poor Declan was far too sensitive for his own good, but then again, that's what she loved about him – so different from Bella, who attracted people like a magnet. For the past few years, Declan had seemed to repel friends until, of course, Lucie had unearthed the reason. But all that was sorted now. Finally seeing him gain a little confidence was what she'd been hoping for for years, even if his blossoming spirit had come at a cost to herself. Still, she supposed, if she was to look at "the incident", as it was politely referred to, from a glass half-full perspective, it had had the desired effect, if not the best outcome. If only . . .

The thought was interrupted by Declan's excited voice.

"Don't forget, Mum. I'm going to Noah's after school today."

"Copy that, Dec. I'll pick you up later."

"And I'm going for smoothies in Cali Press. Sandy's mum is dropping us," Bella added.

"Okay. Well, be safe and call me when you need to be collected. Not too late, all right?"

Lucie waited for the car in front to move off before pulling into the space she'd prayed for. Perhaps it wasn't going to be such a bad day.

She looked over to see Amanda Garth, one of the other mothers, standing with her arms crossed, a brazen look of defiance on her face. She could see Amanda's sidekick, Roberta Williams, too, hanging back, looking everywhere but in Lucie's direction, the shame visible across her features. Lucie ignored them, got out of the car and kissed Declan before he fled inside.

"Are you okay, Mum?" Bella stopped briefly on the steps of the school, put her hands on her hips and scowled at the group of women.

"I'm fine, love, honest."

Lucie could see the look of angry rebellion on her daughter's face, so familiar to how she'd once faced the world herself. They were so alike, sometimes it frightened her.

"Fiery hair, fiery soul," Lucie's father used to tell her.

"Spirited," she'd reply. "Passionate."

"Just make sure you manage that fire well. Hot heads never solved anything."

Didn't she know that only too well . . .

Lucie swallowed the lump that had formed in her throat at her daughter's attempt at support. No matter how terrifying Bella was at times, she adored her. They all said it, didn't they? – that the teenage years are a challenge. Of course, you don't believe it until you're there.

Had she been the same with her mother? she wondered. There was no one to ask. She didn't think she had, but maybe she'd forgotten. She wished she could call her mother now, apologise for how she may have acted during those years. Perhaps her mother could have talked to Bella, or assured Lucie it would pass.

But it wasn't just that. It was watching her daughter grow up and begin to question the world. That was what scared her the most – the thought that Bella was clever enough to figure out someday that Lucie didn't know it all, was just as confused by life as she'd always been and, worst of all, that her fire had gone out.

"Screw them," Bella whispered and then ran up the steps to school.

"Screw them," Lucie repeated and then, "I love you, Bells." Her voice caught.

Bella bounded back down the steps to her.

"I'm sorry I said what I said a while back. You know . . ." She looked at the ground, visibly ashamed of the argument a few months before. "About you ruining my life here. You didn't. I . . . I would have done the same. All of my friends think you're cool." She bent to kiss Lucie on the cheek.

"It wasn't cool, but thanks. Now go – you'll be late." Lucie brushed her away, knowing that the moment of solidarity, the glimpse of the softer side of Bella, had the power to make her crumble.

Glancing back over her shoulder, Lucie could still see them standing there, watching her – Amanda scowling in a way that made her look constipated, her sweet smile anything but.

"Not today, Amanda, not today," Lucie muttered.

She could ignore the stares, the whispers, the glances, knowing what she was witnessing from them was an enormous display of false courage. What she couldn't ignore was the thought of letting her kids down, the repercussions that just kept coming from "the incident". Perhaps she should take a leaf out of Amanda's book – false courage was undoubtedly what she'd need when she was finally forced to admit what she'd been avoiding.

Lucie pulled the door of the school open, staring up at the familiarity, wondering how she was going to break the news to Bella and Declan that this would be their last term at Woodfield Grammar.

Chapter three

"I didn't think you'd answer," Lucie exhaled.

She was back sitting in the car outside the school. She had the phone cradled between her shoulder and her ear and was leafing through the brochures she'd just been given by Mr Downey, the school principal. Her hands were shaking. She still hadn't eaten anything today, but it was more than hunger.

"I've just finished my round of golf. What's up?"

Her husband's tone was bright, considering they'd had yet another argument the night before, where both had hissed through angry whispers. But then, Hamish was an expert at pushing things aside as if they'd never happened. It was starting to rub off on Lucie.

"I've just been into Woodfield. Bella needed something signed . . ."

"And how was it?" Hamish was quick.

"What do *you* think?" She closed her eyes and tried to breathe through a wave of nausea.

Lucie had thought she might be able to avoid John

Downey this morning. Seeing his door firmly shut to the right of the entrance, she'd sneaked up the steps and edged left into the office.

"Lucie! It's so good to see you." Stacy, the school secretary, always dressed immaculately, her greying hair tied neatly off her sallow skin, came out from behind her desk to hug her. "How are you?" She leaned back, holding Lucie's forearms in her hands. "You look . . ."

"Like death?" Lucie finished.

"Not quite, love." Stacy smiled kindly. "Sit down. I'll grab you a coffee."

Lucie plonked down on the chair in front of the older lady's desk. It was where she'd spent many hours over the years, doing administration, having a moan, giggling about the delicate nature of the children – and the sensitive disposition of the pushy parents of Woodfield.

"I need to sign some form for Bella, apparently," she exhaled.

"Teenagers, huh? They'd forget their heads if they weren't screwed on. I'll get it for you now."

"Not just teenagers," Lucie grimaced. "I'm the bloody same. It was so much easier when I was here all the time. I always knew what was happening, or at least you were able to tell me. That way, Bella didn't realise that I did actually have a clue what was going on in their lives."

Stacy set the cup of coffee and the form in front of her. "There you go."

Lucie picked up a pen and scribbled her name at the end.

"So, how's the life of leisure? You must be loving the freedom. I bet you're doing all sorts of fitness classes, cooking those recipes we always talked about. You'll be playing golf next . . ." Stacy grinned and leaned forwards. "I believe it's all the rage to have an affair with a gym instructor, you could try that."

"No, thanks. I can hardly make it to the gym, let alone carry on with someone who's young enough that I could have given birth to them. Besides, my bikini line looks as though someone fired a seventies deep-pile bath mat at it and it stuck."

Stacy giggled. "You could get the gardener to trim your bush! Talking of gardeners," she continued. "Remember Mark Byne's mother? The one who was always dropping us in fresh flowers . . . nice woman. Wait till you see her! Apparently she's spinning, as in on a bike and not round in a circle. She came in yesterday to drop off the money for the trip. Says she's lost twelve kilos. Twelve! I'd say the poor bike is thrilled she's lighter now! . . . Lucie?" Stacy looked up suddenly to see Lucie's eyes filled with tears.

"Oh, God. I'm sorry, Stacy. What am I like? Being back here just reminded me how much I miss it. Miss this . . ." Lucie shook her head.

"There, there, love." Stacy put her hand out and rested it on Lucie's. "Sorry if I was babbling. I miss you, too. I thought . . . well, I suppose I thought, you know, sometimes out of something bad comes something good.

"I thought when I hadn't heard from you in a while that you were living the life, making the most out of all the free time you said you've never had. Didn't we always say that's what we couldn't wait for? Not to have to listen to all the mothers any more. No more Beige Brigade . . ."

Lucie closed her eyes and smiled at the made-up name for the group of mothers who were intensely focused on their children being "the very best they could be", all while wearing every shade of mushroom under the sun.

"I haven't heard that in a while."

"Every cloud has a silver lining." Stacy patted her

hand. "No more listening to how little Bobby is suffering from anxiety because of the pressure to play the clarinet at orchestra level at the same time as coming up with a cure for cancer."

Lucie laughed. "I know, I know. I think it's all the free time that's the problem. I'm not used to it. I don't know what to be doing with myself." She rolled her eyes. "Far too much time to think. But it's good to see you, Stacy. I needed a giggle."

For the last few months, Lucie had done everything she could to avoid setting foot back in the school. The thought of everything still made her face burn. And then, in typical Lucie fashion, she'd gone and made a big deal of being thrilled to have time to herself finally, telling anyone who'd listen that it was all her choice.

It hadn't been, not really. She'd been backed into a corner, making it far less a decision and more a dismissal. Albeit one wrapped in pretty paper, with a leaving party. One where she'd got so drunk that she'd barfed out of the door of the taxi on the way home and then sat sobbing on the steps of her house.

"Maybe I will take up golf. Seems to work for Hamish." She tried to smile now.

How could she tell Stacy, or anyone, for that matter, that since finishing work, everything had gone from manageable to berserk? Her initial determination to make the most of a bad situation had never materialised. Yes, she'd talked of doing all the things she'd never had time to do before. Isn't it what we all dream of – more time, more freedom, grasping an opportunity to breathe? This was going to make her a better mother, a better cook. She'd be fitter, more energetic, calmer, and the children would thrive.

In reality, Lucie had plunged into despair, or was it

irrationality? Sometimes she felt as though she were losing her mind. Constantly worrying, thinking about things that may never happen, waking to feel as if she had a boulder pressing into her chest. Her confidence was at an all-time low, as if she were always waiting on something else to go wrong. Honestly, what else possibly could?

"Listen, Lucie. What's happened, happened. There's nothing you can do about it now. A mountain out of a molehill. It still boils my blood. I can't even look at that woman and that little shit of a son of hers. At least he's on a warning here. They're keeping a close eye on him. That's one good thing," Stacy encouraged. "I'm still shocked how it all escalated so fast. In my day, it was exactly how anyone would have handled it. Well, mostly. You know that as well as I do. Times are so bloody different – everyone's so darn sensitive," she paused. "How are you feeling in yourself? How's all the other business?"

"Terrible."

"Why don't you go and see the doctor? I told you about when I was going through the change . . ." Stacy circled her hand in front of her stomach. "When I finally got round to seeing the doc, all I needed was a good blast of hormones to see me right. I tell you, HRT equals a new me! I'm never coming off them. I feel amazing." Stacy shimmied her shoulders and laughed.

"And you *look* amazing," Lucie giggled. "Ah, I will. It's on the list. Honestly, the change of life is the least of my worries at the moment."

"They still haven't replaced you, you know. There's a temp, with a face like an arse, who has no interest in gossip or chipping in elsewhere like you did. Maybe, when the dust settles, you could come back. You never know what's round the next corner . . ."

"Don't remind me. That's exactly what I'm afraid of."

Funnily, it had been the "chipping in", as Stacy described it, that had been Lucie's favourite part of the job. Truthfully, the school could have done without an "in-house" nurse. Much of Lucie's time spent "nursing" had been nothing more than placing a cold compress on a forehead, tending to a graze from the playing field, administering a little affection when someone had had a fight with their best friend, or letting them lie on one of the beds in the infirmary. But she'd made herself a valuable member of staff, often doing the donkey work that no one else wanted to.

Helping to organise sports day was a favourite of hers, making tea and coffee for parents' day, jumping in to supervise study when a teacher was ill, doing whatever needed to be done. It was better to be busy than idle, and who was she to decide that her position wasn't actually necessary? The parents paid the fees for all the bells and whistles you wouldn't get at any old school, and she'd been happy to chime along.

The first bell signalling the start of class rang out. In previous times, it was when Lucie would be receiving her first patient of the day, usually with a chronic case of "didn't study for the science exam"- or "forgot to do my homework"-itis.

"Now, listen, there's an unofficial staff night coming up. I'll text you. You're coming. No excuses . . ."

They both stopped and looked towards the door to see the principal standing there.

"Morning, Lucie."

"Hi, John."

He looked almost as uncomfortable as she felt.

"Do you have a minute?" He gestured towards the

door of his office as Lucie nodded unsurely.

Of course, he'd seen her come in. There was very little John Downey missed from the confines of his office, always keeping an eye on the superior-level CCTV system that spanned the back wall of his office. Though he was a quiet man, he was the eyes and ears of Woodfield, and Lucie had always liked him. She still did. It was just that she knew what he wanted to discuss with her.

"He wanted to know if we'd made a decision about next year," Lucie told Hamish now.

"What did you say?"

"What do you think I said?!"

Hamish said nothing. She could picture the vein at the side of his head starting to protrude, see him roughly run his hand through his sandy hair and grit his teeth.

"I said that we wouldn't be back next term."

"Why the hell did you do that?" His tone had changed, now far too even to be anything but irate.

"Because it's true, Hamish. There's no way we can pay the fees. I mean, even managing them when they were subsidised was becoming a strain."

She could hear him breathing.

"I can't keep having this conversation. Why can't you just listen to me? I told you, this is a temporary situation. We're in a period of growth. This new business is . . ."

Lucie closed her eyes and exhaled slowly, tuning out the words she could repeat verbatim. Count, Lucie, count. One, two, three, four, five. Nah, feck it . . .

"What?" she interrupted his monologue. "Please tell me, Hamish, what the hell will be the difference between this new business and the bloody last one that failed to take off? I can't do this any more. Not when it's going to affect the kids. We have to make the transition to a new school as easy as possible for them. We have to be honest with ourselves."

"Really? Honest?"

"Yes, honest." What was he on about?

Hamish gave a short, humourless laugh. "I wonder which one of us is being more honest . . . Okay, let's be honest. So, we've had a terrible few months. Things outside our control. And you're acting like the world is over." He tutted loudly. "It's temporary. We're just waiting on that money to come through."

"And what if it doesn't?"

"It will. We're weeks away. As soon as I have it, I can complete the investment and then we'll be earning more than we ever did. This is a no-brainer."

Lucie wanted to scream at the phrase she'd heard her "entrepreneurial" husband utter so many times, making her want to shout that he was clearly the one with no brain.

"Haven't I always come up trumps in the end? Trust me. What happened was *not* our fault."

At least he'd had the grace not to attempt the Chicago mob accent.

"No, I suppose not."

Lucie still found it hard to think about the fact that "the incident" had been preceded by what she now called "the shitstorm". So, the shitstorm hadn't been their fault – that was something, at least.

"Besides, I never liked that pushy prick Downey. Can't he cut us a bit of slack?"

That pushy prick had already given them more slack than they deserved, allowing the children to stay for the remainder of the year on the "staff" rate and paying Lucie to the end of the school year. He'd even kept her on the health insurance plan, owing to her voluntarily handing in her notice, to save him the discomfort of firing her. Yes, Downey had been more than fair, considering the pressure he'd been placed under to have Lucie tied to the school flagpole and stoned in the centre of the courtyard. Luckily, they'd avoided that.

"I have no income now, Hamish. You've barely had any for a year now. We can't keep carrying on as if we're in the same league as these people. We're not."

"There's the pessimistic Irish coming out in you, Lucie. Always ready to rub salt in the wound. And whose fault is it you have no income? Whose fault is that?"

She couldn't listen any more. She ended the call and threw the phone on the passenger seat then stared straight ahead. There was nothing more to say. She winced suddenly, bowing her head and clenching her teeth as another pain shot across her stomach. Then her face crumpled like paper and a sob escaped her lips. Her shoulders shook as the reality of her situation hit with force.

For far too long, she'd been in constant pain, almost perpetually bleeding, terrified that there was something more sinister going on than the change of life, and she was far too afraid to face it. This was bigger than painting on a smile, as she'd done many times before. Why wouldn't it just go away? Didn't she have enough to deal with? Why did everything keep coming at her?

The truth was that Lucie couldn't bear to answer her husband's rhetorical question, because she knew the answer all too well. Catching a glimpse of her face in the rear-view mirror, she said the words, "It's my fault. It's all my fault." Then she took a breath, wiped her tears, turned on the engine and willed herself to drive out of the gate, back towards the bay.

Lucie didn't have the luxury of giving up. That just wasn't how it worked when you had children. She'd made a promise to herself long ago that they came first, always, no matter what that meant for her. A promise was a promise.

Chapter four

Doug

It had always struck Doug Offer how one action led to another and another and another. It was precisely what he was thinking while sitting on the decked veranda of the coffee house, beneath the blue-and-white striped umbrella, watching the movement on the beach. A group of divers were hoisting on wetsuits, jumping up and down in bare feet to loosen the neoprene. Their masks were up on their foreheads, squashing their eyes downwards to meet smiling cheeks.

Doug grinned at the memory. Afterwards, the mark from those masks would remain visible on their faces as they drove towards home in dry clothes, their hair still wet, matted with salt as a reminder of what they'd just witnessed in the clear ocean. God, he missed it – that feeling of instant calm, total immersion, silence, tranquillity. Of how it could make you feel instantly small, insignificant, literally a drop in the ocean.

Doug hadn't been diving for some time now. Tilting his head to one side, he tried to remember when he'd last been. The official decision to stop had never been formally addressed. He would have remembered that, confident that he might have attempted to object. He supposed it must merely have happened upon him – like old age. But wasn't that always the way? Regardless of whether or not you were ready.

Age had certainly caught up with him. Then again, it had been inching towards him slowly for years before he'd accepted its unfaltering presence. Before having to admit that his dodgy knee was no longer a passing niggle that faded as the day progressed. Or that his painful knuckles were simply an ailment with which he woke.

Doug squeezed his hands into fists to test them. Still sore, and it was already mid-morning. But then it happened to us all, didn't it? No matter how fit or young at heart you are, one day, your reflexes, your reactions, your joints are not quite what they once were. What a cruelty it was, to have a mind so sharp trapped within a declining body. Still, he'd been lucky to arrive at his early seventies without too many issues. No, he wasn't doing too badly, he supposed. He was alive, wasn't he?

"Shit could always be worse." Doug chuckled to himself, remembering what was intended to be an inspirational quote. It was what the other police divers at work used to say when something out of the ordinary occurred. When four went down and only three came back up. It was better than saying aloud what they'd been silently thinking: thank fuck it wasn't me.

Over the years, they'd lost good guys doing what they'd done. Too many. But they'd known the risks. It had been part and parcel of it. Each time they'd gone out, sitting with their backs against the inflatable RIB, feeling the boat crash up and down over the waves, Doug was sure they must all have been thinking the same. This could be it. This time, it could be me.

They'd never discussed it, but he'd witnessed the fear in their eyes. It was the same dread he'd often felt himself, mixed with adrenaline blended with grit. No matter if it had been in the sea, in a river, in a lake, the risks had been ever-present. Every action on those jobs, each movement had been as significant as the one before, impacting what came next. Nine times out of ten, they'd all come back together. Most jobs had been routine, non-hazardous, it had all worked out. But there was still that one other time. Afterwards, they'd talk about whoever it had been, raising a toast in their honour.

"He'd just made a down payment on a new house for the wife and kids." Or, "He told me he'd just sorted things out with his son. Never been happier." Or, "At least he got to make that trip a few months ago that he'd always wanted to." As if establishing a connection between what had occurred and everything that had gone before would make it easier to fathom! But Doug had understood it. They'd been trying to make sense of it – that's all.

In fact, it had often made Doug wonder if there was an endless trail of actions, all somehow linked, suspended somewhere, connecting the inexplicable. Mind you, having been a police officer for close to thirty years, he'd seen the detrimental results of some actions, rarely resulting in what he'd imagined might have been the desired outcome.

Even then, when a trial was over, a case closed, Doug knew that there was never really a tidy conclusion to anything. The effects of action went on and on: a child left without a father, a mother alone, broken lives that went on to shatter those that came after. Then again, in his chosen field, it was rare that the result was ever anything other than what was feared.

Sometimes the cases had been straightforward – the recovery of items relating to crimes: firearms, vehicles, valuables. And other times, more often than he liked to admit, Doug had spent his years recovering people. He'd never liked referring to them as bodies. To him, they'd been people, no matter who they turned out to be, or what action had found them submerged in often inky water, waiting to be recovered.

Doug had treated all of his recoveries with the utmost respect, bearing in mind that to their loved ones, he had, in fact, been hunting for buried treasure. No matter what thoughts those souls might have harboured as they sank to their aqueous shelter, there had always been someone willing them to be found. If there was ever a reason for having spent half of his life underwater, searching blindly in murky conditions, Doug liked to think it was to offer some form of closure to the families left behind by those swallowed by rivers or oceans.

It hadn't always been pleasant, but it had been worthwhile. Besides, Doug had mostly preferred being under the water instead of above it. While he'd faced difficult situations underwater, he'd also spent his happiest times there. His team had never been able to understand how Doug could come off a job and almost as soon as he'd peeled off the specialist diving gear, he was back in the water, tanks strapped to his back, heading out to explore the Australian coastline.

"Don't you ever get enough, Doug? The only thing I want to see after one of those jobs is dry land and a few bevvies. Here . . ." Doug would catch the can of beer thrown at him by one of the lads. "Get that into you. Today was tough."

The truth was, though, if Doug hadn't been able to glimpse the alternative view – the marine life, the rainbow of colour underwater – he'd never have been able to keep doing his job after those sadder cases. Sometimes what they'd witness would be so earth-shattering that it had the potential to drive you to sink into the depths, never to return.

"Where there's darkness, there's infinite light, fellas," he used to reply, throwing the can of beer back before grabbing his bag and heading off.

Of course, the light to which he'd often refer wasn't the turquoise blue waters, nor the myriad of sea life, but the person who was at his side during all those recreational dives. His Rose – with her underwater camera strapped around her neck. Her mouth smiling even from behind her cumbersome regulator, her eyes twinkling inside her mask. Rose had been the light below the water for Doug all those years, as well as above it.

It was meeting Rose in the early years of being a police officer in New South Wales that first introduced Doug to his lifelong theory of connected actions. Unable to get her out of his head, he'd conjured the notion the very evening after their initial encounter. Pacing the floor at home, alone, he'd tried to map backwards to what had caused the effect. It had been hard to know where to stop, or how far back he should travel to figure the singular action that had led him to her. The more he'd thought about it, the more confused he'd become, but in the end he'd settled on a string of events commencing almost three days prior.

If Doug hadn't had that awful day out on the beat. If that young boy hadn't chased his ball out in front of that car. If the driver hadn't taken his eyes off the road for just a second. If Doug hadn't witnessed the mother of that child screaming in terror. If that same driver hadn't crumbled afterwards in Doug's arms. If the thought hadn't crossed Doug's mind that perhaps he'd chosen the wrong career path, then he may never have stopped to look at the notice back in the station calling for a new opportunity as trainee police divers.

Doug hadn't thought about it long before booking the diving lessons off Shelly Beach to investigate if diving might be something he'd like to pursue. If his car had started that Saturday morning, he wouldn't have been late, missing the entire lesson. If Doug hadn't been raised to be respectful of other people's time, he might not have gone along anyway to apologise to the instructor. If that same instructor hadn't loved the sound of his own voice so much, Doug might have missed the person emerging from the sea, to stride up the beach, remove the hood of their wetsuit and in doing so, release a storm of bright red hair.

"What? Never seen a woman in a wetsuit before?" She'd shaken her hair until it settled like flames around her face and then flashed a smile, just as dazzling.

"I . . . sorry . . . I thought you were a man." He'd stumbled over the words.

She'd thrown her head back and laughed. "I get that a lot. You dive?"

By then, the instructor had slunk away.

"Thinking of it. Sorry, I didn't mean . . . you don't look like a man or anything. Well, not now, anyway."

"Thanks." She was nonplussed. "You should give it a go." She dropped her mask on the sand and unclipped her air tanks. "Always preferred being underwater myself. Not witnessed a whole pile of great things above it."

"Have you been doing it long?" Doug helped her with the tanks from her back.

"Five years. Mind you, where I come from, the water is different. Never thought I'd see water so blue. But here I am, making a career out of it now." She pointed at her camera.

"Funny. That's what I'm thinking of doing."

"Really? You shoot?"

"Well, not cameras. I'm a police officer. They're looking for divers . . . I thought I'd give it a go."

"Doubt in that line of work you'll see anything other than what people don't want you to. I've heard those waters can be even blacker than where I left behind." Something crossed her face and she turned back to look at the sea.

"And where's that?"

"Can't you tell?" She was bright again. "Everyone says my accent is thicker than a turkey."

"Are turkeys thick?" He issued a lopsided grin.

"Thickest animal in the world, apparently. Ireland. Wexford, to be exact. Don't suppose you've heard of it?"

Doug shook his head.

"Well, good luck with your career. Give it a try, what have you got to lose? Just remember, there are two sides to the ocean. Make sure you get to know both."

It was the best piece of advice he'd ever received and Doug had taken it, getting to know both the ocean and Rose, at almost the same time. Although it was Rose who stole his heart first – his Irish Rose, the very best result of any action, ever.

Doug's thoughts were disturbed by high-pitched cackling from behind. Turning, he glanced over his shoulder at a group of young women huddled together over two little round tables pushed close together. A woman in her thirties with coiffed blonde hair and a beaky nose was holding court, throwing her arms about for emphasis, while the others giggled along. Rose would hate her. Mind you, Rose had never cared much for the company of any woman.

"I should have been a man. I never got the constant gossip, chatter, analysing. It was never my thing. Besides, I've spent my whole life in the company of men. They're just less . . . complicated."

If you didn't know her, it might have made her sound masculine or gruff. On the contrary, Rose was one of the most feminine women Doug had ever met, in her own unique way, fighting to survive in the stereotypical male career path she'd chosen. In those days there hadn't been many female divers, especially not ones forging a career underwater.

In her words, leaving Ireland behind for Australia had turned out to be the only way she'd ever have made it in those days. Over time, Rose became one of the most admired underwater photographers in her field. Here in Australia, they'd encouraged women, unlike 1980s Ireland, where they'd made ignorant assumptions, trying to keep her grounded, continually asking when she was going to pack it all in to get married and have babies.

"They all thought I was a lesbian at first," Rose would laugh, regaling them with stories of when she'd head off on one of the boats that would chug out of the small harbour in the fishing village of Kilmore, County Wexford. Hair tucked up under a woolly hat, Aran sweater on to combat the chilly conditions, ready to dive the many shipwrecks scattered around the coast, in the hope of capturing stills of the tranquillity beneath the surface. "They used to call themselves bounty hunters," she'd told Doug. "Searching for antiquities to salvage. Pirates more like! I had no interest in taking anything. I just wanted to see it, photograph it.

"I suppose, looking back, I was with the wrong crowd. I wanted to preserve it, they wanted to disturb it. We respected each other, though, and I could look after myself below the water as well as above it. I was well able for them.

"Eventually, the other divers started treating me like one of the lads." She'd stopped to roll her eyes. "They didn't even bother trying to hide it when they were taking a piss over the side of the boat, or changing with all their treasures hanging out! What other women would want to be hanging out with them, necking pints in the pub? So, they thought I was gay . . . well, all but one."

The "one" had been one of the reasons she'd left Ireland eventually. The other was to follow her calling. Secretly, Doug had always liked that part of the story, believing that Rose following her dream had commenced a similar trail of actions leading her to him.

"You old romantic," she'd tease. "You were the added bonus. The great surprise. And at my age! Who'd have thought it?" She'd almost sing the words in her thick Irish accent, then toss her red hair to the side and grin.

Her accent never faded, nor did her hair. Even as she got older, her hair had remained the passionate colour it always had been, like her. Although, with age, it had softened a little, taking on a pinkish hue as it blended with the strands of white.

Yes, if Rose were sitting here with him now, Doug was sure she'd be in among the group of divers on the beach – flip-flops on, colourful blouse over the swimsuit she always wore, just in the case an opportunity arose to dive straight into the sea.

"Talking for the sake of talking," she'd be saying about the women at the tables behind.

Doug grinned, shaking his head. Rose had never been one to mix her words.

Glancing up, his smile faded as he noticed a woman walk in. He had to blink and look again. It was her hair that he saw first – a familiar coppery haze around her face, almost the exact colour that Rose's hair had been when they first met.

"Less than two per cent of the population has red hair. Did you know that?" Rose would say smugly. "I'd say that will always make me stand out in a crowd."

The woman who stood out now was wearing sunglasses, keys in one hand, phone in the other. She looked frazzled, unkempt, dressed in a creased-looking T-shirt and black leggings, a far cry from the groomed women behind. When she reached the veranda, someone dropped a fork. It clattered to the ground and the woman started, dropping her keys. Her hair fell in front of her face as she bent to retrieve them. Standing, she brushed her hair aside and continued inside to the counter.

Doug turned to watch her order a coffee and then point to something on the blackboard above the till. At the same time, there was a sudden hush from the table of women behind, as if someone had held up a cue card for quiet. Their heads bobbed up like meerkats, jerking left to right. One leaned in to whisper and their heads moved in unison to the inside of the café – to her. The circle closed tighter, all leaning forwards in a huddle, invisible armour at the ready. Then the blonde woman, the loud one, leaned back in her seat, crossed her legs and arms at the same time, and tilted her chin upwards.

"We'll drop that out to you," Doug heard the man inside say.

The woman with the red hair turned, called something

over her shoulder and then made her way back outside, to where it was already reasonably crowded. Looking ahead for somewhere to sit, she glanced to her right, straight at the table of warriors who'd all turned to smirk. The woman barely paused before immediately whipping her head left, keeping her features neutral. But Doug saw it. It was quick, but it was as clear as day – a fleeting look of panic.

She edged forwards, ignoring the high-pitched laughter that erupted from the beaky blonde in what seemed a frantically forced display. Doug watched the redhead clasp one hand around her phone. The keys in her other hand shook slightly. For a moment she looked like she was going to flee, then her eyes met his. Without hesitating, he stood, pushed his chair back and beckoned to her.

"Please, sit here. I'm almost done." He smiled warmly and moved around the table to pull out the other chair.

Her face changed and she nodded gratefully, flashing an all-too-familiar smile – far too sunny for such a small act of mercy. The last dazzling smile from a redheaded stranger had changed his life. Yes, it had always struck Doug Offer how one action led to another and another, no matter how insignificant.

Thank you, she mouthed, placing her phone and keys on the table in front of her.

Something told Doug this was one of those moments.

Chapter five

Lucie's back was to them so that Amanda Garth and her posse couldn't see her face. In hindsight, she should have gone straight home, except she hadn't felt like it after the impromptu meeting with Mr Downey, followed by another argument with Hamish. Besides, the thought of mindlessly tidying the house, only to watch it unravel as the day unfolded, hadn't seemed terribly enticing. Lately, everything felt like one endless cycle of pointlessness leading nowhere.

Instead, spurred primarily by the incessant rumbling in her stomach, she'd driven to the bay, to her favourite low-key coffee shop. It was, after all, the last place she'd imagined running into the mothers from the school, who usually frequented somewhere far trendier than beachside.

Lucie smiled awkwardly at the man sitting opposite, trying to deduce if he'd been offering her a place to sit, or if he'd witnessed the playground display and come to her rescue.

"Friends of yours?" he asked eventually, indicating towards the other table.

So he *had* noticed. His lips were thin, as though age

had sucked them back inside his mouth, but he was smiling wryly. It reminded Lucie of a smile that a child might draw – a sort of lopsided semicircle.

"Not exactly," Lucie hesitated. "See, I was going to get a takeaway coffee, but they do the best almond croissants here and I thought I'd have one. Not that I need one, but you know, it's Monday and there's not much an almond croissant can't fix . . . well . . . not everything." Lucie jerked her head back at the table of women and rolled her eyes. "Sorry," she laughed suddenly. "It's been one of those mornings."

Doug took a sip from his coffee and looked back at the women, who'd started to gather their bags, rooting in their pockets for change to fling on the table.

"Looks like the party's over."

Lucie stole a glance over her shoulder and then looked back at Doug. He was perhaps in his late sixties, maybe a little older, she couldn't quite tell. His skin was weathered-looking as if he'd spent much of his life outdoors. The typical Australian granddad, she guessed – silver hair neatly brushed to one side, beige trousers, neatly pressed short-sleeved blue shirt that perfectly matched his eyes, sunglasses tucked into his breast pocket. His keys, phone and brown leather wallet were in front of him on the table, a notepad and pen beside them. He appeared organised, together – a far cry from how Lucie felt or indeed looked that day.

Reaching up, she brushed her hair from her face, tucking it behind her ears, and smoothed her T-shirt, looking down at the now orangey stain. Note to self: the darned T-shirt was going in the bin as soon as she got home. She glanced over her shoulder again, tensely awaiting the group to disperse.

They ignored Lucie as they passed – except Amanda, who paused momentarily, jutted her chin forwards and smiled. The smile didn't reach her eyes. She'd always admired that about Amanda: how she could smirk and scowl simultaneously. Lucie focused on Amanda's chin. It was what her mother would have called a weak chin. Lucie had always found the description amusing. It was probably the reason why Amanda held her face at such an awkward angle. With nerves, Lucie let out a shaky giggle and then made a pained apologetic face with her teeth clenched. Amanda's eyes narrowed, making her look like she was silently passing wind while having an interrogation lamp shone at her face.

"How are you finding not working?" She looked pointedly at Lucie, then turned to Doug. "Be careful of her. She's dangerous," she drawled before walking away, chin in the air.

She was followed closely by Roberta, who smiled clumsily, went to say something and stopped when she saw Amanda watching her. As soon as they disappeared around the corner, Lucie's shoulders dropped with relief.

"Interesting woman."

"That's one way of putting it," Lucie laughed. "I'm not, by the way."

"Not what?"

"Dangerous." Lucie turned to thank the waiter, who'd placed her coffee and croissant down. "Another coffee?" she smiled at Doug. "On me."

Doug nodded. "Thanks. A cappuccino, please."

Lucie pulled off a bit of the croissant and popped it in her mouth. "Sorry. That was embarrassing. Did I look terrified? I can't believe I laughed." She covered her mouth as she chewed. "Pathetic! I'm still shaking. Look." She held up her tremoring hand.

"Let's just say I don't think you'd win any acting awards. Not sure you'd be able to hide much with those expressions."

"Hah. Mam used to say my face always gave me away, that I couldn't lie to save my life. I thought I'd got better at it with age. Obviously not."

"You're Irish." It was a statement rather than a question. It was the way she'd said "Mam" – the Irish lilt clear, albeit mixed with an Australian twang.

"I surely am." Her face lit up. "There's not many that pick that up nowadays, I've been here so long. Have you ever been?"

"No. Never. I always wanted to, but it was one of those things that we . . . well, it never materialised."

"Never too late. Well, so they say. I find myself saying that a lot lately and yet there's plenty I never got round to doing."

"If it's not too late for me, it's certainly not for you. A young woman like you, the world at your feet."

Lucie looked up and laughed. "Christ, I'm not that young." She took a sip from her coffee and tore off another piece of croissant, covering her mouth again. "I'm Lucie, by the way. Lucie Woods. Spelt with an -ie and not a -y, just to be difficult. Bane of my life. I always wanted it to be just a -y at the end. I spend more time spelling it out for people."

Doug's eyes flicked up suddenly upon hearing her name, his smile fading momentarily. She didn't notice through her babble.

"Doug." He recovered quickly and stuck his hand out to shake hers.

"Nice to meet you, Doug." She took his hand. He reminded Lucie of someone, although she couldn't think who. It would probably come to her in the middle of the night, waking her and then making it impossible to get back to sleep. "Thanks again for saving me there. Very chivalrous." She bowed her head with mock reverence.

"No problem. My Rose always says to be careful of the woman surrounded by a pack. She usually bites."

"Oh, I like that! Your Rose sounds very wise, but maybe I deserve it."

"Doubt that. I'm a good judge of character. You can tell a lot about someone by their general demeanour. You don't appear to be a confrontational sort."

"No. I don't seem to have it in me any more. My parents were always saying that I was as fiery as my hair." Lucie picked up a strand and shook it. "Made snap decisions without thinking. I don't know, maybe they were right. Mam used to say that I was one of those eejits led by the heart and not the head."

"Not a bad way to be. I knew someone very like that once. Maybe it *is* the hair."

They were briefly interrupted by the waiter, who arrived back and placed the coffee in front of Doug.

"I suppose I should explain that . . ." Lucie began once he'd left. "That – how can I put it? – little display."

"There's no need." Doug sat forwards and straightened his wallet and notebook, realigning them so they were equidistant apart. Then he lifted his keys as if thinking about leaving before placing them back down just as fast. "Unless you want to?"

Lucie shrugged. Recently, she'd felt as though she needed to tell someone so much that if she didn't, it might erupt from her at the most inopportune moment. That she'd be standing in a queue in the supermarket telling a total stranger, which she supposed in one way was what she was about to do. So far it was only with Nina she'd discussed it. But, suddenly, she found herself wanting another opinion, an unbiased one.

"There was an incident, you see . . ." She peered up at Doug, whose hands were now clasped in his lap. "Of course, that's the nice way of putting it. You have kids?"

Doug shook his head. "No. No kids."

"Maybe you wouldn't get it, then."

"Try me."

Lucie took a deep breath. "I threatened a child."

Doug didn't flinch. "Go on."

"It was *her* son, that woman, Amanda . . . Blondie. To cut a long story short and get straight to the *accidentally unprotected point* of it all . . . I threatened her kid and got myself fired from my job as the school nurse. Nicely put, I was *advised* to step down. So, here I am. Unemployed, hated – and, I suppose, deservedly so." She shrugged again, then picked up her cup and took an enormous gulp from the black liquid. "Shit," she winced, wiping the excess from her mouth. "That's hot."

Doug leaned back in his chair and crossed his arms. "Now, that sounds like a very watered-down version of events. I like to have all the facts before I form an opinion." Doug leaned forwards again. "And, you've left out the most important part." He paused for dramatic effect. "What was the motive?"

"Whoa! What are you, a cop?" she grinned. "If so, I'm terrified. I'm going to openly admit to my crime and let you make an arrest." She held her arms out straight in front, wrists up. "Take me away, Officer."

Doug chuckled. "As a matter of fact, I am. Or at least I was. I'm retired now."

"Oh!" Lucie looked surprised. "Well, then you definitely

won't agree with my actions, regardless of motive. I've picked the wrong person altogether to hear my confession. Typical!"

Doug tutted. "Come on. Cops are the least judgmental people on Earth. I could tell you a story or two that would make your toes curl and, I'm sure, make whatever you've done seem perfectly normal."

"I'd like that."

"You first." He motioned for her to continue. "I'm going to need to know more before I decide what sort of criminal I'm dealing with." He pointed at his cup. "Look, I have a fresh coffee here *and* I'm retired with nowhere to be. Much lower risk than confessing to a real cop."

Chapter six

It was the part of parenting about which no one takes the time to warn you – the not-so-nice bit. When they're placed in your arms that very first day, all you can hope for is that they'll have a beautiful life, be accepted, loved as much as you love them at that moment. You'll be there to protect them, to keep them safe. It isn't until they go off to school and start to grow up that you realise you can't always be there, not every minute. So you pray that they'll never have to face anything unpleasant, at least until they're old enough to be able to deal with it. Because there will be uncomfortable times, Lucie knew that only too well. Life wasn't always easy.

From the moment Bella was born, Lucie adored being a mother. Finally having a family again, her own flesh and blood, after she'd been on her own so long, it was everything. Despite the circumstances of discovering her pregnancy being a whirlwind. But as soon as she arrived, Bella was the balm over everything, the answer to why life had taken Lucie along an unanticipated curve. Bella was a straightforward baby, the textbook little girl: confident, twirling and singing, adoring the company of others, relaxed. After three years, Lucie and Hamish had been thrilled to discover they were expecting again.

"Let's find out what we're having this time," Hamish suggested when they went for the scan. "So we can plan."

Lucie had known why Hamish wanted to know. Waiting another six months to see if he was going to have a textbook son to match the textbook daughter who adored him would be too much to endure. Bella had idolised her father almost from the moment she'd been born. They were like two peas in a pod and a son would be the icing on the cake.

"You see that . . ." The nurse had pointed at the screen while Hamish grinned broadly.

"Unless that's another umbilical cord, I'd say he's his father's boy." Hamish had clapped and rubbed his hands together.

"A boy," Lucie had whispered delightedly. "Our boy."

Declan Woods was going to be an international rugby player, a famed cricketer, an accomplished golfer, an all-rounder. Until it became apparent that Declan wasn't the textbook boy his father had wished for – more interested in stories, drawing, Lego, happy to sit quietly, not craving the attention from Hamish that Bella did. To Lucie, Declan was a joy, preferring to remain indoors with her, away from the heat, despite him sharing his father's sallow skin and sandy-blond hair. By the time Declan reached school age and started asking for the girls in his class to come over to play, Hamish was convinced there was a problem.

"Have him tested. He's not sociable. There's something not right."

"For what? For not wanting to play sports. For enjoying his own company. For not liking rough play. Don't be ridiculous. There's nothing wrong with him. He's happy."

"I don't want my son playing with girls."

"Why? I'm a girl. Bella's a girl. Cop on, Hamish. Don't be another chauvinistic Aussie. He's perfect."

Her husband's criticisms tore through Lucie like a knife, forcing her to become fiercely overprotective. To her, Declan was perfect – sensitive, caring, adoring of his older sister and mother, somewhat wary of his father. Lucie had seen the way Hamish would pick him up and hurl him around the room in an attempt to unleash the boy's rough and tumble. That would frighten anyone!

"It's not normal. You're treating Dec with kid gloves. You'll make him a sissy."

"I can't believe you're saying that. In this day and age! He's just a lovely gentle kid. He is who he is."

They'd fought about it for years, Hamish forcing Declan to play football at the weekends, enrolling him in all sorts of typically "male" classes in which Declan had no interest. Until Declan rebelled, point-blank refusing to get out of the car, making Hamish lose interest.

"You deal with him."

"Delighted to," Lucie had grinned, thrilled that Declan had a mind of his own and wasn't afraid to use it.

Lucie had hated her husband for thinking that their perfect little boy was anything but. In turn, Hamish doted even more on Bella, creating a sort of invisible divide in the family – Bella and Dad, Declan and Mum. It was how they sat when they went to the cinema, how they arranged themselves when out for dinner, how they walked when they went to the beach. Lucie supposed maybe she'd allowed it to happen. It was more comfortable – less painful than delving into the reasons.

And to be fair, Hamish wasn't entirely dismissive of his son. Lucie knew he loved Declan. Of course he did – and he was a good dad – but there was an underlying disappointment always present. It made Lucie overcompensate, make a bigger deal out of Declan's achievements, trying to pump him up where she could.

Then, after starting at Woodfield Grammar, Declan seemed to flourish and everything was great for a while. He was being challenged academically and it seemed he'd found his place. Working at the school, Lucie always made a conscious effort to stay away from her children in their day-to-day school life, to let them forge their own path. Where Bella played every sport under the sun and stayed on the radar academically, Declan played the minimum amount of sport yet soared above the academic radar, winning prizes for projects, awards for excellence.

"See," Lucie persuaded her husband. "I told you. He's not the typical boy. He's better."

"But does he have friends?"

Lucie had wanted to scream. So, Hamish had been Mr Popular in his day. Not everyone needed thousands of friends. Couldn't Hamish just leave him be? "Declan *has* friends. Plenty of them."

Lucie had seen Declan playing outside at break with the other children. She'd seen it with her own eyes. So what, Declan didn't want many play dates . . . that was normal, too. To be honest, Lucie was only too happy to go home on a Friday afternoon and have the children all to herself. She didn't want streams of children traipsing through the house after the working week.

"Do you want to have someone over to play this

week?" she'd encouraged, just in case. "Anyone you like. Hell, you can have four or five. We have room . . ."

"No, thanks, Mum."

"Do you think he's overweight?" Hamish asked another time. "What are you feeding him? Cut back on the snacks."

Again, she'd wanted to throttle her husband. Declan had gained some weight over the past few months, but it was a phase. He was only ten, hadn't quite grown into himself yet. She'd gone through a chubby stage herself before puberty. It was all normal. Wasn't it?

Lucie had hoped to prove Hamish wrong once again, but something did seem different this time. For weeks, Declan had been tucking into extra snacks, withdrawing to his room alone, not wanting to spend time with any of them, saying he was working on projects. At the same time, her mind had been occupied with Hamish and his business, or lack thereof, worrying about money and about Bella, who seemed to be taking the lion's share of attention with her mood swings. Declan had somehow slipped out of focus, but Lucie would get to the bottom of it – as soon as she had a minute. Declan got there first.

"Mum, am I weird?" he'd asked one day, observing her.

"Is everything okay with your brother? He has friends, right?" Lucie had asked Bella casually one Friday evening.

They were making pizza in the kitchen, just the two of them. Declan was staying with Hamish's mother, Granny Vera, in the city for the weekend. Bella looked up and paused as though wondering if she should answer.

"Seriously? He has *no* friends, Mum. There's a group at school who ghost him all the time. They say he's . . . weird."

"He's not weird. He's just . . ."

"*Weird*?" Bella raised her eyebrows.

She said it so nonchalantly that Lucie froze. For a moment she couldn't speak. Was he weird? No. Declan was *different*, if different meant that he was more studious, but he wasn't odd.

"You're there at the school all the time," Bella continued, scattering cheese on the pizza base. "He sits on his own."

Did he? Lucie felt sick.

"Bella, what's ghosting?"

"The other kids, they pretend he's not there. Like he's invisible. They walk through him. Pretend they can't hear when he speaks. They call him fat, weird, gay . . ."

"What?" Lucie was starting to panic. How the hell had she missed it?

Bella watched her mother nervously, noticing her face change, her breathing grow ragged.

"Whenever I see it, I tell them to stop, but I can't be there all the time, Mum."

"Why didn't you tell me? Why didn't you do something?" Lucie was shouting. "Bella!" Lucie pleaded, her eyes filling with tears.

"I'm sorry, Mum. I . . . I thought he could fight his own battles. Dad always says he needs to toughen up." Realising her mistake, Bella stopped what she was doing and stared at the ground.

"Don't you dare!" Lucie spat. "Don't you dare use that as an excuse. He's your brother. He adores you – worships the ground you walk on. And *you* call him weird? That makes you no better than *them*."

Bella frowned, startled by her mother's unexpected aggression.

"I thought you knew," she tried to explain. "I'm sorry. I don't know why I said that about Dec. I'll fix it."

Lucie shook her head and put her arm around her daughter, softening. "Love, it's not up to you to fix, but you *have* to tell me, please. You know you can tell me anything and I'll do whatever I can to fix it. That's my job. We're a team. We stick together, remember?"

Bella nodded and then glanced at her mother. In barely more than a whisper, she added, "It's *awful*, Mum. At first it was just one kid, but now the others are doing it, too."

Lucie had to put her hand on the kitchen worktop to steady herself.

"Who? Give me a name," she asked through gritted teeth, feeling the ground move beneath her feet, the room begin to swirl – along with the contents of her stomach.

Declan was being bullied practically before her eyes. Lucie had been right there and she'd missed it. What else had she missed? What else had she pretended wasn't happening?

"Jack Garth."

She should have known. Amanda Garth was a ringleader in her own right. It made sense that her son – an all-rounder like Jack, gifted at sport, popular – might be the same. Was Jack the type of son Hamish would have preferred?

Lucie thought about it all weekend, formulating the best way to deal with it. She'd go to John Downey, the principal, first, and then she'd meet Amanda and speak with her calmly, ask her to get Jack to stop. As a member of staff, she'd have to be careful to go about it the right way.

Lucie was going to speak to Declan, too, as soon as he got back home. Reassure him. God, she was going to hug him tighter than she ever had before. Even Hamish had been shocked when she told him what had been happening and how she planned to deal with it. For once, he hadn't taken his usual line of blaming her for being too soft on their son.

"It's not right." Hamish had shaken his head in dismay as they sat in bed discussing it on Sunday night after a somewhat eventful day to put it mildly.

"Poor Dec. I feel responsible. Maybe I pushed him too hard to fit in. I'm . . . I'm sorry, Lu."

It was the first time that her husband had looked remorseful.

"I know Dec and I don't always see eye to eye, but he's my son. I do know that. It's taken me a while to realise, but Dec is one clever kid. I may not get the rugby player, but I bet we get a doc or a scientist out of the kid someday. Do you want me to come with you to talk to Downey?"

Lucie had almost crumbled at the words she'd wanted her husband to say for so long – the longed-for solidarity in protecting their son. They were finally on the same page. There was no point in being angry, for pointing the finger of blame, or for agreeing that Hamish *had* been too hard on him. If anything was going to come out of this awful situation, perhaps it was this – a better future for Declan. Going about it the right way was precisely how to fix it all.

Chapter seven

"So, you didn't go about it the right way." Doug leaned back as Lucie finished.

"*Definitely* not." She shook her head. "I broke just about every rule in any parenting textbook on Earth. Got myself fired. Lost every friend I thought I had at the school . . ."

"And your son?"

"I've never seen him so happy. Once it all stopped, Declan started to come out of himself again."

"Well, then. Sounds to me like you broke a few rules but got the results."

"But that's the thing, I'm not a rule-breaker." Lucie sighed. "Imagine, I worked for almost fifteen years at Sydney General Hospital and never once got in any strife. Then, I get myself fired from being a school nurse. The shame. If only I'd—"

"You can waste an entire life thinking 'if only' – there's no point." Doug held his hands out and shrugged. "Sometimes you've just got to move on. Accept that things happen for a reason. They're a doorway into the next phase. It might not always be a better phase, but life is a series of stages and like it or not, they're coming.

"The worst thing you can do is dwell. Dwelling is just hesitating and if there's one thing I've learned over the years, it's that hesitating for too long only makes things worse. In fact, hesitating can get you killed," he warned, laughing. "So they say."

Lucie felt a chill run up her spine as she watched him. It sounded a lot like what she might tell someone in the same situation. His words made a lot of sense, so much so that it was as though he'd read her mind. For a moment she wanted to tell him more, admit it all, confess that what she'd told him today was only the tip of the iceberg.

Hesitating, dwelling, it was precisely what she was doing. In fact, it was what she'd been doing for years. Lucie was more stuck than a fly on one of those revolting orange spiral strips her mother used to dangle from the kitchen window in summer. Lucie still remembered being fascinated, watching the flies stick to the paper, their wings still humming until they slowly ceased, never to move again. Now, she was the one who was caught – skulking into the school like a criminal to drop off Bella and Declan, returning home to lie on her bed with those constant pains in her stomach but doing nothing to make it right.

What if she really was sick? What if her wings eventually stopped buzzing like those flies? What if everything she was feeling lately was her body shouting at her to pay attention and she was ignoring it? It was time to address the physical symptoms she'd been experiencing, at least. There was no way Hamish would ever be able to manage the children, not on his own, regardless of their financial situation, which in itself was worrying. Hamish wasn't going to make everything better. It was up to Lucie to take charge for the sake of Bella and Declan.

She'd had the thought months before when everything had started to go wrong. Back then, Lucie had made a sort of contingency plan, but she hadn't seen it through. At the last minute, she'd stalled. Talking to this man now, Lucie had the feeling that everything was about to get worse before it got better if she finally decided to face facts. Maybe this stranger was right – the next stage was coming, no matter how much she tried to ignore it.

"Am I allowed one 'if only'?" Lucie closed her eyes and smiled.

It was the part of the story that had almost made Doug spit out the last mouthful of his, by then, cold cappuccino.

"See this." Lucie had pointed the shiny weapon under Jack Garth's nose. "If you so much as look at my son again, call him names, threaten him, breathe near him, I will shove this so far up your arsehole that you won't sit down for weeks. Understand?"

Jack Garth's mouth had dropped open as he stood staring with round eyes at the usually chirpy school nurse, whose nostrils were now flaring as she hissed the words. His head nodded robotically. Straightening up, she tucked the object in her pocket and rearranged her uniform.

"Now," she smiled sweetly. "Get to class, you little shit. Tell anyone about this and you'll have to deal with worse," she finished, repeating the same threat Jack had used on Declan to keep him quiet.

Lucie patted her pocket containing the maths compass for good measure and eyeballed him. Jack scarpered, skidding as he rounded the corner, his shoes squeaking on the floor.

It was so far removed from how she'd imagined dealing with the situation, it was laughable. Then again, Lucie had never expected to witness Declan being held against a locker, an object to his throat, being spat on.

Lucie had been keeping an eye on a sixth-grade class while the teacher went to have a quick word with the principal. She, too, had made an appointment with Mr Downey for later that day to discuss Declan and all he'd finally told her the night before.

For months, Jack Garth and his friends had been teasing him, calling him names and far worse. Lucie had had to close her eyes to stop herself from exploding as her son revealed that Jack and his group, but namely Jack, had repeatedly stabbed Declan in the leg with a maths compass. He'd shown her the marks. Little mottled bruises here and there on his smooth, creamy skin.

They'd pushed Declan over in the toilets, making him wet his trousers, taken his clothes when changing for gym. Then there was the constant "ghosting". To Lucie, this was perhaps worst of all. They'd made her son invisible, disappear, vanish.

"It was after I won the science fair. It started then."

Declan's much talked-of volcano project had erupted in more ways than one, spilling hot lava all over her son's life at school, igniting a fit of jealousy in Jack Garth with his mediocre grades. Listening to it, Lucie had known what she'd like to do to Jack Garth, but she'd been determined to go through the correct channels.

"Kill the little prick," her friend, Nina, had said to her the night before on the phone. "I've been through this, Lucie, with my boy. All his life, he's been teased for being different, for having an Asian mother, telling him I'm the cleaning lady, asking does he have noodles for lunch, making funny faces at him. I called the parents – they do nothing. 'Not my son. He'd never do that.' So, I got them on their own and I told them I'm watching them, and if they keep doing it, there'll be trouble."

"You didn't?"

"I bloody well did. You have to go straight to the source."

"Didn't they tell their parents?"

"No. They got such a fright, they nearly pissed their pants!"

"I can't do that, Nina. I work at the school."

"Then trip him up when he walks past."

Lucie hadn't imagined for one moment that she'd take Nina's advice literally. Not until she'd rounded the corner after the sixth-grade teacher returned, to see her son surrounded by a group of boys pretending they couldn't see him. They were holding their arms out like zombies and pushing at Declan blindly. Declan had pushed back, making Jack trip over. Lucie had secretly applauded before noticing Jack right himself and produce something from his pocket.

At first, Lucie hadn't been able to tell what was in Jack's hand. She'd tucked herself close against the wall to watch the exchange, hoping to gather ammunition for her meeting with the principal. The other boys had edged backwards when they saw what was coming. Declan had been pushed against the locker, the object raised, and in slow motion, Jack's head had jerked back, his lips pursing to produce a foamy lump of saliva that travelled towards her son's face.

"Stop!" As she'd shouted the words, something had torn inside her. Perhaps some resentment that she'd been harbouring for years also erupted. "Go, Declan, *now*," she'd shouted, moving towards the group.

Declan stared in shock, wiped his face and ran. The others followed as Jack backed into the row of lockers, in the same position Declan had been moments before. Seizing the weapon from his sweaty hand, the blue protective lid of the geometry compass dislodged and flicked through the air, landing at Lucie's feet.

It never occurred to Lucie until afterwards that the insignificant piece of blue plastic may have been the very thing to save her, if it had remained on the compass and not flown through the air. But then, in the heat of the moment, she could never have imagined that the point of the compass without its safety cover would somehow catch the light from behind, making it appear as though the school nurse was primed to stab young Jack Garth with the maths tool. Nor did she anticipate what would happen next as Jack Garth ran away from her as fast as he could after dismissing him.

Back in her office, she'd shut the door and rested her body against it, trying to catch her breath. What she'd witnessed had forced her to defend her son in an almost primal way. It was what anyone would do if they saw someone spit in their child's face. It was disgusting. She let out a nervous adrenaline-fuelled laugh and then jumped when she heard her own high-pitched menacing tone.

What if Jack told?

No. He wouldn't. Bullies were always the same – as soon as they're confronted, they back down.

Lucie sat at her desk and stared ahead, suddenly wondering what could be so bad in that boy's life that he was projecting it onto her son. Again, she had to stop herself. That wasn't her concern – her priority was Declan. Jack had his own parents. But now what was she going to tell Mr Downey? Should she cancel her meeting with him?

Lucie couldn't think straight. If she went to him, he would undoubtedly want to speak with Jack Garth and Jack might tell. Still, it was her word against his and Lucie had no intention of actually doing anything to the boy. She'd just wanted to frighten him – and by the look on his face, she had. Maybe she'd casually mention to the principal that she had concerns and could he keep an eye out. Yes. That's what she'd do – play it down. She was panicking over nothing.

It felt good to have some sort of control, especially after the day she'd had yesterday. She was still reeling over such a memorable weekend. Sunday had been an absolute nightmare.

Grabbing her mobile, she quickly tapped out a message to Nina, then threw the phone into the drawer of her desk:

Did what you told me. Grabbed that little shit Jack Garth and told him if he ever went near my son again that I'd shove a geometry compass so far up his arsehole that he'd never sit down again. Is it bad I was holding the compass?

Perhaps Lucie shouldn't have come into work today. After what had happened the day before, it would have been understandable for her not to. Maybe she should head off early, go home and sort out the mess at home. Lucie sat for what seemed like hours, too distracted to do any work. She eventually picked up the landline on her desk and dialled the number.

Nina answered straightaway.

"Well, are you proud of me?"

"For what?"

"Didn't you read my message?"

"What message? I've been sitting here waiting to hear what happened. Also, why are you at work? After yesterday, don't you think you should be home?"

"There was nothing I could do at home. Besides, I felt weird being there."

"Well, what happened?"

Lucie filled her in quickly.

"What a shit! The fury of Lucie Woods! Remind me not to cross you any time soon. This perimenopausal business has unleashed a peri-monster," Nina joked.

Lucie almost laughed, then something stopped her in her tracks.

"Hang on, why didn't you get my message?"

Reaching into the drawer of her desk and retrieving her mobile, Lucie flicked open WhatsApp before dropping the phone on the table as if it had scalded her hand. Picking it back up, she then scrolled through the eighty-seven messages. Eighty-seven!

"Lucie? Are you there?"

"Oh, fuck. Oh, Christ. Nina."

The realisation that she'd sent the message to the wrong group was accompanied by a sharp knock on the door. The next three hours were spent in the principal's office as Mr Downey flicked through the CCTV screens.

There it was – the image of Lucie threatening a ten-year-old boy with a pointed compass, the light glimmering off the shiny tip, the angle hinting at something far more sinister. Lucie went over the story, again and again, while John Downey shook his head in dismay. Then Amanda Garth burst through the office door, launching directly at Lucie, blonde extensions flying, while Mr Downey tried to pull her off.

Tears. Screaming. Accusations. Threats.

Jack and Declan were interviewed separately. Jack smiled sickeningly at Lucie when he left the room. It genuinely frightened her. The child was pure evil.

When it was over, Lucie went to her office to collect her things, exhausted by everything, flat after being suspended from work, pending investigation.

Then came all the legal correspondence from the Garths, threats to call the police, enduring stares, nasty comments . . . In the end, Lucie decided to make it easy for them. She left, handing in her notice, while Jack Garth and his mother walked away unscathed.

John Downey moved Declan to another class, which was something, she supposed, and one or two mothers *did* show secret support, but what was done was done. There was no going back.

Lucie shouldn't have done it – nor should Jack, nor should Roberta Williams, who'd broadcast her message to all the other school groups, standing firm behind Amanda, regardless of what Jack had been doing. But then, Roberta had always been a lick-arse.

The issue of Jack's bullying was lost in translation. John Downey knew, deep down, that Lucie was telling the truth, but his hands were tied. And Hamish . . . he'd almost delighted in telling her that her actions had now placed them in dire financial straits, his earlier solidarity suddenly evaporating. Lucie made mistakes, too, just like him. She wasn't perfect. The fall from her pedestal was going to hurt.

"I guess I made a mess of it all." Lucie smiled sadly at Doug. "But thanks for listening to me today. Meeting you like this, I suppose I really needed someone impartial to talk to. You might call it a stroke of good fortune. And you're right. I need to move on. I've been dwelling and there are other more pressing issues that require my attention."

"It'll blow over." Doug hesitated for a few seconds. "Can I ask you something?"

"Fear not." She held up her hands. "I'm unarmed today. My geometry days are over. Compasses are now no longer allowed at the school – thanks to Amanda."

Doug laughed before turning serious. "No. Not that. You said a few times that something happened the day before . . ."

"Oh. Didn't I say? I can't believe I forgot that part. What is it they say? Things happen in threes . . . I'm on two, so watch out."

Doug waited.

"Our house was burgled. Ransacked, in fact. Everything of value, gone. Just like that, in broad daylight." Lucie stopped. "I honestly thought things couldn't get much worse."

Doug smiled knowingly. "That's the funny thing about life – things always can."

Chapter eight

Doug

Pulling into the driveway of the cottage, Doug then switched off the car engine and removed the keys from the ignition. Tossing them from hand to hand, he stared ahead, moving his jaw from side to side. He'd taken his time on the drive back home along the coast, lost in thought, rehashing the morning. Honestly, he could have sat there chatting to Lucie for hours longer, if the waiter hadn't started to hover as the lunchtime rush filtered in. After a while, she'd picked up her phone, glanced at the time and made a face.

"I'd better get on. I've kept you here long enough listening to my woes. It was nice to meet you, Doug. I enjoyed it," she'd smiled.

"Me too."

He'd wanted to say something more profound, to conclude their meeting more eloquently, but he'd felt lost for words.

"Thanks for the advice on the . . ." Lucie had pretended to point her keys at him threateningly, screwing up her face.

"Thanks for telling me."

She was an open book. Doug had been able to glean that immediately. There weren't many who'd reveal the story of their downfall so readily with minimal prompting. She'd obviously needed to get it off her chest. It was sweet how utterly ashamed she was of how she'd threatened that boy. It was unfortunate that she'd lost her job, but Doug could see how that had happened, too – right was right, after all. He'd always believed in doing the right thing, heeding the law, following protocol. Then again, he'd never had kids.

Her face had lit up when speaking about hers – even when telling Doug about the trials of raising a teen, the constant doubts you feel as a parent, wondering if you were doing your best.

"Watching Bella grow up, it's terrifying. It's almost like watching my own life wither away as hers begins. It's the most bittersweet thing in the world."

That part had interested Doug, how someone as young as Lucie could see her life as withering away. It had sounded . . . sad. Lucie was only a few years older than Rose had been when Doug first met her, yet Lucie seemed hell-bent that her life was over.

"I'd do anything for them, literally *anything*, as long as they're happy. Life stopped being about me a long time ago."

They were noble words, soaked with some other sentiment that Doug couldn't decipher – a trace of defeat, or perhaps resolve. If it were any other person, it might have sounded like martyrdom, but that wasn't it, either.

Without those undertones, Lucie seemed to be the type of mother who perhaps Rose might have been, given the chance – protective, loving, proud, accepting. Rose always said that the most significant thing you can *ever* do for another person is to take them for who they are, forgive their mistakes, embrace their differences.

Doug smiled to himself. He never usually sat for so long in the car outside as he was doing now. Typically, coming home to their little white cottage, yellow rose bushes flanking the blue front door, felt like breathing sunshine. Lately, he'd noticed the matching blue paint had started to crack on the window shutters, splitting apart and flaking away. He'd need to sand them down soon, apply a fresh coat of paint as they did every year following the hotter months, in preparation for the chillier time of year, when Rose liked to sit on the veranda out back, watching the waves.

Doug never had to ask what she was thinking. The answer was always clear on her wistful face as Rose closed her eyes, letting her mind travel to a faraway ocean – to the one left behind in Ireland. Even after all this time, painting those darned blue shutters year after year, it was where she'd call home.

Doug got out of the car and ran his hand over the flaking paint, watching it come away in his hand. After brushing it off, he opened the front door.

"I'm home," he called, dropping his keys on the table in the hall and making his way into the kitchen. Opening the fridge, he looked at the sparse contents before closing it, unenthused. He wasn't hungry anyway.

As an afterthought, he opened it again and took out a beer. He reached behind to grab the bottle opener and cracked it open before making his way through the connecting door to the living room. It was the reason they'd bought this house – for the perfect view of the sea from the big window at the back.

"Interesting day." He glanced to his left. "I met someone who reminded me so much of you. Same red hair," he chuckled. "Same fiery spirit. Irish! Isn't that a coincidence? You'd have liked her."

Doug moved forwards and reached his hand out to the narrow neck of the urn before running his fingers over the rounded body, then brushing away the particles of dust that had gathered on the lid.

"What did I miss here?"

He scooped up the vase and walked out to the veranda, placing it beside him on the table along with his notebook and pen.

"I know. I know." Doug rolled his eyes. "I promised I wouldn't do this."

Rose had made him swear that afterwards, he wouldn't hold on. It was the same thing he'd told Lucie Woods not to do – to dwell, hesitate, sit in the past. But as yet, he hadn't been able to bring himself to free that blasted urn of its contents. Besides, wasn't it always easier to tell other people what you should be heeding yourself?

"Dump me in the sea. Do you hear me, Doug? Don't be hanging on. Remember our motto – hesitating can get you killed."

Rose had been referring to the safety measure they'd always employed when they were out diving, hoping it may influence her husband not to stall for too long after the inevitable. The motto had seen them well over the years until then. Until they'd received the news that there was nothing more to be done but to accept the next stage, where Doug would be left alone.

As they'd grown older over the years, Doug secretly used to wish that it would be him who'd be the one to go first. He'd told Rose about it towards the end. She'd laughed.

"The likelihood of that happening was always slim.

What did you expect when you married an older lady? I did try to warn you, all those years ago. Ten years is ten years, but you wouldn't listen." She'd placed her hand on his. "Promise me, Doug. When the time comes, you let me go. Don't trap me. Set us both free."

"Hush now," was all he'd said, trying to ignore that she was fading faster than they could have anticipated, each one of her glorious petals dropping off day by day. "Besides, I always liked older women."

"Hah! Well, you have one now, that's for sure." Even up until the very end, her youthful humour was still as present as the day he'd met her.

"Nothing you could ever have told me would have stopped me from being with you."

Sure enough, Rose had tried to deter him at first, all those years ago, after their initial meeting on the beach. Doug had been tenacious. He was going to have Rose if it was the last thing he ever did. It was Rose who eventually taught him to dive, after hounding her, turning up uninvited at the beach week after week. If it hadn't been for her, he probably never would have pursued his police diving career. But he had.

"I'll be back," he'd smiled the day he was leaving for six months of intensive training in Melbourne.

"What do you want – a medal?" She'd tried to sound dismissive. "Anyway, I've a contract up the coast for a few weeks. I won't be here," Rose had teased, still wrestling with falling for someone ten years her junior.

"I'll find you."

"In the sea? Well, I suppose by then you'll be specially trained to find anything."

"The only thing I want to find is you."

He'd kissed her then and she'd finally given in.

Months of trying to convince him that she was far too old for him at forty-five – that the ten-year age gap would eventually gape open when one day he decided he wanted children.

"All I want is you."

Rose *had* been all Doug had ever wanted. Their non-traditional life together, breathing their passions in unison, had been enough. Not having children, missing out on that side of his life, had never really bothered Doug. And the expanse of years between them had gone unnoticed until it finally tore open. When Doug realised that he'd have to endure his twilight years without Rose. It was only then that he'd wished they'd had a child – a living legacy.

"Here." Doug had flicked open his wallet earlier that day before Lucie stood up to leave. "I wanted to show you this." He'd taken the picture from the plastic case and handed it to her.

"Your Rose?" Lucie looked at the photo of the woman with the red hair, smiling at the camera. "Oh my God. She looks like—"

"Like you," Doug finished, nodding. "I noticed it as soon as you walked in, then when I heard you speak . . ."

"Wow. That's . . . that's really weird. Was she Irish, too?" She ran her fingers over the image.

"She was. From Wexford. She was here for thirty-eight years. Mind you, she still couldn't bring herself to say she was an Aussie! Meeting you today . . ." He paused and frowned. "I suppose you remind me of her. Not just in looks – must be the spirit of the Irish. Always a bit of fight in them. Rose used to say that nothing in life was ever as bad as you thought it was. That there was nothing that wouldn't eventually be all right . . ."

"In the end . . ." They said the words at the same time.

"My niece, Ann, says that. That things always work out. I used to believe it, too. Lately, I don't know what I believe any more." And then, "Is she still . . . ?"

Doug took the picture back and tucked it in his wallet.

"She passed away. Eighteen months ago."

"I'm so sorry, Doug. From the way you spoke, I thought she was still alive."

He nodded. "I still find it hard to talk about Rose in the past tense."

It was hard to believe it had been a year and a half since Doug had seen her face, touched her hand, heard her give out! He wondered if Rose would be disappointed in how he was now filling his time, but he already knew she would. He'd retired at sixty-five from the force, having spent years underwater, then his latter years as a detective-cum-supervisor to the younger crew of divers.

His diving pastime was no longer an option, not any more. It dawned on him then, the thing he'd been trying to remember earlier – when his last dive had been. How could he have forgotten? It had been with Rose. Together, they'd waded straight into the sea from the beach in front of the cottage, holding hands. Afterwards, Rose had hosed down their gear, carefully storing it in the shed beside the house and locking it. That evening, she'd poured them both a glass of wine, holding hers up in the direction of the sea, and whispered, "For all the years."

For all the years. They'd gone so fast.

"Find something that interests you. Give back," Rose had coached, over and over. "Just don't give up."

Doug *had* kept his promise, he supposed, finding something that gave some form of structure and purpose to each day. That it didn't interest him in the slightest was neither here nor there – nor did he imagine that it helped other people. In fact, it probably did quite the opposite.

He thought of Lucie again. In truth, he hadn't stopped thinking of her all day, her image becoming entangled with that of Rose's in his mind. Earlier, when she said her name, he should have politely excused himself, but something had glued him to the seat, making it impossible to move. When Lucie had started talking, he'd been hypnotised. Should he have said something more? Hinted? No, that would be breaking the rules – and Doug was a stickler for the rules, despite what he'd said to Lucie earlier about bending them to get the required result for her son. That had been more like something Rose would have said.

"You're infuriating," Rose used to tell him. "The heart can't always follow the rules, Doug. Remember, if you ever have a chance to help someone, *really* help them, then help, at whatever cost. Bend those rules – that's what they're there for."

He could hear Rose's words clearly – his wife with her heart so full, ready to do whatever she could for another person. Doug often wondered if she was that way because they'd never had children – if Rose had had a surplus amount of nurturing inside her to give and nowhere to direct it.

"And another thing, you're far too bleedin' strait-laced. Loosen up – think with your heart and not that stubborn head of yours."

Doug let out a laugh. Even from beyond, Rose was still keeping him in check. Lately, he wasn't sure if he thought for himself at all any more, or just replayed all the things his wife had once said. Now, it seemed everything she used to tell him had been to guide him when she no longer could.

Yes, perhaps he should have left when he realised who Lucie was. Of course, he hadn't imagined that he'd meet her in person when he'd driven towards Double Bay that morning. It was hugely coincidental, almost serendipitous. Maybe, he was meant to come into her life. Even stranger, perhaps *she* was meant to encounter him. Having now met the person who up until that moment had been simply a name on a file he'd been handed a few weeks before, well, it changed everything, making it more real than the version he'd read about.

"Help her."

He tilted his head, hearing what his wife might have said.

"Look at you. Your jaw is going again. You must be bothered."

Doug stopped moving his jaw from side to side as he often did when he was lost in thought.

"Shh, Rose. Let me think."

"So, you were a police diver? That's fascinating," Lucie had said when they reached where her car was parked.

He'd known before she took the keys out to press the unlock button which one was hers. Black SUV, almost brand-new, shining with supposed prosperity.

"So, if I'd disposed of my maths weapon that day in the sea, you might have been searching for it?" She raised her eyebrows and grinned.

"And I'd have found it, too. I always did."

"Well, then I'm glad I didn't bury the evidence. Must have been a tough job all the same."

"It was. Unearthing things that people want burying isn't always easy. It was sad."

Lucie nodded knowingly. "They say that though, don't they? Things can't stay buried forever. The truth will always out."

"That's what I've usually found," he nodded, trying to read her expression.

"Your wife . . . how did she . . . ?"

"Cancer – ovarian."

She'd remained silent, her brow furrowing, some look he couldn't quite decipher crossing her face.

"I'm sorry." And then, "I'd tell you it gets easier, but it doesn't, not really. Grief is always there." She tried to smile. "It affects everything that comes after."

"You lost someone?" Doug asked.

"Everyone. I lost everyone – except my niece. She's back in Ireland. In the space of six years – Dad, Mam, my brother, my best friend . . . my . . ." She trailed off. "Makes you wonder what it's all about. You learn to live with the life you're left with, I suppose. There's no other option, really."

"You have your husband, though, your kids?"

"Yes. I have my kids."

Doug flicked open his notebook and lifted the pen. In large letters, he wrote the name Lucie Woods in the centre of the page. Drawing a circle around it, he then drew lines emanating from it.

Lost job. Adores kids. Marriage in trouble?
Financial problems? Honest.

He paused then before writing the final words.

What does she know . . . ?

Doug felt sure he knew the answer to that final question himself. You learned to read people in his line of work – especially from things they say that seem irrelevant. He could be wrong, of course. Some people were smarter than they let on, but he was sure that on this occasion, Lucie Woods knew very little. Doug put the pen down and looked at the urn beside him, then frowned upon hearing Rose again.

"The real question is, Doug, what are you going to do about it?"

Chapter nine

"You came." Nina was at the bar, a bottle of beer in front of her, legs dangling off the bar stool. "I was having a bet with myself that you'd cancel, *again*."

"Sorry I'm late." Lucie leaned in for an air-kiss. "I lost track of time brushing my moustache into place," she joked, pretending to smooth down the invisible hairs on her upper lip.

"Oh, I know. I wasn't sure whether to French plait my beard or leave it loose. I went with loose." Nina rubbed her chin and grinned.

"Suits you," Lucie smiled. "Very youthful."

She sat down beside Nina and gestured at the barman. "Gin and tonic, please."

"Starting on the hard stuff. That bad, huh?"

"You have no idea."

Lucie *had* been about to cancel, *again*. Standing in front of the mirror earlier that evening had almost made her lift the phone and tap out some lame excuse as to why she couldn't meet Nina after work. Staring at her underweared reflection in the mirror, Lucie was sure this wasn't what Doug had meant when he'd told her to face things.

She'd squinted at her reflection, trying to decide what it was she looked like. She settled on an upside-down water balloon, where all the liquid had gathered at the bottom, leaving the top part "flaccid". She despised that word. It was so . . . weak, up there with "moist" and "curd" on her list of most-hated words.

Lucie put her index fingers and thumbs together, making a circle, before placing the shape over her belly button and watching the white flesh ooze out like an untoasted bagel. "Bulbous" – another horrid description.

She tried putting her shoulders back and standing on tiptoe to elongate her droopy form, tilting her head back. Better – but it gave her a turkey's neck, the skin no longer able to snap back to its original form. She must remember to do those exercises where you smiled like you had no teeth and nodded your head up and down.

Lucie sighed and gave up. It was a far cry from her past routine of getting ready for a night in the city with Nina, giddy with excitement at the thought of an evening spent huddled at the bar, laughing and eating tapas. This felt more like a chore. Before, Lucie might have booked a blow-dry, hurled a frozen pizza in the oven like a frisbee for the kids, burning it while attempting to master a smoky eye. Then rushing out of the door without a backwards glance as soon as she saw Hamish pull up outside.

This evening, she'd showered, half-heartedly dried her hair – perhaps this is what they meant by the "undone" look – and thrown some make-up at her face. Her fail-safe jeans had failed her at the last minute. Lying back on the bed to close them, she did a reverse limbo to stand up.

Watching the zip come slowly undone again could hardly be considered a success. Unless she wanted to spend the evening trying to tuck the excess flesh back into the now restricting waistband and have her bullet-proof knickers on show, she'd better wear something else. In the end, she'd settled on black trousers and a blouse, which made her feel like she was going for a job interview.

Catching a glimpse of herself in the mirror now behind the bar, Lucie felt as uncomfortable in her choice of clothes as she did in herself.

"It'll catch up on you someday," her mother, Tess, used to warn. "The old spare tyre. It's a middle-aged thing. It gets us all. I like to think of it as padding in case I have a fall. I'll bounce straight back up unharmed."

Tess Maguire had been thin her entire life, but sure enough, as the years came in, she'd gained a blockiness around her middle, exaggerating her twig-like arms and legs. Lucie used to giggle, confident that the spare tyre of belly fat her mother used as protection would never catch up with her. Lucie had never had to worry much about her weight, not until lately. Now, she felt as if her flesh moved without her moving. And sure enough, there it was – an "in case of emergency" circle of flesh, exactly like her mother.

"You look great, Nina." Lucie smiled at her tiny Filipino friend approvingly.

Nina still looked twenty-five, her clear, unlined skin and minuscule frame belying the fact that she was beyond her mid-forties. Dressed in jeans and a fitted T-shirt that on Lucie would have emphasised every lump and bump.

"Look at them." Lucie gestured behind at the table of girls in their twenties. "I'd say we're old enough to be their mothers."

Nina glanced back and shrugged. "Maybe, but we're not their mothers. Won't be long before they have hair sprouting from their faces, too – varicose veins, saggy knees, flat arses, the lot! Anyway, who'd want to be that age again?"

"Me. I would." Lucie raised her hand and laughed.

"Stop." Nina smacked her arm playfully. "We're not quite at the age where we sneeze and fart at the same time. Or worse still, the ones who fart and don't even acknowledge that they've let one slip! Do you think they can't hear it, or is it that they just don't give a shit?" Nina laughed.

"I think they don't give a shit," Lucie giggled. "Remember when we worked at the hospital. They'd be farting away as they told you all about their grandchildren, not a care in the world. God, wouldn't that be great?"

Nina spat out her beer. "The farts?"

"No, not a care in the world," Lucie chuckled before turning serious. "I almost *did* cancel tonight."

Nina patted Lucie's hand again and smiled encouragingly. "But you're here now. Besides, if you'd cancelled, I would have come to your house and dragged you here by the hair on your chinny chin chin. Now, what's up? Spill."

It was almost two weeks since Lucie had had the awkward conversation with the principal about her children's future at the school before bumping into Doug at the beach café. After that morning, she'd gone home, plonked herself on the sofa and thought about the encounter. Telling a total stranger all of her woes had seemed like a good idea at the time, briefly releasing her from the immense pressure she'd been under. For a few hours, it had given her a lease of life, a sudden flurry of strength. So much so that she'd picked up the phone and made an appointment with the doctor.

"Hesitating can get you killed." She'd replayed Doug's words.

Of course, Lucie recognised he'd been reiterating his old diving motto, but nonetheless, it was true. What if her symptoms were more than just stress and the change of life? At times, the pain she experienced in her abdomen was so intense that it was difficult to breathe – that couldn't be normal – as well as feeling totally emotionally out of sync. Lucie knew only too well, as a nurse, that ignoring the problem for much longer would only make things worse.

"I've an appointment next week with Professor Stone." Lucie was turning a beer mat over in her hand as she spoke.

"Why?" Nina frowned.

"My doctor referred me. I've been having some . . . pain. It's nothing." She took a sip of her drink, shrugging it off.

"What sort of pain?"

Nina was the one person Lucie should have been talking to about these things but for some reason hadn't. She felt stupid now. Once the appointment had been made, Lucie briefly felt relieved before starting to think the worst again. Maybe the parallels between Doug's wife, Rose, and her might transpire to be more than freckles and red hair.

"Well, I was trying to pretend it wasn't happening," she sighed.

"Jesus, Lu. We all know how that ends."

It was something they both remembered well from their nursing days – people who came in with illnesses having neglected them for months before doing anything about it. Lucie and Nina had often quipped about it in those early days of invincibility, acknowledging that *they'd* never be so ignorant as to dismiss an obvious problem.

"Remember Grapefruit Man?" Nina raised her eyebrows, referencing the case they'd encountered in theatre years before – a man in his early thirties who'd allowed a lump develop for close to fifteen years.

By the time he'd decided to do anything, the growth had been almost the size of a grapefruit. Grapefruit Man became the butt of many of their jokes. Thankfully, the grapefruit-shaped appendage resting on his shoulder like a second head developing from his neck had been nothing more than a pus-filled cyst. They'd watched aghast as the surgeon drained it, both silently questioning how anyone could be so negligent – playing Russian roulette with something so easy to solve.

Staring at the pile of what looked like a generous helping of mashed potato on the surgical tray, Nina had whispered to Lucie, "You want a steak with that?"

They'd exploded in laughter, thankfully concealed beneath their surgical masks.

"It all worked out for Grapefruit Man in the end, though, didn't it?" Lucie smirked. "I wonder where he is now. Must have been a massive weight off his shoulders," she giggled before turning serious.

Of course, there had been plenty of other not-so-fortuitous cases over the years – inoperable tumours left to fester until it was too late. Bodies so riddled with cancer that it was a wonder they didn't evaporate to dust as soon as they were opened. It was a hard lesson – a mistake the friends had promised never to make, not when early intervention was so successful.

"Ah, I just thought it was menopausal stuff. You know. Night sweats, feeling anxious, piling on a load of weight, niggles, bleeding . . ." Lucie went on to explain.

"What sort of bleeding?"

Lucie bit the corner of her lip before answering, keeping her eyes on the bar. "Irregular, but I thought normal. Well, at first I thought it was. I mean, we all know what stage I'm at. You're at it, too. And they say that, don't they? That your periods get irregular before they disappear and—"

"What sort of bleeding?" Nina persisted, forcing Lucie to look up.

"Constant. Almost constant. Oh, shit, Nina," she exhaled suddenly, dropping the breezy act. "I'm terrified. I thought I could hack it. Not only that, but I'm also sporting this bloody thing." Lucie reached down and wobbled her stomach up and down. "Maybe it *is* a grapefruit. A mouldy old one. Anyway, I've made an appointment and—"

"Jesus, Lucie." Nina was shaking her head, looking at Lucie's stomach, which indeed looked far fuller than it usually did. "How long?"

"A while. A few months . . ."

Nina frowned. "How long, Lucie?"

"Maybe six months." Lucie looked down again.

"What did the doctor say?"

Lucie was shaking her head like she had a twitch. "He said it could be nothing. Could be fibroids. But it could also be, you know, something more."

"When did you go to the doctor?"

"Early last week."

"And you got an appointment with Stone for next week?"

Lucie knew what Nina was implying. It was virtually impossible to get an appointment with Professor Stone, not unheard of to wait months unless it was considered a high priority.

"Well, he just thought it was better to rule anything out."

"Yes. I mean, absolutely, yes, of course," Nina nodded encouragingly before asking the question they'd always been taught to consider carefully at the hospital. "What does your gut say?"

Lucie patted her stomach again. "Well, I'm not pregnant, that's for sure. That would be truly immaculate."

Nina waited for more.

"My gut says something's not right." Her eyes welled.

There, she'd said it – faced it. That wasn't so bad.

"You must be feeling awful, Lu. Six months? For fuck's sake. But you have been under a lot of pressure, with everything else going on. Have you told Hamish?"

Lucie swallowed her tears and rolled her eyes. "No. Things aren't exactly great there, either."

"Oh, Lucie. I'm sorry you're going through all this. It's one thing after another, isn't it?"

Lucie nodded, looking back down again. "Sure is. Christ, Nina, I feel like I'm in a cycle of doom."

"Look, it's probably nothing," Nina reassured. "And if it is, it can be fixed, right? You may need to have a—"

"Don't say it, Nina! I can't even think about it. With everything else going on. How would I manage?"

Of course, the doctor had mentioned it straightaway – the possibility of a hysterectomy. At her age, with these kinds of problems, it was something to consider. It just seemed like one more thing to add to her list of dread.

"It may not come to that and besides, nowadays, it's better. It's not *as* big a deal as it used to be. And you're not working, so it might be a good time. I'd help, and Hamish will just have to chip in."

"Hmm." Lucie doubted that.

Ever since meeting John Downey and yet another fight erupting, relations with Hamish had become even more strained. In fact, they were barely able to look in each other's direction without passing a snide comment. It had all started, Lucie supposed, after the burglary and when Lucie was dismissed from work.

Perhaps she'd try talking to Hamish again this weekend about everything, or maybe she should wait until she saw Professor Stone next week. There was a strong possibility that none of their other problems would even matter if Lucie received terrible news.

"I suppose anything would be better than this pain. It's bad, Nina. I know I'm not one to complain normally . . ."

"Well, then this is a good thing, if you think about it," Nina smiled. "Hey, and remember, every cloud has a silver lining. You said you wanted to lose some weight. I mean, how much does a womb weigh nowadays? And a grand big Irish one at that! That's gotta be at least two and a half kilos, straight off." She clicked her fingers. "Better still, you'll get loads of lovely new artificial hormones. You won't be able to keep your hands off Hamish. You'll be like a horny old lady, swinging from the rafters."

Lucie laughed at her friend and her hilarious way of looking at things. Losing weight would be nice, but she doubted an influx of hormones would fix the other problems they were having – their lack of bedroom athletics being the least of them.

"It's going to be okay. You did the right thing making an appointment," Nina assured. "And remember what we discussed before. Why not do that back-to-nursing course next year? They're crying out for nurses like you and the kids are older now. I'd love to have you back at the hospital. We could run riot, be nasty to all the young nurses. We'd have a ball!"

Lucie nodded. It was something she'd been considering.

Now, more than ever, she needed to get back to work. "We'll see."

There was so much more Lucie wanted to tell her friend, so much she hadn't. Telling Nina everything, as she once had, had ceased over the years – the reality of some of Lucie's choices too challenging to admit. Instead, she told Nina all about the lonely old man she'd met with the deceased Irish wife and how it had made Lucie think she'd encountered him for a reason.

"It was weird. I haven't had a connection with someone like that in so long. A lot of what he said made sense and before you say it, it was nothing like *that* – he was just a sweet old man. Easy to talk to."

"Yeah, but you always find the ones who aren't easy to talk to! They gravitate towards you. Talking of which, that reminds me. There's something I meant to tell you . . ."

Lucie narrowed her eyes.

"It's nothing bad. Well, I wouldn't have said anything, only you'll be in the hospital next week and you probably won't, but just in case you *did* bump into him, forewarned is forearmed . . ." Nina babbled.

"Spit it out, Nina."

"Max is back."

Chapter ten

Getting out of the taxi, Lucie thanked the driver and watched him drive off. Standing alone in the empty street, she looked up at her home and exhaled raggedly. Sometimes it was still hard to believe that she lived in a house like this with its sloping driveway, veranda all the way round, swimming pool, glass balcony off her bedroom from where she could glimpse the bay. Beautiful as it was, part of Lucie just wanted to turn and head off up the street after the taxi.

The house stood in total darkness, aside from a single light glowing next to the double front door to guide her. After letting herself in, Lucie closed the door gently behind her and exhaled raggedly once again. She'd tried really hard to enjoy herself earlier. But hearing Max's name, Lucie had felt her stomach lurch, immediately reaching for the bar to steady herself.

"Really?" She'd tried to act cool, picking up her phone and flicking at the screen as if the name wasn't reverberating in her ears.

"Yeah. It was good to see him. It's been, what . . . ?"

"Fourteen years," Lucie answered fast, her voice too even. She coughed to try to hide it.

"Wow. It *has* been a long time. Do you think Max will get in touch with Hamish?"

"Doubt it."

"Suppose. I just thought, well, you know. Blood is thicker than water and all that."

"They're only cousins. Anyway, wine is thicker." Lucie tried to laugh. It sounded forced.

"I'm sorry, I didn't mean to . . ."

Lucie had waved her hand and grimaced. "Will you stop! You're right, water under the bridge."

After that, the evening had fallen flat, despite Nina trying to carry on as usual. If nothing else, it confirmed one thing. Max made four, quashing Lucie's theory that bad things occurred in threes. First, the burglary, then being fired, followed by the suspicion that she was in fact dying and now this.

Lucie had hung on for as long as possible before calling it a night, not wanting to insult Nina. But in the end, no matter what she drank, it seemed to have had the opposite effect – each drink sobering her further, making her feel even more detached. Even sitting forwards on the bar stool so her feet could touch the ground – which might anchor her, cease the spinning sensation – hadn't helped. It had been happening a lot lately, the feeling that everything was moving around her and that if she were to give in to it, she'd tumble over.

Reaching down now and removing her shoes, she allowed her feet to flatten and absorb the coolness from the white marble tiles. She walked into the living room and shivered when her eyes settled on the uniform obscured shadows on the wall. To an outsider, it might look as though the place had been stripped back in preparation for a fresh coat of paint – the antique rugs rolled up, vases removed, paintings taken from the walls to be stored away. Even the television was gone. The television?! Who the hell in this day and age stole a TV? It was plain cruel. The rest she could get her head around, but the television? What value did that hold, really? It hadn't even been a particularly good one.

She'd almost become used to seeing the room this way – devoid – so different from the homely space it had been before the burglary. Her favourite place in the house, in fact, now barren and bereft. It had been *her* room – in many ways *her* sanctuary. The kids rarely came in for fear of disrupting the calm she'd created and being murdered in doing so. It was what Lucie's mother would have called a "good room" – reserved for Christmas, entertaining and "gloating", Tess might have added. Back in Ireland, they'd never had a "good room" growing up – every inch of each room had been utilised to its full potential in their little terraced house.

If she closed her eyes for long enough, Lucie could still envisage the stolen paintings within the slightly grubby-looking rectangular shadows. It had been three months already – she really should have painted over them by now. But there was something about their presence that grounded her, reminding her of what once had been. Never, not for one moment, could she ever have imagined that she, Lucie Maguire, hailing all the way from Knockmore, Ireland, would become an art enthusiast. She could imagine her older brother, Sammy, if he were still alive, never allowing her to live that one down.

"You, who covered your room in posters of Duran Duran and topless fellas holding babies, an art lover! Notions!" he would have said, especially where the more modern pieces were concerned.

"Pass me a pot of Dulux and a canvas, and I could knock one of those up in the garage. Art?! Would you go on outta that!"

"Investments, dear brother," she would have told him in her best connoisseur accent.

Sammy would have choked if she'd divulged how much they'd paid for some of them.

"Investments, my hole."

Turns out, Sammy would have been right. What bloody use were investments when they were gone? Deep down, Lucie knew it was all a load of codswallop, really. Growing up, the closest thing they'd had to art in their house had been the charity calendar in their kitchen filled with Irish landscapes, or her mother's miniature figurine collection of creepy ladies holding umbrellas and old men whittling wood.

It was a far cry from Hamish's upbringing. His mother, Vera, owned what had become a successful gallery in Sydney and was an avid antique collector. Of course, it hadn't always been a successful gallery. Apparently, being the son of a single-mother art dealer hadn't been all it was cracked up to be.

"My childhood was smoke and mirrors," he'd uncharacteristically admitted once. "Vera was the typical 'fur coat and no knickers'. Ming vases and an empty fridge. If it hadn't been for Auntie May . . . let's just say, I may have eaten one of those paintings."

"Notions!" Lucie had echoed Sammy's fictitious insult when Hamish told her about it, immediately picturing

Vera as Dame Edna, the Australian comedian with purple hair and winged glasses similar to his mother's.

She hadn't been far wrong, either. Lucie could only imagine what her own family might have thought of Vera, her mother-in-law, let alone what they might have said about Hamish. She could almost imagine them rolling around laughing if she'd ever had the chance to tell them she was after marrying an entrepreneur.

"An *entrepreneur*? Aren't they just wasters who can't find themselves a decent job, so they go and make one up? Society sponges," her father, Paddy, would have told her. He'd never had much time for people doing anything he couldn't fully comprehend.

"Would that be like an inventor?" Tess might have asked. "Do you know what I've always thought would sell really well? Like, a bag that you didn't have to carry around with you. One that frees up your hands."

"Like a backpack?" Sammy would have teased as they all clutched their stomachs in hysterics.

Lucie plonked herself on the sofa and focused on the blank spaces on the wall. Here she was again, dreaming up imaginary conversations while staring at her now imaginary art collection. Thank goodness her family weren't around for it all. She'd never have lived it down.

It was all Vera's fault, really. It was she who'd educated Lucie on the Australian greats as soon as Lucie had trained herself not to giggle at Vera's crazy glasses. But behind those glasses, Vera had an eye for picking out obscure pieces, which in time would become sought after. It was the reason Vera now lived in the lap of luxury, never having given up on her dream, despite her son's apparent suffering as a child. Lucie couldn't decide if it was admirable or plain selfish.

Lucie had never been able to put her finger on the draw she felt towards the paintings, the inexplicable way they made her feel. At first, the price tags these sometimes enigmatic pieces carried had made her giggle nervously, but she'd soon got to grips with the appreciating value – not that she'd ever have sold them. It was silly, of course it was. Who the hell did she think she was? They were just paintings – and it was still a hobby of which she was somewhat embarrassed. It certainly hadn't been to be boastful or flashy. No one, except Hamish, knew about her interest in art, her secret passion.

Hamish had loved Lucie's enthusiasm so much, the common thread connecting his mother and his wife, that soon they'd been ploughing money into paintings. Mind you, at the time they'd *had* the money. Whatever entrepreneurial thingy Hamish was working on at the time had paid off, bringing about one of those periods where everything was wonderful – where they'd do everything they'd been starved of in the previous months of waiting for money to come in.

Lucie smiled wistfully. She supposed, at first, it had been an appealing way of life. When the money came, it came big. But slowly, Lucie began to understand that as the highs got higher, so, too, did the risk of plummeting, when it all went wrong. Soon, Hamish investing in start-ups that mostly failed to start became a way of life she came to despise. She'd happily have given it all up . . . aside from those darned paintings.

Lucie could have sat staring at them for hours. Losing them, above everything else that had been stolen – coming home that evening after collecting Declan from Granny Vera to discover that everything she'd adored had been taken – was harrowing. She could still remember staring with confusion at the disarray in the hallway, thinking that a bomb must have gone off. Then it had torn her in two, walking into the living room to see the empty spaces on the wall. She'd never felt so angry in her entire life. At that moment, everything had turned red and all she could think was why, why, why . . . why me? In hindsight, was it any wonder that she'd reacted the way she had the next day when she'd witnessed Jack Garth spitting in Declan's face? Someone had figuratively spat in hers. How it stung.

"We'll replace everything," Hamish had promised. "Your jewellery, everything. Are you sure they got everything? Maybe you should check again. It might have fallen down the back of the chest of drawers . . ."

Lucie had shaken her head woodenly, staring at the ground, her arms limp by her side. "I checked. It's all gone. Everything. Mam's bracelet – everything."

"I didn't hear you come in."

Lucie looked up to see Hamish standing in the doorway. His eyes drifted towards the empty spaces on the wall and then back to her.

"I just got back." She leaned back from where she'd been resting her elbows on her knees, cupping her face.

"Good night?" He sat opposite her and looked at his watch. "You're early."

He was still wearing his work trousers, a white shirt open to his chest, the tie probably removed in the car on the way home amid some high-energy phone conversation. Lately, he looked tired – a grey tinge dulling his features. In all of their years together, Lucie had rarely seen her husband look tired. Not Hamish, with his boundless energy, always ensuring he got eight hours' sleep.

Hamish took marvellous care of himself – forever at the gym, out running, dangling from the pull-up bar he'd installed in the garden, playing golf, eating well, drinking litre after litre of water. He'd always been the same – image was everything. It was so far from Lucie's way that she hadn't particularly warmed to Hamish when she first met him, regardless of his pristine looks.

"Flashy git," she'd whispered to her companion following their first encounter. "He's all over himself like a rash! State of him. Someone give me an antihistamine, quick. He's going to cause a breakout of smarmy dick!"

Perhaps she should have paid closer attention to her first impression. Hamish was the first man Lucie had ever encountered who used moisturiser – and not just any moisturiser, the proper stuff. Lucie often dipped into it when she ran out of her own. When they were first married, he'd revealed unashamedly that he went for regular manicures and had his eyebrows threaded. By then, it had been too late. *Threaded*? Lucie still plucked her eyebrows in the car with a tweezer she'd had for so long, she was sure it was the one she'd swiped from her mother's minuscule make-up bag decades before.

"It was okay," Lucie yawned now. "Nina was working all day, called it a night early," she lied.

"Not like her."

"No. I suppose not. Then again, none of us is getting any younger. Are we?"

Hamish didn't answer.

Lucie was wondering if she should tell him about her appointment with the doctor, when suddenly he put his hands to his face and exhaled loudly.

"We need to talk." He finally looked up.

The words carried an unfamiliar tone – uncertainty. Hamish rarely doubted himself. It was actually the thing about him that changed her initial opinion. Back then, she'd found it reassuring.

"Okay," Lucie answered unsurely.

His face was stern but still handsome. Hamish had got better-looking with age, if that was possible, but wasn't that always the way it was – the men improved, the women lost elasticity.

"What's up?" she prompted.

"I've been offered a sort of consultancy role . . ."

"Hamish, that's fantastic!" Lucie jumped in straightaway. "That's exactly what we need. Stability. You in a stable job. And I spoke to Nina – I'm thinking of doing the back-to-nursing course. With both of us back in employment—"

"Hold up, Lucie." He put his hands up, frowned. "This is just for a couple of months. I told you, this tech start-up I'm working on is the real deal. That's what I'll be doing as soon as the money I'm waiting on comes through." He laughed humourlessly. "You know I'd never make enough going back into a nine-to-five. This is the life you wanted, Lucie. It's not easy to maintain it for you."

"For me?" Her head jerked back defensively.

"Yeah. The house, the cars, the school." He gestured around the room.

"I never asked for any of *this*." She mimicked his action. "I told you, where I was brought up, we never—"

Hamish stood abruptly, rolled his eyes and made for the door. "Oh, Jesus, spare me, will you? For once, spare me the talk about Knock-bloody-more and how fucking perfect it was."

"It *was* perfect," she scowled. "Simple. None of these complications. The ups and downs." She undulated her hand.

"Yeah." He walked back towards her. "Except you're always happy with the ups, aren't you? As soon as the ups come, you're perfectly happy with a new car, buying a new painting . . . Oh, and remember when you took off to Ireland on a whim that time to see your niece? And if that wasn't enough, you went and bought her flights to come here when we couldn't bloody afford it. Some flashy birthday present that was!"

Here we go again. Hamish would never stop mentioning how Lucie had dropped everything to go and see her niece, Ann, in Ireland, eighteen months ago. They'd lost touch for years before that. Ann had reconnected unexpectedly with Lucie after Ann's marriage had crumbled.

"That's not fair, Hamish. I hadn't been home in years. Ann needed me that time. I had to go to Ireland. She's family."

"Yeah, and where is she now? She never bothered to come here, did she? Maybe we should ask her for a refund on those flights." He shrugged exaggeratedly.

Lucie ran her fingers through her hair and gritted her teeth. "Please, Hamish. Let's not make this about something else. Lately, things have been such a strain. So the burglary couldn't be helped. Me losing my job – my fault." She put her hand on her heart. "But we *can* control what happens from now on. What we need is a change, to face things head-on. I told you what happened in the supermarket the other day . . ."

Lucie's bank card had been declined again.

"Temporary glitch," he interjected. "It's what happens sometimes when you work for yourself like I do. Get real, will you? Or *you* go get a job if you're so concerned."

Lucie closed her eyes for a moment. "I intend to. It's just lately, I haven't been feeling great. I've had—"

"Yeah, you're moping." He didn't let her finish. "Feeling sorry for yourself."

"That's not it, I . . ." What was the point? "We could sell the house," Lucie tried again. "Move. Start over. You could get a job at the bank again. Everything was fine then. Remember? Or maybe we could make a go of it in Ireland. Things are good again there. The economy is flying. It might be a—"

"A step back," Hamish hissed. "That's what it would be. And you think the kids would cope moving to a country where we know no one, where we're outsiders?"

"I did it." She stood. "I moved here. I knew no one. All this . . ." She held her hands up. "This doesn't feel like what I signed up for. This isn't who—"

Hamish walked towards the doorway again then stopped. "What?" He smiled cruelly. "You know what I always wanted to know? If Ireland was so bloody wonderful, why did you stay here all these years? Why didn't you go home? What kept you here? And if this . . ." He thumped his chest. "If this isn't what you signed up for, then maybe you should have signed up elsewhere. To some great big safe, boring person. Does anyone spring to mind, *Lucie*?" He spat her name.

Lucie sat back down and stared ahead. Tonight, she didn't have it in her.

"We'll finish this conversation when you've calmed down," she suggested.

"Oh, I'm calm."

He wasn't.

"You think it's not normal to go through a rough patch? That's all this is. Maybe it's you who needs to take a long look in the mirror and answer some of those questions, Lucie." He turned and stalked away.

Lucie grabbed a cushion from the sofa and hugged it tightly, curling herself around it as she lay back, thinking of his words. No matter how hard Lucie tried, she couldn't answer all of his questions. Except the answer that deep down she'd always known – the one that still hurt the most.

Chapter eleven

"I'm sorry about last night." Hamish was sitting up in bed, looking sheepish.

Lucie had eventually fallen asleep on the sofa, trying to order her thoughts. Broken sleep was something she'd become accustomed to lately, often waking every hour on the hour, like a news bulletin. The early morning sun had started to edge across the living room floor when she'd forced herself up and made her way upstairs to their bedroom.

"The kids will be up soon." She sat on the edge of the bed, put her head back and exhaled.

Hamish reached out and put his hand on hers. She didn't stop him.

"It *will* be okay. Trust me, this is just a phase – a lull. We'll be riding high again in a few months."

Lucie nodded, far too exhausted to argue – and desperately wanting to believe him. She turned her head towards him and swallowed.

"Give me a timeframe," she pleaded. "If everything

isn't okay by then, then swear you'll listen to me – consider some of the changes I mentioned."

"Three months. But it won't come to that."

It was enough, for now.

Afterwards, they'd had a pleasant lazy Saturday, extending into the evening. Hamish seemed present, instead of the usual distracted checking of his phone every two minutes and staring ahead as if in a trance. Aside from one phone call where he'd mouthed, "Work," rolling his eyes and rushing into the house, it had been a good day. When he'd returned, he'd been full of energy and Lucie hoped it was because he'd received some positive news. She'd decided not to ask – leaving him to play basketball with Declan and lovingly tease Bella. It had felt normal.

The next morning, Lucie offered to take the children to Sunday sports at Woodfield. Despite hating being at the school, she decided if Hamish was willing to make an effort, then so should she.

Sitting in the car park, safely inside the car, Lucie pulled the rear-view mirror towards her. She put her finger under her left eyebrow and hoisted it up. Taking her finger away, Lucie watched the skin fall slowly back over her eyelid. That eye, in particular, had started to crease lately in such a way that even if she opened her eyes wide, it didn't seem to iron itself out. It made one side of her face appear older. Perhaps it was the side she slept on – firmly facing away from Hamish.

"Do you ever feel really old, like *really* old?" Lucie had asked Nina on Friday night, unable to stop herself from gazing at the girls behind them.

"What is this *obsession* with age? It is what it is," Nina had laughed.

"I know. It never bothered me before, but everything is starting to droop."

"And it'll keep drooping," Nina had laughed again.

Interrupted by a squeal of giggles from the girls, Lucie glanced back again and smiled before admonishing herself.

"Christ, look at me. I'm one of those old ladies who smile like an eejit at young people," she'd paused. "I was fun, Nina, wasn't I?"

"You were." This time Nina didn't laugh, registering the look of doubt on Lucie's face. "You were the most fun of all. Everyone said it."

"I miss her," Lucie had said wistfully.

Nina had smiled sadly. "You'll come back. I know you will."

Lucie lifted the other eyelid. That one was better. Was she obsessed with ageing? Perhaps it was the fear of being ill that was driving it. Mind you, even without that worry, all the other little telltale signs of being "over the hill" were present – singing the wrong lyrics to songs in the car while the children laughed. Not having a clue what band they were talking about, or what slang to use. Up until recently, Lucie had started saying that everything was "sick". She'd heard the kids at the school use the term. As a nurse, she'd found it most confusing at first until she got to grips with the fact that it actually meant "cool". Then Bella had asked her stop, telling her she sounded like a granny. Then, to add insult to injury, this morning in the car, Bella had reached over and yanked a hair from Lucie's chin as she drove them to school.

"Jesus!" Lucie's hand had shot to her face.

"Holy crap. Look at that!" Bella held the curled hair

up to the light. "That's a big one, Mum. That could have come from your—"

"Yes, thank you, Bella." Lucie had stopped her in time.

Lucie looked down to see that the blasted hair had landed in the leather pouch near the gearstick. Bella was right. It did look like it could have come from elsewhere. How on earth had Lucie missed that?

Picking it up, she held it up, marvelling at the length, before opening the window and flicking it away. Lucie rubbed at the spot from where the curly white hair had been on her chin, making sure it hadn't come from a party with other friends. It felt too familiar.

"Pluck my eyebrows for me, will you, love?" her mother used to ask. "I can't bloody see anything any more."

"Only if I can do your chin, too," Lucie had joked.

"You're some rip, Lucie Maguire! I tell you, I hope you end up with a daughter as honest as you. Someday you'll be past it, like me!"

"I won't, Mam. I'll be forever young."

The memory made Lucie smile for a moment before it faded. How the worm had turned. If Lucie had her time over, she'd be telling Mam how beautiful she was instead of teasing her, highlighting the insecurities her mother must have felt about growing older. Maybe Lucie should have told her mam that her hair was fabulous that day she'd come home after having cut it short. Instead, Lucie had said that she looked like she was wearing a mushroom made out of candyfloss. But then, was that not what every daughter did? Not realising that one day, out of nowhere, the hairs would sprout from their own chin, no matter how much you plucked them away. Or that they, too, might succumb to "old lady" manageable hair.

"I sincerely hope you *will* be young forever, Lucie – in mind, at least. The other bits, there's feck all you can do about it."

Mam had been right about that. Tess Maguire *had* stayed forever young. Her body had aged, but her mind remained as fresh as it had always been – ever the one to dance at parties, giggle along at their jokes, take the relentless slagging from Lucie and Sammy, give back where she could. Tess Maguire had loved her life – her family – simple as it had been.

Lucie often wondered what Mam would make of Bella and Declan. Would she have doted on them, as she'd doted on her other granddaughter, Ann? Of course she would. And how Bella and Declan would have adored the family in Ireland that they'd never had the chance to meet. Sometimes, Lucie felt as if her children had missed out dreadfully, not knowing the people who'd made Lucie the person she was. There was only her niece, Ann, now as a point of reference and she was so very far away, back in Ireland.

That said, getting to know Ann again, after being separated for so long, had been fantastic. At first, Lucie had thrived while supporting Ann, who'd gone through a painful divorce and ended up back at their childhood home in Knockmore. But recently, a distance greater than the oceans that divided them had developed again. Was Lucie to blame? Probably. Lucie didn't want to trouble Ann with her own problems. She'd tried to convince herself that that was it, anyway.

In truth, Ann's presence back in her life had made Lucie pine once again for all the other Maguires. And then every time they spoke, Ann kept asking Lucie what was wrong. Not knowing how to answer, it had become more comfortable to avoid Ann's calls. Also, there were those stupid flights Hamish kept harping on about. Buying Ann return flights for her thirtieth birthday, so she could come and visit them in Australia, and then putting up every excuse in the book as to why it wasn't a good time, had generated an awkwardness. Lucie didn't want Ann seeing her life as it currently was: a disaster. Besides, she was terrified that in person, Ann might begin to want answers to some of the questions that Lucie had worked hard at to avoid – especially one.

"After Mam died, why didn't you come back for me?" Ann had asked when Lucie first returned to Ireland to find her niece.

"I never would have been allowed to take you to Australia. You were still a minor. I did come back for your mam's funeral, but you were gone by then. It was such a mess."

It wasn't entirely true.

The real story would undoubtedly shatter the illusion of Lucie as the caring aunt. Ha! what a joke. The loving aunt who'd left her seventeen-year-old niece in Ireland, with no other family, to fend for herself? After they'd reconnected, Lucie had hypocritically flung upbeat advice at Ann, who'd been at an all-time low following her separation. Ann had listened, finding strength in her aunt's sanctimonious words to plough through her troubles and come out the other side. Almost as soon as she had, the baton of hardship had shifted to Lucie, making Lucie edge away.

"Lucie?"

Lucie jolted at the knock on the half-open car window.

"What are you doing hiding away in there?"

It was Stacy from the school office.

"Sorry, Stacy. I was a million miles away. How are you?" Lucie opened the car door and climbed out.

"I'm fine, love. I pulled the short straw to make tea and coffee this morning for the parents."

"I was wondering why you'd be here on a Sunday. Sorry," Lucie grimaced.

It was usually Lucie who volunteered to serve refreshments.

"Fancy giving me a hand?"

Lucie looked over at where the other parents were watching the games and chatting on the grass – the usual group of mothers present like a middle-aged girl gang.

"Mind if I don't?"

"Ah, come on, girl. You're still a parent here. You can't hide away forever. And I wanted to talk to you about something." Stacy shifted awkwardly from foot to foot.

"What about?"

Stacy's smile didn't quite reach her eyes.

"Well, maybe it's not my place, but I wanted to give you the heads-up. Believe me, there are more of this kind of letter than you might imagine, so don't go thinking you're the only one, but—"

"Stacy?"

"I'm sorry, love, there's no easy way to say it. I just didn't want you getting the letter, knowing that it had technically come from me. Well, not really, I mean it's Accounts that issue it—"

"Oh, God." Lucie's hand flew to her mouth. "I totally forgot."

"It happens." Stacy looked relieved. "As soon as the fees are two months in arrears—"

"What?" Lucie dropped her hand. She could feel her face burning hot, her limbs hollowing. "I thought you were talking about the money for the school trip. What do you mean the fees are in arrears?"

"You didn't know? There would have been an email sent first."

"No." Lucie shook her head. "They're definitely paid. I mean, they have to be. I pay them right after I get paid by the school each month and I'm still being paid by the school . . ."

"Oh." Stacy didn't look convinced. "Maybe there's been a mistake. Do you want me to check it for you again?"

Lucie bit her lip, trying to think, before the thought hit her. Surely not?

"Stacy, can I ask a favour? Could you take the kids for a few hours? There's something I need to do."

"Of course." Stacy could see the look of panic on Lucie's face. "You go. I'll drop them back later." She inched away, knowing she'd gone and put her foot in it.

Lucie climbed back in the car, a sudden heat passing over her entire body. What was going on? First, their joint account card had been declined at the supermarket, now this? Reaching for her phone, she opened the bank icon and watched it spin. Entering her passcode, she prayed that there was some mistake. When the amount flashed up, she gawked at it. Running down through the recent transactions, she could see various amounts here and there transferred to Hamish's account. What the hell?

At that moment, Lucie looked up to see Priscilla Trott, trotting towards her. With a shaking hand, she put the keys into the ignition as Priscilla approached. This was the last person she needed right now. Priscilla was Brent's wife. Their children also attended Woodfield but were in different years. Hamish and Brent had first met while working at the bank years before. Brent was still there and now looked after all of Hamish's business accounts.

"Shit," Lucie muttered, pretending she hadn't seen her and trying to start the engine.

"Lucie. Cooee, Lucie."

Lucie took a deep breath and stuck her head out of the window.

"Hi, Priscilla, how are you?"

"Great, just great. How's that dishy husband of yours?"

Priscilla had always had a thing for Hamish, never leaving him alone whenever they were out together socially, perpetually hanging off him, rubbing her hands over his chest.

"Great, just great," Lucie mimicked. She, too, couldn't wait to get her hands on Hamish, but in a very different way.

"Listen, Brent has been trying to contact Hamish. For quite a while now, apparently," she tutted. "I'm not sure what about. You know how tight-lipped they are about business. I said if I saw you, I'd ask you to get Hamish to call."

Lucie could feel the oxygen leaving her lungs.

"Any idea at all what it's about, so I can tell him?" she managed.

"Afraid not. Well, Brent did mention something about the insurance company, the one that's owned by the bank. That ring a bell?" Priscilla waited for an answer and then held up her hands. "Oh, of course. Oh, Lucie, I haven't seen you since the house was burgled. I heard there was a spate of burglaries up around your way. They always go for the nice houses, don't they? I said to Brent, that's one good thing about living further back, in the cheap seats." She laughed at her own bitterly edged joke.

Lucie eased a little. "It must be that. The insurance

company have been dragging their feet. Isn't it terrible? We pay all that money year in, year out and then they make you jump through hoops."

"Disgraceful. Anyway, why don't you come over next weekend for a drink. And by the way, I heard about all that other stuff at the school here and I just wanted to say that I'd have done the same," she whispered out of the corner of her mouth. "Not that I'd admit that aloud. Whatever were you thinking of, putting it on the group chat, though? You must be loving not having to work. I would."

"Yes, it's fab." Lucie plastered a fake smile on her face. "Mind you, I'm still always chasing my tail. Talking of which, I have to dash."

"Sure. Sure. You tell the handsome Hamish to call," Priscilla winked.

"Oh, I will. Take care now."

Lucie started the car and was just about to drive off, when a familiar pain shot across her stomach. She winced, trying to breathe through it. *Typical.* Then her face changed as she gritted her teeth.

Hamish had better hope that one of the pieces of news Lucie had been gifted that morning cancelled the other. If that insurance money was on its way, Hamish needed to replace what he'd obviously taken from her account. Which posed another question in itself: just how bad was everything?

Chapter twelve

Lucie seized the steering wheel, feeling a surge of anger shoot through her veins. Her stomach was now churning, the niggling feeling of what felt like contractions starting to build.

"Not now," she muttered.

She was furious with Hamish. What the hell was he playing at? She supposed she had only herself to blame. Recently, Lucie had checked out of life, become so wrapped up in losing her job and her health issues that she'd taken her eye off the ball.

Driving out of the gates of Woodfield and back onto the winding roads, she wasn't entirely sure if the agony she was experiencing was whatever was going on inside her, or if it was pure unadulterated fury at Hamish. Lucie stopped the car suddenly, pulling into the side of the road to calm herself.

Clutching her stomach, she felt something rip inside her, then a rush of nausea, followed by a pain so intense that she had to close her eyes and will herself to breathe.

What was happening to her? Tears smarted at the thought of what the doctor was going to reveal next week. Her symptoms were getting worse by the day. Was her time up?

She'd always been fearful that she, too, might be tarnished by whatever curse had taken all of her family well before their time. Perhaps Lucie would be the same, dying young, leaving the world behind before she was ready. The thought terrified her. Lucie wasn't prepared – she hadn't done all she was meant to yet. Most of all, she hadn't faced all she ought to – and maybe now she wouldn't have time. What sort of mayhem would Lucie leave behind? How had time suddenly caught up before she'd had time to tell the . . . She couldn't even say it.

It struck her then how we're told almost from the day we're born to tell the truth. Children must speak the truth, no matter what it is. Out of nowhere, the childhood memory flooded back.

"Was it you, Lucie? Was it you who ate the cookies?" Her mother had stared at her, trying to hide her smile.

"Nope."

Despite the crumbs around her mouth, the remnants still inside it, Lucie had attempted to lie. There'd been no further treats for Lucie that week while her mother strove to teach her right from wrong.

"I don't care what it is, all I ever want from you is the truth."

In the end, Lucie had come clean and she'd learned her lesson. Or, indeed, she'd learned what can and can't be hidden. How there are often little indicators pointing directly to the truth. Over time, we *mostly* learn that it's better to tell the truth. Or at least, we come to understand how to conceal it – to wipe away the crumbs before answering, to swallow the evidence.

Sitting here in the car, shaking, the reality of her life hit Lucie hard. She'd hidden so much over the years, only sharing one side of herself with the world. In this way, perhaps she was no different from Hamish. He, too, had been hiding things. But now, the truth was becoming as visible as the crumbs around his lying mouth.

Lucie took a deep breath and started the engine again, preparing for the confrontation. There was so much *more* they needed to deal with, but currently, the root of their immediate issues, the same problem that had thwarted their lives for the past few years, was money. Stupid money! Now there was a cold truth . . . Right then, it dawned on Lucie that their main problem wasn't *lack* of money, nor their financial struggles, but her husband's perpetual need for *more* money. But then, he'd always been the same. From the moment she'd met Hamish, he'd wanted more – a bigger life, always on a mission to prove himself.

At first, Lucie had concluded that it derived from what Hamish had considered a deprived childhood. She'd soon learned that that had been widely exaggerated, too. He'd always had a roof over his head and food on the table, despite his dramatic tales of childhood misfortune. One thing he *had* lacked was perhaps nurturing. Vera was an odd sort, never particularly motherly – not heartless, just unmaternal.

By the time Vera became successful, Hamish had already left home. Lucie often suspected that Hamish had felt hard done by about this as if he'd missed out on the monetary rewards. He'd suggested a few times that his mother should now provide him with what she'd failed to in his youth. As far as Lucie was concerned, it was Vera's money. She could give it to a cat sanctuary, if she so desired. And Lucie had to hand to her – she'd worked hard for it. In Hamish's case, the apple fell *far* from the tree. He was far too proud, with a misguided sense of privilege, to believe in old-fashioned graft. Hamish wanted to be handed everything on a plate.

Then again, perhaps Lucie was responsible, too. Becoming a mother had distracted her from the real world. As much as she'd adored working at the hospital, she'd been happy to give it up at the time, no longer wanting to pay the extortionate price of childcare. So, she'd given up her beloved career in favour of Hamish's pipe dreams of the suburban life: a big house, fancy cars, private schools.

Lucie had enjoyed working at Woodfield, but it had given her a hazy view of reality – listening to the stories of endless holidays and parties, making her believe for a while that *this* was normal life. In a way, Lucie supposed, she'd become caught up in it, too.

Then the bubble had burst. Holding that darned compass in her hand that day and pointing its spike at that child, Lucie had popped the fake balloon of her life. Hamish had blamed Lucie, tried to make her believe that it was *she* who'd destroyed everything at that moment. When all along it was Hamish who'd filled that balloon with so much hot air that it was only a matter of time before it popped. Now, it had.

Lucie had known almost as soon as Stacy said it who was responsible for those unpaid school fees. Like she'd told Stacy, she was still being paid by the school until the end of term. Technically, nothing had changed for her. It was Hamish who had them under pressure – *he* was the reason they were where they were. Perhaps where they'd always been.

Lucie gripped the steering wheel, watching her knuckles turn white as she pulled onto the short stretch of motorway that would take her to the turn-off for Double Bay. Blaming herself – that's what she'd been doing. Punishing herself for that stupid incident at school.

Lord knows she'd experienced far greater life-defining moments than saying she was going to shove a compass up a child's arse! Of course, she hadn't *meant* it. It was a figure of speech. Okay, not the best choice of words, but she'd darn well repeat it to protect her son. What did she care if there was a group of mothers at the school who hated her? That sort of nonsense would never have bothered her before.

No. There had been far more significant moments in Lucie's life. Moving to Australia in her early twenties, for one. Then there'd been those awful years – six years of hell. Losing her father had ripped Lucie apart with grief and hidden guilt for not having been there in Ireland with him. As if that hadn't been enough then her mother had left, dying peacefully in her sleep a year later.

After that, Lucie hadn't been sure she'd ever recover. And then – oh, God, the thought still caught her when she least expected – her brother, Sammy, had been killed in a car accident. In one way, she supposed it was the correct order of things: her father, then her mother, then her older brother. Except Sammy had only been thirty-four years old. Bit by bit, as each one of them had left, a part of Lucie had died with them.

Then came Felicity.

Yes, that had been the real moment that Lucie's life had splintered. Losing her best friend, her sister-in-law, her soul sister, that was when everything had changed – driving all the godawful decisions Lucie had made afterwards, leading her to where she was today.

Lucie's breathing grew ragged thinking of Felicity's

death and that time afterwards in her life. It was a place she'd promised never to revisit. And she hadn't, not until Ann had sought Lucie, who was living out in Australia. Had Lucie been hiding? Maybe – concealing herself far from the truth. Perhaps it was time to face it.

But first, Lucie needed to face Hamish, to stop allowing him to handle their lives like some sort of antiquated housewife. No. This was no lull as Hamish kept implying – this was something more.

Another pain shot across Lucie's stomach. At least she had the hospital appointment next week. Right now, she couldn't think about that. All she had to do was speak with Hamish. It was time to do things her way – talk it out, reach a solution, which is precisely what she would have done, had she not pressed the accelerator hard, eager to face at least one truth.

Chapter thirteen

Doug

It was one more thing that had changed since Rose died. Sunday mornings were now spent with his brother, Nick, and his wife, Irene. Irene liked to call the eclectic mix of food "drunch". The idea was to fill Doug with a combination of breakfast, lunch and dinner, in one sitting, making Doug feel like some sort of charity case.

His intake would be closely monitored by Irene, who'd nudge Nick to refill Doug's plate as soon as it was nearing empty. Afterwards, Doug wouldn't be able to move for the rest of the day, sustained by what could have lasted him a week. Perhaps that was the idea. Still and all, the weekly meeting was a chance for him to chat about Rose. He could almost picture her sitting opposite him, rolling her eyes at Irene's incessant chat.

"Won't you stay the day, Douglas?" Irene asked. "No point in going home just to sit there alone. Have a drink, relax. The grandkids are coming over later. I'm sure they'd love to see you."

His brother's wife was the only person who insisted

on calling him Douglas.

"I promised Rose I'd look after you. Jeez, I miss her. Like sisters, we were."

Doug nodded, spearing a sausage and popping it in his mouth so he didn't have to reply. They *hadn't* been like sisters. At first, Rose and Irene hadn't really got along, not in the way Irene had wanted, anyway. They couldn't have been more different.

Irene had expected a comrade-in-arms in her sister-in-law. One prepared to moan and tut about the two brothers, the trials of marriage, the challenges of motherhood. With no children of her own, it had been trying for Rose to partake. Mind you, she soon became the "cool" Irish aunt with the exciting diving career, doting on her nieces and nephews who adored her, never forgetting a birthday or an occasion.

Irene had appreciated that and over the years, the unlikely pair learned to respect the other for who they were. Rose with her red hair free, fresh-faced, dressed in some sort of tie-dye kaftan, sandals, a myriad of colourful beads around her neck. Irene: a rigidly set puff of hair, neat trousers and blouse, sensible shoes and thick glasses complete with a gold chain. Irene was never without a shock of bright pink lipstick, no matter the time of day – the type that would remain on whatever vessel she was drinking from long after it had been through the dishwasher.

"You don't like her, do you?" Doug had asked Rose years before when he first introduced her to Irene. They hadn't been together long then.

"Do you, *Douglas*?" she'd giggled, mimicking Irene's high-pitched Australian drawl.

"She's family," he'd shrugged, offended. Perhaps he'd imagined the same as Irene – the four of them sitting around, teasing each other in the way only family can.

She'd stopped smiling when she saw his face. "It's not her I don't like. I suppose she reminds me of my sister," she admitted.

"You have a sister? I thought it was just you." Doug was shocked. She'd never mentioned a sister before.

"Well, it *is* just me now. We fell out."

"You know if you ever wanted to go to Ireland, make amends . . . We could."

"Nah." She shook her head. "I left all that behind. She didn't agree with my life, my choices." A dark look passed over her, different from her usual demeanour. It made her seem so distant that Doug decided not to question her further.

"You're wrong." He'd taken her in his arms then. "It's not just you. It's us now."

After that, Sundays had always been spent the same. Rose and him, taking a drive up the coast, stopping at a little café, going for a walk before idling back home to sit on the veranda, chatting, laughing, debating their differences of opinion. That had been Doug's favourite part – watching Rose grow irate when he'd refused to agree with her, shaking her head in dismay, tutting loudly at what she called his Aussie chauvinism. How he'd adored teasing her, noticing her nose scrunch up in annoyance before he'd laugh and tell her he was set in his ways and there was nothing she could ever do to change it.

"Too darn strait-laced," she'd mutter. "And I thought by marrying a toy boy, I'd be avoiding the antiquated opinions of my own generation."

Of course, it was mostly the same argument. Doug filling her in on whatever case he was working on – the black-and-white version – and Rose trying to argue the case of the underdog, find the grey area between the details.

"But why?" she'd always ask. "What you have to ask is *why*, Doug. What makes people so desperate that they do what they do?"

Becoming a detective in the latter part of his career, when police diving had become too risky, had given them plenty to debate on Sunday afternoons.

"I can't take on every person's problems. The law is the law, Rose. If you break it, there are consequences."

"Bullshit!" Head back, eyes alight. "The only place where there are hard and fast rules is below the water. For safety," she'd repeat time and again. "But above it, on dry land, well, there are times when the rules are meant to be bent, where the law doesn't always protect you . . ."

"The law is there for a reason, Rose. Even you have to see that."

"Never mind," she'd said once, "you wouldn't understand." She'd stared out at the waves beyond them on the beach and without looking at him, had muttered, "People do things, sometimes – make decisions, choices that tear life into before and after. After, nothing is the same."

Back then, Doug felt sure she'd been referring to her reason for leaving Ireland – to the one who'd encouraged her diving – the man who'd unintentionally broken her heart. Again, Doug hadn't pushed her, knowing how intensely Rose hated talking about the past. It instantly made her retreat into herself.

Lately, with Rose gone, Doug often wished he *had* taken the time to press her further. Perhaps Rose had been trying to hint at something from "before". Something that may never have come to light without a gentle nudge. Now, he'd never know. Back then, Doug had never considered that one day there would no longer be an opportunity to ask, to delve deeper. But then, everyone had their secrets, didn't they? Maybe you weren't meant to know everything.

"Don't you think, Douglas?" Irene interrupted his thoughts.

"What's that?' He looked up, baffled. They were sitting at the plastic table and chairs on the porch outside their house, having finished eating.

"I was just saying you should join a club. You're still young – younger than me, anyway," Irene guffawed. "I'm sure Rose would approve. You could have years left yet. What are you? Seventy? I forget these days. I always thought I'd go first, before Rose. Didn't I always say that, Nick?" She turned to her husband, who was sitting back, picking at something lodged between his teeth. "She was always so youthful, even though she was that bit older than me. Don't you think?"

"I . . . well, yes, I suppose."

It was sometimes challenging to follow Irene's train of thought. It jumped from place to place before you had a chance to consider her first statement.

"And I told you about Tom. You remember Tom? Friend of Nick's from work. Well, his missus died a year ago and he's been seeing a lovely lady. Dating, he calls it. Met her at boules. Boules! Who knew pushing your balls up and down the lawn might result in an affair of the heart.

"Now, Tom says that it's like he has a second shot at life. That this one is much livelier than the wife ever was. Can you imagine? Seventy-three and dating. Mind you, I did always think his wife was a funny one, more to her than met the eye. Don't we all have a past, though? Hmm?"

Doug's brother, Nick, turned towards him, casting his

eyes upwards at his wife's babble, and then winked. "All except Doug. No skeletons in his closet." Nick patted his brother's arm. "What was it Rose used to say about you? Squeaky clean. Nothing dodgy from your past."

Doug rolled his eyes and laughed. It was a running family joke how much Doug had always been a stickler for the rules. Even as children, it was Nick, older by a couple of years, who was forever getting into trouble.

"Funny, because it's true," Nick added as Irene got up to clear the plates.

"Help me, you big lump. Douglas, you stay there. I insist." Irene turned to Nick, who reluctantly pushed back his chair, leaving Doug alone.

Funny, because it's true. And it was true, Doug supposed. Before Rose, Doug had had no past. Well, at least nothing worth discussing. Brought up in suburban Sydney, his parents had run a grocery store. They'd had a pleasant childhood – very run-of-the-mill. His brother left had school to become a carpenter and Doug had eventually joined the force.

He'd had friends, a good life, if not terribly exciting. The truth was that until he'd met Rose, nothing significant had occurred in his life. Aside from losing his parents from old age, Doug had existed, happily and inconsequentially. For him, it was Rose who'd spilt *his* life into before and after.

"How's the new job, Doug?" Nick sat back down again. "You never told me much about it."

Doug leaned back. "Not much to tell. Actually, I packed it in. Wasn't really a job, so to speak. Paperwork, mostly. I handed in the final file last week. Done now," he grimaced. "Maybe I should join a club."

Taking a sort of casual role with a company had been

another of Irene's bright ideas. She'd heard about it through her son, who worked for one of these big corporations in the city. She'd suggested it to Doug and it had made sense at the time, giving him a purpose.

"I'm beginning to think there's more to people than what you see on paper," Doug added soberly.

He didn't elaborate that he'd thought about nothing else for the past few weeks. Nor that he'd wrestled with whether or not even to complete that final file before submitting it. In the end, he'd finished it. It was, after all, what he was being paid to do.

Nick reached over and smacked his arm playfully. "You're getting soft in your old age, little brother. I don't know how you did what you did all those years. You know how *I* feel about the law."

Doug laughed. "Hah. Don't I know only too well. Remember that time you were caught stealing beer when you were seventeen!"

"In my defence, they wouldn't let me pay for it. There was no other way," Nick laughed.

"You were underage!"

"I was six foot two. I was a man, for Christ's sake! What man doesn't want a bevvie with his buddies?"

Doug shook his head and smiled. "I'm thinking of taking a trip, actually."

"Really? To where?"

"Ireland."

It had been on his mind for a while. Perhaps as a way to stay connected with Rose, as if being there might help to capture her spirit again. At times lately, he could feel her starting to slip further into the recesses of his memory. At others, it was like she'd never left. Still, it frightened him.

"Ireland?" Irene was back. "Whatever for?"

"I thought I'd see where Rose came from," he stopped. "Maybe sprinkle her ashes there."

Irene made a face. "Do you think she'd like that? I mean, don't you think it's odd how Rose never went back? Not once. I often wondered did something happen, more than she'd already told us. Imagine never seeing your sister again . . . But then, I suppose she had me." Irene looked pleased with herself.

Rose had told them the story once, the reason she'd left so suddenly, and then had never spoken of it again.

"I don't think it was odd," Doug responded. "What happened was tough and I think she just needed to leave it behind, but there was a big part of her that never stopped missing Ireland. I'd like to bring a piece of her home."

"You see that, Nick!" Irene tilted her head and smiled. "That's why they were so bloody happy. Doug must be the *only* romantic Australian man alive."

It was what Irene had said next that was still playing on Doug's mind as he drove away shortly after.

"'Perfect,' Rose used to say of you. Except that you're far too black and white, Douglas. That was the one thing she'd have changed about you. She wanted you to see the colour in between, and not just the grey parts. To look between the lines. I still remember her telling me. She said, 'Doug sees the colour in the sea, but above it, he needs to understand that sometimes there's more to life than right and wrong.'"

It was the most profound thing Doug had ever heard Irene say. Had he missed something in life? Indeed, Rose had filled his life so completely that he'd never felt the need to ponder the meaning of existence. Not until now. All of a sudden, Doug felt as though he were right back at the start – searching again in the depths of muddy water, only this time for sense, fulfilment, the meaning of life. Without Rose, what the hell was it all about?

For the last couple of weeks, since meeting that woman, Lucie, Doug felt as though he were drowning in his thoughts. Each time he thought of her, he'd try to eject her from his mind. Exactly as he'd told Rose, he couldn't take on every person's problems. Then today, Irene's words had delivered him a blow. After Irene had said what she had, told him to look between the lines, find the colour, Doug had decided not to stay the day, after all. Instead, he'd excused himself early.

He wasn't sure why he'd decided to drive home along the motorway. He usually took the scenic route. Turning onto the smooth stretch, he replayed his sister-in-law's words. They were so close to how Rose would have spoken that they couldn't be anything but straight from her mouth. Was Rose trying to tell him something? He shook his head, sure he was losing it, and without knowing why, he indicated left, taking the slip road with the sign for Double Bay.

It was the squad car he noticed first, pulled into the side of the slip road, a car parked just ahead of it. A police officer was standing beside it, routinely taking notes. The other officer was inside the squad car, talking into the radio. Doug slowed his speed as he passed, enough to glimpse what looked like an abandoned jeep on the side of the road. Inching past, his eyes flashed over the number plate and he jolted.

"Can I help you, sir?" The officer standing at the car approached as Doug pulled in, stopped the engine of his car and got out.

There was a hard-nosed look on the young officer's face. Doug retrieved his wallet from his pocket and flashed his retired police detective card at her. She glanced at it before her face softened. Doug couldn't help but think that she looked like a teenager dressed in uniform playing cops.

"Afternoon, sir," she nodded respectfully.

He was glad. She could easily have told him to take a hike.

"What's happened here?" Doug walked towards the vehicle and glanced inside.

"All under control, sir. Usual stuff. Middle-age woman, she was—"

"Where is she now?" Doug turned to look ahead, to where the slip road veered left.

He didn't need her to explain. He was able to guess what might have happened.

"She went that way, on foot." The girl pointed matter-of-factly. "I offered a lift, but she was distressed . . ."

"Okay." Doug walked away, not waiting for the girl to say more.

He got straight back in his car and stared ahead. At the top of the hill ahead, Doug could either go straight, getting back onto the motorway to head for home. Or he could turn left, towards Double Bay. Left or straight? Right or wrong?

She hadn't got far. Doug could see her up ahead, sitting crouched over on a bench, her hair hanging over her face. He pulled in again, turned off the engine and watched for a moment. She had her phone in her hand and was staring blankly at the screen. Tapping at it, she put the phone to her ear, then just as quickly took it away again. Then she wrapped her arms around her stomach, squeezed her eyes shut and went to stand before thudding back down on the bench.

Doug got out of the car and walked towards her. She turned upon seeing him approach, recognition mixed with surprise visible on her features. This time she stood awkwardly, roughly tying her sweater around her waist as she did so. Doug's eyes flitted over her, dismally taking note of the colour in the otherwise black-and-white situation. He averted his eyes quickly. She'd noticed. Her eyebrows furrowed and she attempted to conceal it further with the sweater. Then, in slow motion, her head rolled to one side, her lungs issued a short puff and she collapsed.

Rose was right. Life isn't always black and white. There's plenty of colour there if you choose to look. If only the colour hadn't been Lucie's blood-soaked trousers, the tinge of blue to her lips, or her red hair blowing listlessly in the breeze as he caught her.

Chapter fourteen

"Lu, Lucie. Are you okay?"

Lucie opened her eyes from where she'd briefly dozed off, stretched out on the bed in the emergency department. Looking up to see Nina's concerned face, she grasped for her hand, tears smarting.

"What the hell happened? I just got here. You poor thing. Are you all right?"

"Never been better," Lucie said sarcastically and attempted to sit up, then stopped when she remembered the drip in her arm. "Oh, Christ, Nina. What a day! I think the high point was collapsing on the side of the road. The low point was . . . Hang on, how come you're here?"

Nina hesitated, leaning over to brush Lucie's hair away from her face. "Max called me," she admitted. "He saw you being brought in. He was worried."

"Oh, Jesus. Could it get any worse?" Lucie closed her eyes and sighed loudly. "I thought I saw him, but I was otherwise occupied at the time. I was half hoping I was hallucinating."

Lucie didn't elaborate further. It certainly wasn't how she'd imagined re-encountering Max. Being rushed into the emergency department in a wheelchair clutching her stomach, her hair drenched with sweat, face whiter than snow, wasn't exactly the vision she'd had in mind. Lucie flinched, catching a glimpse of the green plastic bag on the chair beside her containing her now ruined trousers. Nina followed her eyes.

"Super choice of colour." Nina gestured towards the bag.

Lucie threw her eyes to heaven. Having had a few days' respite, of course, she'd chosen to wear white. What the hell had she been thinking?

"I thought it would add to the drama. A more striking contrast," she responded wryly. "What did Max say?" She could barely meet Nina's eyes.

Nina smiled sympathetically and patted her hand. "Just that he'd seen you being brought in and you looked a little worse for wear. When he didn't see Hamish with you, he thought he'd call me to make sure you weren't alone. Also, he thought I might be able to help get you seen quicker. So, here I am. Ta-dah! Medical fairy at your disposal." She splayed her hands out then picked up the bag from the chair, dangled it for a moment in front of Lucie. "Honestly, white?" she grinned, throwing it to the corner of the cubicle and pulling the chair closer to sit. "Forget it. Don't worry. I think Max is the least of your worries at the moment. Don't you?"

Lucie nodded. "You have no idea."

Nina was right. Lucie currently didn't have the headspace to let Hamish's first cousin, Max, add to her concerns. Ever since Nina had mentioned that he was back in Sydney, Lucie had thought a lot about how she'd react if and when she finally bumped into Max. With the family connection, she supposed it was only a matter of time before their paths crossed.

Max and Hamish had been raised like brothers, albeit ones who'd never really seen eye to eye. They hadn't seen Max in a very long time. He'd all but disappeared years before. Over the years, they'd tried to ensure that they didn't attend the same family gatherings, Hamish's mother, Vera, always giving them the heads-up if she knew her nephew would be in town, which was rare. With Max living in Melbourne last time she'd heard, it had been easy to avoid him. Lucie often wondered if time had healed everything like Hamish had always said it would – like putting balm over the "episode", as he called it. Lucie doubted it. Time wasn't always a healer, she knew that first-hand.

"I spoke with the nurse." Nina interrupted her thoughts. "You were very dehydrated." Nina gestured at the fluids line connected to Lucie's arm. "They've given you something for the pain. And the bleeding is heavy, obviously." Nina gestured to the green bag again. "They've done your bloods, as you know. My professional guess is you're anaemic – note the fainting. They've called Professor Stone. He's going to be here tomorrow to run those tests, so they're keeping you in—"

"Tomorrow! I can't, Nina. The kids! Stacy from school has them. I need to call her." Lucie went to grab her phone from the table beside her. "I need to get home. I'm fine now, honestly. Nothing that I'm not used to." She attempted to sit up again.

"Don't you dare, Lucie Woods. *I'll* call Stacy." Nina gently pushed Lucie back down. "Stop worrying. If I have to sit on you, I will. Better still, I'll restrain you with those godawful brown leather straps. You're staying put. Now, this has gone on long enough." Nina was getting impatient. "You were due to see Stone next week anyway, but it looks like your body has announced it needs to be sooner. So stay the hell there. Let Hamish get them. Where the hell is he, anyway? Is he playing golf or something? I tried his phone—"

"He's gone." Lucie inhaled slowly, trying to remain calm.

She could still barely comprehend the phone call she'd had with him earlier, sitting on the bench at the side of the road. The line had been poor, but she'd heard enough to grasp the general gist. It wasn't good.

"What do you mean, gone?" Nina looked baffled. "Gone where?"

"Gone. He took a contract role for a few months. He left today for Singapore."

"Singapore!"

"Yeah." Lucie put her head back, scrunched her eyes shut, feeling a shudder of dread ripple through her body. "With no warning. Oh, Nina. It's all gone so horribly wrong."

Nina registered the look on Lucie's face. "Okay. Just breathe. What's happened? Tell me."

The whole thing had been horrible, humiliating – one of the most demeaning moments of her life thus far. Earlier, driving towards home, Lucie had been in a world of her own – ultimately fuelled by a determination to get to the bottom of their problems. She never usually drove fast. As someone who'd lost a brother to a road accident, Lucie was a careful driver. She genuinely hadn't realised she was speeding until she heard the sirens and glanced at the speedometer. She jumped at the sound, immediately slowing her pace, still uncomprehending that the flashing lights behind were signalling for her to pull over.

Lucie had almost reached the slip road for Double Bay when they caught up. Panicking, she indicated and took the slip road before pulling the car to the side of the road. It wasn't until she was stopped and looked down that Lucie noticed the red stain in her lap, feeling a sudden warmth between her legs. Flustered, she'd grabbed her sweater from the passenger seat, laying it across her lap to cover it. Indeed, the earlier pains she'd felt in the car had been an indication of what was about to occur, but she thought she'd be home by the time it materialised.

Lucie had reached into the glove compartment to retrieve her licence, resolving to accept the slap on the wrist and a possible fine, and be off with a profuse apology. The injustice of this unexpected addition to an already shocking day had made her squirm as she'd looked in the rear-view mirror at the two police officers approaching and sheepishly rolled down her window.

"I'm so sorry, officers. Really, I never speed. I'm dreadfully sorry." She handed her licence out of the window. "I only noticed that I was going faster than I should have been when I heard the sirens." She smiled submissively, hoping to admit fault and in doing so, hasten the process.

The male officer issued a somewhat charitable smile, while the woman craned her neck inside her vehicle, all business. Lucie edged back to allow the inspection. She didn't look that much older than Bella – hair in a tight bun under her hat, mouth downturned.

"Lucky you have no children in the car." The female officer shook her head in alarm.

"Yes, I'm sorry," Lucie repeated. "I was on my way home. I've got to be back to pick up the children from Sunday sports. I forgot something at home," she explained.

"Not a reason to be speeding, Mrs . . ." The woman glanced at the licence and then back at Lucie. "Woods." She looked at the photo again.

"Not the greatest snap of me," Lucie grimaced. "I think it smudged, there, see . . ." She pointed feebly at the card. "Makes me look like I have a moustache."

The male officer grinned somewhat, while the woman made her way to the front of the car, inspecting the licence plate.

Lucie's eyes followed her, noticing how her eyebrows had suddenly knitted together. The officer looked back through the windscreen at Lucie, then made her way slowly to the driver's window.

"Mrs Woods, not only were you speeding today, but we were able to see from our patrol cameras that both the registration and insurance on this car expired six months ago."

"What?" The artificial smile slipped from Lucie's face. "I . . . no . . . are you sure? I had no idea. My husband usually looks after it. Oh, God, I'm so sorry. I'll sort it straightaway."

"Your husband?" The officer looked unconvinced. "Is this your vehicle?"

"Yes, but I . . . I'm not working at the moment," Lucie babbled. "See, I'm a nurse. I was working at Woodfield Grammar and, well, I unexpectedly lost my job and you see, things haven't been great and . . ." Lucie stopped herself. "Look, I didn't know. That's the truth. I'm sorry. I *should* have known." Was this really happening? Lucie felt sick.

"If this is your vehicle, then it's up to you and not your *husband* to ensure that everything is up to date." The smug look on her face was palpable.

Lucie could feel tears smarting, desperately attempting but failing to swallow them back.

The male officer shuffled awkwardly, noticing her distress. He turned his back on Lucie for a moment, whispered something to his colleague and swivelled back.

The female officer put her hand up. "I'm sorry." She eyeballed her partner, stepping in front of him, then took a breath, speaking evenly as if reading directly from a manual.

Lucie could barely understand her but heard enough in the evidently well-practised recital to know that they were seizing her car.

The rest was a blur. Stepping out of the car, her legs had nearly faltered, the mortification of the situation making it difficult to stand. Catching the curious glances from other passing drivers, all Lucie had wanted to do was get away as fast as possible. She remembered them offering her a lift, to which she refused. Lucie could feel the blood rushing in her ears as she pulled her sweater around her waist in an attempt to conceal her drenched trousers as they made arrangements to have her car towed away. The tears flowed freely with every painful step as she fled the scene, head down, shame and rage filling her body. When she reached the bench just after the slip road merged for Double Bay, Lucie sat down, shaking, and lifted the phone to call Hamish.

"The fucking car has just been seized," she spluttered into the phone. "What *is* going on, Hamish? I was on my way back to talk to you. The school fees haven't been paid, either. Stacy just told me. You took money from my account. What the hell, Hamish. I'm on the side of the fucking road. What is going on?

"Oh, and I met Priscilla. She said Brent has been trying to contact you for days. What's that about?" It poured out of her. "Not only that, but I'm also here in chronic pain and I've bled through my trousers. Come and get me, *now*."

Silence. And then – and this was the part that still got her, of everything she'd just said – he asked, "Did Priscilla say why Brent was looking for me?"

Lucie held the phone away from her face, staring at the screen in shock before putting it back to her ear.

"*No*!" she shouted, not caring who heard. "Jesus Christ, Hamish. Didn't you fucking hear me? Come and get me. We need to talk. *Now*," she screamed.

"I can't."

"What?"

"I can't. I'm at the airport."

"You'd better be joking." The oxygen exited her lungs.

"I had to leave early. They want me in Singapore tomorrow. There was a flight today—" The line crackled.

"Singapore? Singapore! And you didn't think to tell me. What, did you expect that I'd come home and you'd just be gone? Were you not going to tell the kids?"

"I told you on Friday."

"You never bloody said Singapore."

"I did. You've been distracted, Lucie—" The line broke again.

He hadn't told her.

"Hamish, you'd better tell me what the hell is going on."

"I can't talk right now. It's just for a few months. We need the money." His voice was going in and out. "And maybe . . . some time apart. Things haven't been good between us. I need space to think—"

Lucie caught that part. "Space to think? Space to fucking think? Are you leaving me or something?" Lucie couldn't believe what she was hearing. "Hamish, I've no car. What the hell is happening?" She was suddenly terrified, her hands starting to shake uncontrollably.

"I have to go . . ."

"Hamish? Please. I'm . . ." She was about to say frightened.

"I . . . sorry . . . explain—"

The line had crackled before going dead as Lucie sat staring the phone, wanting to hurl it into the street. Then she'd looked up to see that man – the one she'd met in the café. She'd stood . . .

"I fainted. The next thing I remember, I came to in the back of his car. Remember that man I told you about before? Doug? The one I met with the Irish wife? Well, he was passing and saw my car on the side of the road."

"Idiot!" Nina exclaimed, shaking her head. "Hamish, I mean. What on earth, Lucie? Has he left you?"

Lucie shrugged. "I don't know. I really don't know what's going on."

Nina squeezed her hand. "What a mess. I met Doug outside earlier. One of the nurses pointed him out. He was waiting to see if you were okay. He left his number. What a sweet man. He looked worried. Thank God he was there when he was. Here . . ." Nina passed her the piece of paper with Doug's number on it then paused. "Lucie, I had no idea everything was so bad."

"Neither did I."

Tears pooled in Lucie's eyes before escaping in thick streams. Nina leaned over and rested her head against Lucie's arm.

"Do you think Hamish is in some sort of trouble? It all sounds a bit surreal."

"I don't know, Nina. I don't know anything any more. He's obviously got us into some sort of situation where everything is coming crashing down all at once. Or maybe I've been ignoring it, but I need to face things.

"We're broke – clearly." Lucie wiped away the tears. "The accounts are dry. The car is gone. What the hell else don't I know? Oh, God, I've been such a fool."

"We'll get it sorted, Lucie. I promise. I'll do what I can, but I still have to work, so you need someone else to help out. And we don't know what the doctor is going to say. What about Hamish's mother?"

"No." Lucie shook her head. "Not Vera. The Woods have brought me enough trouble over the years. I'm sick of them all. Whatever's going on, whatever is coming, I have to do this alone."

"You're going to need help with Bella and Declan. Look, we'll figure it out. But right now, I need you to concentrate on getting better. That's all for now. I'll call Stacy and collect the kids. They can stay with me for a few days."

At that moment, Lucie wanted the hospital bed to swallow her whole. Years before, she'd promised herself that she'd never again let everything crumble apart as it once had. Marrying Hamish, leaving behind broken, grieving Lucie Maguire, she'd sworn never to let everything get on top of her again. Back then, she'd laid the past to rest, become a different person – a mother, a wife, with a new family. It was what she'd needed to do to survive.

But now, the seams were coming apart once more. Lucie could feel it happening and she was terrified. Lord knows, once upon a time Lucie had been the strong one, the one who could make it on her own. Nina was right – she needed help. Lucie had avoided asking for it for so long, but now, there was no other choice.

Chapter fifteen

It was strange. Almost as soon as being admitted to hospital, Lucie began to feel a little more at ease, no longer able to deny that she was in dire straits and needed help. Propped up in bed in a private room, being cared for, her thoughts began to settle somewhat. For now, there was nothing she could do about Hamish, who still wasn't answering his phone. He had no idea that his wife was even in the hospital, or that reality had begun to dawn on Lucie now that she'd finally had time to catch her breath.

Nina was right. Right now, all she needed to focus on was her health. She had Bella and Declan to consider – and trying to mask them from unnecessary worries. Lucie knew one thing for sure: after this, whatever happened, life would change, for them all. In time, she'd have to tell the children more, but all she had to do in the meantime was ensure they were cared for, get better then solve it all. Those were the steps. One, two, three. Put that way, it seemed more manageable.

Professor Stone, the gynaecologist, had been pragmatic when he came to see Lucie on Monday afternoon after she'd been taken for ultrasounds and spent the morning being prodded. Lucie had always liked the straight-talking doctor in his mid-fifties. Despite his perceived gruff nature and looking more like a rugby player, he was very in tune with the female condition. She'd assisted him in theatre on many occasions, always admiring his candour.

"Fibroids, Ms Woods. Huge fibroids. From what I can see, you have the contents of a fruit basket inside you – maybe some veg, too. There's a few of particular concern. One about the size of a small head of lettuce." He'd tilted his head, counting on his fingers. "A large apple – a cooking apple, let's say – a peach or maybe a kiwi, depending on what season, and two strawberries." He finished his analogy. "Which would explain the constant bleeding, exhaustion, pain . . . Have you had difficulty with intercourse?" he'd asked bluntly.

"Yes," she lied, not wanting to divulge that recently – actually, for longer than she could remember – intercourse hadn't featured on the "Specials Menu".

"I'm not sure how you managed for so long, to be frank. I imagine you've been cultivating them for some time now. But these things always come to a head."

"Of lettuce," she joked, to which he'd looked at her strangely. And then, "I thought it was the onset of menopause."

"Well, there's that, too. I imagine from what you've told me, and from your age, that your oestrogen levels are low, which would attribute to some of the other symptoms like night sweats, flashes. It can be hard to differentiate exactly what's causing what, but those fibroids need to come out. Then we can get to the bottom of the other symptoms – try to manage them, give you back some quality of life," he smiled encouragingly.

Quality of life. The irony wasn't lost on her as she sat listening. This was only the first hurdle of what would be many before there was *any* quality of life. His words came as a relief, though. She hadn't been losing her mind, all those months suffering in silence. There had been an issue all along – and one that could thankfully be solved.

"You're too young to be feeling this way. We'd like to see that chirpy Irish nurse back." Professor Stone smiled reassuringly from where he was standing at the foot of the bed. "I always liked you, Lucie. You were a great asset to the hospital."

Lucie hadn't meant to start blubbing, but she gulped back a sob.

"There, there . . ." He came round to the side of the bed and patted her arm. "Now, there are a few options, as I'm sure you know. We could try a myomectomy – removing the fibroids from your uterus – but the size worries me." He shook his head. "They can, in some cases, grow back and since you *are* approaching menopause—"

"Whip it out," Lucie said suddenly, to which Professor Stone looked taken aback. "I mean," she composed herself, "I can't run the risk of this happening again. If you think a hysterectomy is best, do it."

She'd already considered all the possible options, but in the end, she knew there was only one choice, especially with all of her other problems. Her private health insurance with the school was going to run out in the coming months and if this operation was going to happen, it needed to happen now.

"I don't need to tell you that it's a tough surgery, Lucie. Two weeks off your feet. Six weeks not driving, a lot of rest."

"That won't be a problem." She thought of her car being impounded and not having enough money to have it released, let alone tax it, never mind meet the loan repayments.

"Well, then it's settled. I'm hoping we can retain your ovaries. Losing them at this stage would bring about other problems with hormones, et cetera, but I'm confident from the scans that the fibroids are contained in your uterus. To make you aware, this is going to be an abdominal surgery. They're too big for any other method of removal."

"I understand," she nodded before adding, "And thank you. I thought . . . I was convinced I had cancer."

He nodded. "We'll be checking for cancer, but I'm hopeful that *this* is all it is. Keep the faith. Do you have help with your children? You're going to need it."

"I'll make sure I do."

"Right!" He clapped his hands together and turned to leave before glancing back at her. "I'll be back later to schedule the procedure. In light of your past with us here, I'll see what I can do to get it done by the end of the week. Stay put there for a few days. Relax. I want you in top condition," he paused. "Like I said earlier, I've good memories of your time nursing here. You know who I ran into . . . ?" He stopped, batted his hand. "Ah, never mind. I'll see you later."

Lucie had known precisely who he'd been about to say. She'd been thinking about *him*, too. Being back at Sydney General had flooded her mind with bittersweet memories of the past, of working at the hospital. For so many years, she'd practically lived here, adoring every second. It was impossible not to visualise herself as she'd once been, in her starched uniform, satisfied smile on her face, head bobbing with duty.

It was just as difficult not to picture Max – white lab coat open, head stuck in a clipboard, a smile spreading across his face as she passed. Had it all really happened? It was hard to imagine the life she'd once lived before Hamish and Bella and Declan – one that would now be so very different if it had continued back then.

Lucie's mind plummeted back to the present as Bella and Declan trundled through the door, followed by Nina.

"Mum! Are you okay? Where's Dad? How long do I have to stay at Nina's?" Bella was all questions as she approached the bed.

"Mum," Declan hugged her. "Are you sick?"

"No." She patted his head and smiled at Bella. "It's so good to see you both." She swallowed her tears. "I'm okay. I have to have an operation. It's serious but not *too* serious and I'm going to be fine," she assured. "Dad is away with work for a few months. Urgent spy business." She winked at Declan, who opened his eyes wide.

Bella looked unconvinced. "I had to miss school today."

"It's just temporary. Here . . ." She handed Declan a few dollars. "Go and get something from the shop. I need to talk to Nina."

Bella grabbed the money from Declan's hand and dragged him out of the door.

"Quite the madam lately." Nina rolled her eyes. "Isn't she? Sorry, I couldn't get them to school this morning. It was a bit frantic. Well, what's the update?" She looked concerned.

"Don't worry. Yep, Bella is a handful. I don't know how I'm going to keep certain things from her. So, I spoke with Professor Stone."

* * *

"Oh my, you're like Grapefruit Man! Or at least Lettuce Lady," Nina giggled after Lucie filled her in on what they'd found harbouring inside her. "It's no wonder your trousers won't close. Talk about taking your five-a-day to the next level, literally, in your trousers. It's good news, though. You must be minorly relieved. It could be far worse."

Lucie nodded. "I *am* relieved. And yes, it's the best of a bad situation. Professor Stone says I've to stay here before surgery."

"Well, I'm not surprised. Neglecting yourself like that, Lu. Seriously? And don't go being difficult. Listen to him."

"I know, I know. Christ, we're that age, aren't we?" Lucie giggled suddenly. "You know, fully-fledged members of the DVB."

"Speak for yourself! My God, I haven't heard that in so long." Nina exploded with laughter.

It was how they'd secretly referred to patients of a certain age and somewhat tricky disposition. Dry Vagina Brigade, referencing menopausal women who'd allowed the physical symptoms of that stage become their demeanour.

Nina couldn't stop laughing. "Stop. And now, here we are! Karma!"

"Do you remember trying to explain to Max what DVB stood for? For a doctor, he was so bloody clueless sometimes." Lucie glanced at Nina. There, she'd said his name – acknowledged him.

Nina raised an eyebrow. "Are you having a trip down memory lane?"

Lucie shrugged. "Be hard not to. I can still see it all so clearly. We were babies when we started here, weren't we? What? Twenty-four years young – and knew it all.

Our entire lives ahead of us. I wish I'd cut those narky women more slack now I know what they were going through."

"Hey." Nina put her hand on Lucie's shoulder. "You still have an entire life ahead of you. It ain't over yet. You just need to get through this surgery, get better and face the rest. Talking of which . . ." Nina turned sober. "Any word from Hamish?"

"Nothing."

"What is he playing at?"

"I don't know, but I can't think about him. If I do, I'll want to murder him. If, and when, he comes back, I'm going to fire my fruity fibroids right at his head, starting with the lettuce." Lucie's smile faded. "Nina?"

"Yep."

"Do you ever think what might have happened if things had worked out differently . . . ?"

Nina didn't answer.

"It's silly, I know," Lucie said. "Being back here, it has me thinking."

"It's not silly. Would it help if you saw him? Spoke to him?"

"Jesus, no. No. I think it might make everything worse."

"Maybe it would clear things up. It might . . ." Nina trailed off when Lucie turned towards the door to see Bella and Declan coming back laden with sweets.

"So . . ." Bella sat on the bed, flicking her hair to the side. "Are you pregnant or something? I'll kill myself if you are. Morto!"

Lucie laughed. "Well, we can't have that. Nor have you mortified of your mother. I'm quite the opposite of pregnant. In fact, I need a hysterectomy."

"Oh." Bella's face dropped.

"Is that bad?" Declan asked.

"It's okay, guys, honestly. I'll just be off my feet for a few weeks – six exactly. A great big rest. Lots of time to think. The doctor said the operation is this Friday. They want to keep me in until then to keep me out of trouble."

"But who's going to look after us?" Declan asked.

"Well . . ." Lucie glanced at Nina, who nodded encouragingly. She'd already told Nina the plan over the phone. "Now, before you react. Just bear in mind that I had no other choice with Daddy being away and Nina working."

"Not Vera," Bella groaned. "Please not Granny Vera."

"Not quite." Lucie held her breath.

Chapter sixteen

Doug

Pacing. It was something else Doug did when he was trying to think – that and his jaw moving – his mind turning more productively when his body was active, helping him to focus. It was the very reason that Doug now found himself at home on a Tuesday afternoon, pacing the floor, up and down, back and front, side to side.

"Mother of God, you're making me dizzy. Would you sit the hell down," Rose would say. "What's up with you, anyway?"

Doug had always grown addled towards the end of a case. Right before he uncovered the final, often glaringly obvious, piece of the puzzle.

"What have you bloody gone and done now, Rose?" Doug scowled at the vase on the mantelpiece. "You have me in a twist. A twist!"

Even from afar, Doug had a sneaking suspicion that Rose was still trying to harangue him.

"Sending me cryptic messages through Irene, of all people. Really, Rose," he scolded. "So, life isn't black and white. I got the message loud and clear. You couldn't have made it any clearer!" He shook his head, thinking of the sorry state in which he'd found Lucie two days before. "Poor girl, but what do you want *me* to do about it? It's not my concern." He paused again, glared at the vase and held up his hands. "And now look at me! You have me fit for the loony bin."

If anyone could see Doug, pacing the floor and having a full-blown argument with an urn, containing the ashes of his dead wife, they'd have had him committed.

"If it's not your concern, why are you wearing the floor out, hmm?" Doug could almost picture her, sitting there in her wicker chair, arms folded, chin thrust forwards, that self-congratulatory look on her face.

Doug sighed and plonked in his armchair. "Rose, please, you're sending me doolally."

He closed his eyes, sneakily opening one to check if Rose had decided to give him a break. Nope. Her head was cocked, foot tapping. She meant business.

"Go away," he whispered, closing both eyes again, crossing his arms and wriggling his shoulders to get comfortable.

"You know why we met?" Rose had asked once. "You, Doug, were in the right place at the right time."

"And what about you?"

"I'm still deciding," she'd begun. "Some days, I feel like I was where I was supposed to be that day. Others, I think I was in the wrong place at the wrong time. Time will tell," Rose had teased, elevating her eyebrows and wrinkling her nose as he took a playful swipe at her.

Ever since then, Doug had quietly believed in fate. He wondered if circumstance had played a hand in the events of Sunday. Indeed, Doug had had no way of knowing, after leaving his brother's house that day and driving towards Double Bay, that he'd once again happen upon Lucie Woods. Had he been hoping he would? Maybe. But he never could have anticipated finding her in the state he had, perched on a bench, doubled over in pain. Nor that moments later he'd be bundling her lifeless body into the back of his car.

"Lucie, can you hear me?"

She'd come round seconds after Doug had laid her on the back seat and taken off towards the hospital.

"You've fainted. My name is Doug Offer. I met you a few weeks back. Remember? There's no need to be concerned. I'm driving you to the hospital. Stay where you are. You'll be okay," he'd stated calmly.

She'd been disoriented, mumbling words, not making sense.

"The car . . . I . . . police . . ."

"Lucie," he repeated. "Don't worry about that now. Just breathe. Don't try to sit up. Can I call someone for you? Your husband?"

Her voice had been more precise. "He's gone."

That part had shocked even Doug. What on earth had she meant?

Doug's eyes flashed open for a second to register that Rose had decided to leave him in peace – for a while, anyway – alone with his thoughts. Closing his eyes once more, he shuddered as his mind catapulted back to a similar morning two years before.

Sunday's scene had been all too familiar, edging too close to a memory he'd neatly filed away. It had been a morning like any other. Doug had risen before Rose, pottering in the kitchen to make her a herbal tea for her to sip alongside his dark bitter coffee. He'd been standing at the window, binoculars to his eyes, keeping watch on the boats drifting past.

"Doug."

He'd never once heard Rose say his name that way, nor seen such a look of terror in her eyes to accompany her trembling voice. Dropping the binoculars, he'd walked towards her, reaching for her just as she'd faltered. Doug had caught her, laying her gently on the rug. Straightaway, he'd known. Rose had, too.

In the end, it hadn't been a morning like any other. It was *the* morning that changed everything, where normality was interrupted by the extraordinary. As soon as Rose had walked into the living room with her nightdress drenched in blood, her hands tinged red, her face white, Doug had known it was grave.

"The beginning of the end," Rose had poetically called it a few days later.

If only that had been the beginning. Rose had hidden it from Doug for months, trying to avoid what was coming.

"No treatment," she'd said when the doctors revealed in the coming days that it was cancer, an advanced form. "No surgery."

"Please, Rose . . ." He'd pleaded with her to reconsider.

"Would you go away outta that. I'm eighty years old, love – feck that. I'm not spending my final days prodded and poked when I can spend them with you. If you'll have me . . ."

"You stubborn old . . . turkey."

Rose had laughed at the reference to their very first conversation, where she'd told him that people used to say her Irish accent was thicker than a turkey.

"See," she'd smiled, her eyes filling. "It was a good life. I *was* in the right place at the right time, Doug Offer. You gave me the second life I never thought I'd have. If I were cheese, I'd be desperate mouldy by now. Well past my sell-by date. Now, take me home, my love. Take me home and let's look at the sea."

So he had.

Rose fought bravely, lasting almost five months – five almost perfect months before the pain got too much. Then she'd taken her leave peacefully, in the bed Doug had moved to the living room so she could look out at the life she'd always loved.

"I'll always be with you, Doug. You know that. I'll never really go."

Over the months they'd talked, reminisced, held each other. It had been the best and the worst of times.

"Thank you."

It was the last thing he'd said to Rose as he held her. They were the only words that could come close to summing up how she'd impacted his life.

"Thank you. You're like my guardian angel," Lucie had whispered to Doug beneath anxious eyes after the nurse came to wheel her away for triage.

He'd noticed how jittery she'd become as soon as he wheeled her through the doors of the A&E. He'd thought it strange for someone so accustomed to hospitals. And hadn't she said she'd worked there for many years?

It wasn't the only thing Doug had discerned that Sunday. There'd been a doctor standing back observing them. He'd looked shocked to see Lucie. Lucie had looked briefly in his direction, then crouched forwards in pain, letting her hair fall over her face.

Doug had noticed the doctor grab a nurse and point towards them. The nurse had come over straightaway. Doug had explained as best he could and then she'd wheeled Lucie away. The doctor had turned his back then, appearing to be on the phone. Then Doug had been left sitting there, waiting for what seemed like an age until a small woman with dark hair approached.

"I'm Nina. Lucie's friend. Did you bring her in? One of the nurses told me. Thanks for waiting."

"I was passing Double Bay and I saw her in distress . . . I met her before . . ."

"She told me," Nina smiled.

"Is she going to be okay? I didn't want to leave until I knew she had someone with her."

"She's going to be fine," Nina reassured. "They need to run tests. I'll stay with her now." She'd patted his arm.

"My wife, Rose . . . She had similar . . ." He'd stumbled awkwardly over the words. "She'd had similar issues."

Nina had nodded kindly, taken his number and promised to get Lucie to call when she was feeling better. Doug had almost been at the door, when the doctor he'd noticed earlier stepped in front of him.

"That woman you brought in . . . Have you . . . do you know her?" He, too, was struggling to articulate himself.

"Yes, sort of," Doug answered, taking in the giant bald man. He was tall, very much so, in his late forties, perhaps. Or maybe older – it was difficult to tell. He had a youthful face but was somewhat unhealthy-looking – carrying extra weight.

"What happened?"

Doug didn't know how to put it.

"I'm sorry," he said before Doug had a chance to

answer. "I don't work in Emergency. I was just getting a file. I . . . I used to know her."

It was an odd choice of words. Doug looked at the name badge on the doctor's white coat.

"I only met Lucie once before. She fainted. I suppose I was in the right place at the right time. Can't you just look at her file?" Doug asked.

The man nodded. "Yes. Quite right. Her husband? Did someone call him?"

"I'm not sure. Lucie told me he's . . . away." It sounded better than "gone". "Do you know him?"

The man shook his head too quickly. "No."

"Okay. Well, I better go."

It was positive in one way, Doug supposed, how he noticed all the little things that most others failed to see. In another, it was a curse – always being on guard, switched on. One thing for sure, Doug felt confident that the man wearing the badge emblazoned with the name "Prof Max Woods" must surely know Lucie and her husband, and Doug was intrigued. There was more to Lucie than met the eye, Doug was sure of it. But what? Even in her state of distress, Doug had found Lucie endearing. Even in desperation, there was something generous about her.

So he liked the girl. She reminded him of Rose, but was that enough to get involved? Last week he hadn't thought so. After much deliberation, Doug had decided to finish this last job and then move on, just as he'd told his brother on Sunday. Then bloody Irene had gone and said what she had, "Look between the lines." And then seeing Lucie again, in the flesh, so unwell, it made him wonder all over again. Doug was bothered. That's what it was – *worried* about a practical stranger. What if Lucie was sick like Rose had been?

Doug opened his eyes and looked at the urn on the mantelpiece.

"You've gone very quiet, Rose." He tilted his head. "Ah! the silent treatment, I see."

He could guess why. Over the past few weeks, Doug had meticulously gathered everything he'd needed, paid a visit to whoever could shed more light on it all. He'd been thorough.

He'd already handed in his findings and now, suddenly, he wondered if he should have waited. The contents of that file, well, it wasn't pretty.

"Goddammit!" Without thinking, he grabbed his phone from the table beside him and tapped in the number.

"Hi, Doug." The call was answered straightaway. "I was just about to call you. Great work, by the way. I've been over the file and it looks like this isn't our concern any more. Like you advised, I'm handing it over to the appropriate people." The man chuckled. "You went above and beyond with this one. It's a done deal. Christ, some people, huh? Almost admire—"

Doug interrupted. "Listen, on that . . . I was wondering, could you hold off a few weeks? Some more things have come to light. I just need a bit more time. Can it wait?"

"Really? I think there's more than enough."

"Couldn't you just—"

"Hey, you're off the clock now, buddy, unless you want to stay on. We've plenty more where that came from. And the guys are impressed."

Doug hung up with a sinking feeling. Then again, if it hadn't been him, someone else might have uncovered the truth of those files. Darned truth. What was it Rose used to say? "The truth is subjective."

"Okay, okay, Rose." Doug stood and walked towards the window. "So, I've hung the poor woman." He looked back at the urn. "So, what do you want me to do now? I'm all ears." He exhaled gruffly.

Something deep down was telling Doug that the husband might already know that something was going on.

"He's gone." Those had been Lucie's exact words. But where, and why?

Now, Doug felt the need to find out – and also how much Lucie actually knew. Doug could hardly tell her everything, not in her current condition. Maybe he could make her see it for herself. Yes, perhaps that was the answer.

"Happy now?" he asked aloud to the only person whose opinion had ever mattered to him. "I'll do my best to help her. I'll try to find the real truth about Lucie Woods."

Part Two

Past Truth

Chapter seventeen

How often Lucie had wished for a break over the years.

"A little stint in the hospital would do me a power of good," she used to joke.

Now that it was finally here, it felt wasted on her. She was still trying, without success, to contact Hamish and piece together what on earth was going on.

Was he having an affair? Would she even have minded if he was? Perhaps he was some sort of drug mule. Maybe he was in the Mafia. Could it be that he hadn't been playing golf at all and was instead cultivating marijuana? Was he even in Singapore? For all she knew, he could be lying low in the basement, hiding from someone with a name like Vito or Tony. Would they come after her? Would she end up in the witness protection programme with short peroxide hair, a bumbag and cycling shorts . . . ? No matter how hard she tried, it was impossible to dull her outrageous ideas.

"Just forget it for the moment. You need to be strong for surgery," Nina had told her the day before when Lucie revealed her preposterous theories. "Just focus on yourself. I'm sure there's a logical explanation. There has to be."

Lucie had nodded weakly, promising Nina she'd make an effort to relax.

To stop her spiralling thoughts, Lucie allowed her to mind drift backwards. But even there, in what should have been her warm, fuzzy place, she couldn't seem to string the events of her life together in sequence. It was something she sometimes did, whenever she was feeling really alone – tested herself to see if she could still conjure the past, their faces: Mam, Dad, Sammy, Felicity. All no more. And here was Lucie, still here.

Sometimes she wished she could have gone with them, wherever they were. When Dad died first, Lucie had been convinced that he'd forever watch over her from the comfort of a plaid armchair in the sky – a cup of tea in hand, brushing the crumbs from a beloved almond finger from his jumper. Then, when they'd all passed on, Lucie had tried to comfort herself that she now had an army in the sky keeping watch, guiding her from beyond. It had kept her going, at first. Lately, she hadn't felt them so much.

"Jesus, if you're all guiding me, you're making a right balls of it," Lucie muttered to herself.

Maybe it was all a load of crap. When you die, you die. Wasn't that what some said? When the last of the Maguires had died, save Ann, people used to utter soothing thoughts.

"They'll always be with you."

"Aren't you lucky to have them looking down on you."

"It'll get easier."

"Grief is a terrible thing. It passes."

"God only takes the good ones."

Well, then why the hell had God left her behind? Was she not good enough?

It was *all* bullshit. All lies. Grief never passes. It's always there. Some days were easier. Having Bella and Declan had given Lucie a new focus, but the pain had never left her, the injustice of life, or death, always present.

It's not fair. There's no reason. Why did you all go? Why did you leave me?

There had been times over the years when Lucie had wanted to scream it aloud. Once or twice she had, hearing her words echoing, her anguish not enough to fill the emptiness in the room. How she wished she could rewind back to the last time when they'd all been together in her parents' house – to the night before she'd left Ireland for Australia. Right now, if she could, Lucie would have transported herself back there to whisper in her own ear, "Stay, Lucie. Stay with them. Hold on to them."

"You're never coming back. Are you?" Felicity had said quietly, studying Lucie with sombre eyes.

They were sitting at the kitchen table in her parents' terraced house in Knockmore. It wasn't the first time her sister-in-law had expressed the same concern.

"Oh, God, I will, Fliss. Of course I will. It's just a year – two max. I swear on your life."

Felicity laughed. "Jesus, don't swear on *my* life, swear on your own, Lu."

"Oh, yeah," Lucie grinned. "Swear on my own, then. Sure, how could I leave all this behind?"

They both turned to look where Lucie's mother was humming to herself at the worktop, cutting crusts off sandwiches and arranging them on plates. Outside, her father had the barbeque "revved up", as he called it, and was standing over it in the lashing rain, holding a golf umbrella to protect the rows and rows of already blackened sausages.

Felicity and Lucie had burst out laughing.

"The *state* of them." Lucie rolled her eyes then reached over urgently to grab Felicity's hand. "I wish you were coming with me. Imagine the adventures we'd have."

"Hah!" Felicity smirked. "There'd be no adventures with me. An old married woman like me and a seven-year-old daughter in tow . . ."

Felicity and Sammy had married shortly after their daughter, Ann, was born – one of the few teenage faux pas pregnancies that had ended in a happy ever after . . . in Knockmore, anyway.

"What's this?" Sammy pulled out a chair, turned it and swung his leg over as if mounting a horse. Resting his arms on the back, he raised an eyebrow to his sister. "My *wife* is going nowhere, Lu. You're on your own, I'm afraid." Sammy reached over and pulled Felicity towards him, nuzzling her neck.

"I wouldn't trust all the beach bums with her," he said.

Then he looked at Lucie. "Fair play, sis. I didn't think you had it in you to *actually* go." He swiped at one of the corks dangling from his hat and beamed.

Lucie had nearly fallen over when she'd arrived earlier that evening at her parents' home for what was being dubbed the Last Supper. She hadn't eaten all day, knowing she was to be fed enough food to last her for months to prevent probable starvation, as Mam kept saying. After letting herself in, Lucie had flung open the living room door.

"Surprise!"

"Mother of God." It was all she could manage as she took in the scene.

Mam, Felicity and even seven-year-old Ann were dressed in brown aprons, each with a teddy bear tucked into makeshift pockets. They were wearing brown ears, made out of what looked like the inside of cereal boxes, attached to hairbands, their noses painted black.

"Teddy bears!" Lucie exclaimed. "What the . . ."

"Kangaroos!" Felicity corrected, pointing at the teddy dangling from her apron. "That's my baby roo."

"Oh." Lucie burst out laughing and then glanced at her father, who was sitting in his usual spot.

Perched on his head was his old fishing hat, attached to which were several corks dangling from string. He didn't look pleased.

"Good effort, Dad." Lucie walked over and tapped one of the corks.

"Your mother's idea." He shook his head in dismay as the corks bobbed about, one poking him in the eye. "Not mine." He reached up to steady the movement. "She had me down at the Italian restaurant collecting corks last week. I told them I was helping Ann make something for school. They would have thought I was a right eejit if I said they were for a hat."

"Ah, give over, Paddy. It's just a bit of fun. They all wear them in Oz. Keeps the mozzies away," Tess said proudly.

"Suits you better," Lucie winked at Sammy, who was wearing a similar hat, looking slightly more enthused than their father.

He'd even gone a step further, adding pink zinc stripes like a surfer to his face.

"Lipstick." Felicity gestured at the marks.

"G'day, Lucie. Fancy a brewski?" Sammy asked in a believable Aussie accent, passing her a beer.

Lucie giggled. "Cheers, mate. Ah, guys, you shouldn't

have. I feel like I'm already in Australia." She grimaced at Felicity, who was trying to hide a smirk.

"Tess has been watching *Neighbours* on TV for days trying to get a taste for the lifestyle," Felicity revealed.

"Oh, I have." Tess adjusted her teddy bear. "And *Home and Away*. You know, I quite like that Alf Stewart. Solid sort. Lucie, if you could find someone like him to keep an eye on you, I'd feel much better about all this."

"Alf Stewart is a narky old man." Lucie erupted at her mam's description of the patriarchal figure of the fictitious seaside resort.

"Yes, but from what I can see," Mam wagged a finger, "he's misjudged. Heart of gold, he has. Really – always looking out for the schoolkids. Imagine! they wear little checked dresses to school. Short sleeves! You'd be freezing here in that get-up. You'd have to feel sorry for him. His wife is an alcoholic, troubled, so steer clear of her, but if you have any problems, Alf will help you, I'm sure."

Lucie rolled her eyes, putting her arm around Tess. "Mam, it's not real. You do know that? I doubt Australia will be anything like it seems on TV."

"Looks real to me. Ah, you know what I mean. Mix with a nice crowd, won't you, Lucie. Don't get caught up with one of those fellas with long blond hair that needs a good shampoo, even if he does have the biggest surfboard on the beach," she winked. "Sausage sandwich?" Mam thrust the plate under her nose.

Later, when little Ann had gone to bed, they'd all sat around discussing the big adventure, Mam lecturing her on safety, Sammy teasing her about how her fair skin would be lobster red after five minutes on Bondi Beach.

"And don't get in the water, Lucie. I don't want you

coming home without a leg. Sharks everywhere, even in the ponds! Watch out," Mam continued.

Lucie, who was usually bemused by her mother's inaccurate warnings, sat listening nervously to the familiar chatter. God, she was going to miss them. It was only hitting her now just how much. Even though she'd been living in Dublin for the past six years, nursing, she still came home most weekends, depending on the rota at the hospital. At first, she'd loved Dublin, but since turning twenty-four, Lucie had begun to feel the need for something more – fearful she'd spend the rest of her life living in horrible digs and coming home like the spinster sister every weekend.

"Hey, I bet you'll meet someone." Felicity leaned over and patted Lucie's arm now. "Love of your life."

"Well, it hasn't happened so far now, has it? Maybe it's just not on the cards for me, Fliss." Lucie picked at a bit of leftover cake. "Not like you guys."

Felicity and Sammy had met when she was seventeen and he was nineteen. Almost as soon as they had, Felicity had fallen pregnant in what became a huge scandal in small-town eighties Ireland. But the gossip had passed soon enough.

Before that, Felicity hadn't had an easy life by any means. Her mother was unhinged, for a start, and her childhood had been disturbing to the say the least. Lucie still shuddered when she thought about how things might have worked out for Felicity. Felicity had attempted suicide during that awful time, but in the end, everything had worked out, thankfully. Now, Sammy and Felicity were love's young dream.

Lucie would be lying if she said it sometimes didn't bother her, wondering why *she* hadn't been as lucky in love. That was an understatement. Hell, she'd never even had a boyfriend, not one. There had been a few kisses here and there, but it never went beyond that. Sure, Lucie gave off the impression of being all worldly, bang up to date with the latest fashions and music, but in matters of the heart, she was more Mother Teresa.

"Don't be stupid. Would you look at you? You're the funniest person I know, and gorgeous. Just promise you'll come back. I . . . I need you." Felicity's voice broke suddenly.

Paddy and Tess had gone into the living room to watch the news while Sammy was upstairs reading Ann another story.

"I need you too, Fliss. And I will. I promise. We'll all be together again soon. I . . . I just need to do this. I need to see what else there is."

"I know. Go see. Tell me everything and then come home."

If Lucie had known it would be the last time they'd all be together, then perhaps she would have told them more, explained how she'd felt that life hadn't yet delivered. Funny, looking back now, she'd had everything she'd ever wanted right there in that room. But wasn't that how it always was – that you don't realise until it's gone . . . ?

Chapter eighteen

Despite herself, Lucie had dozed off dreaming about it all. Waking disoriented from her sleep and opening her eyes to see that familiar face, blonde hair hanging loose, made Lucie jump.

"Fliss?"

"No, it's me."

The tears came immediately. "Ann!" For a moment, Lucie had thought it was Felicity, imagining for one second that she'd magically summoned her friend. "You came." Lucie hugged her tight.

"Of course I did. Just like you were there when I needed you. We're family – that's what we do. That's how the Maguires roll, remember . . ."

The family motto, drilled into them all from birth, made Lucie smile. Ann was also smiling broadly. It was so natural that for a moment, it pierced Lucie's heart.

"What bloody well took you so long?" Lucie teased from behind glassy eyes.

* * *

Lucie had almost chickened out when it came to it. But she'd realised there was no other choice. Sometimes the only ones who truly have your back, who will drop everything in an instant, are the ones with whom you share blood. Lucie was glad now that she'd made that phone call to her niece on Monday, bringing Ann up to speed on recent events – from the incident at the school, to fainting on the side of the road, to needing surgery, to Hamish's disappearance.

"I knew there was something," Ann had admitted down the phone. "I just knew something was up. Then I thought I'd done something. Why, Lu? Why didn't you tell me before now that you were under pressure?"

Lucie had exhaled loudly. "I was trying to be brave. When everything first started to go wrong . . . well, at least . . . things haven't been great for a long time, but I . . . Ah, I don't know, I was denying it all," Lucie had explained, filling Ann in on her current situation. "I'm used to managing on my own without family and I guess I didn't want to trouble you. I'm supposed to be there for *you*, Ann. Not the other way round. *I'm* supposed to mother you. I mean, I let you down so badly before. When Felicity died, I—"

"Stop that right now, Lu. That's in the past. You said you had your reasons for not coming back when Mam died. That's good enough for me."

"But it's not good enough, Annie. I *should* have dropped everything. I've been thinking about her a lot. I was so broken after Fliss, so bloody lost. And then . . . oh, Ann, I'm lost again." Her voice had trembled.

"Please, Lu. That's for another day. And remember, there are only seventeen years between us. My *own* mother was barely old enough to be my mother! We look after each other. It's not all on you to be there for me. What can I do right now? Just say the words."

Lucie hadn't been able to say it. She hadn't needed to. Ann got there first.

"I'm on my way."

It was Ann who'd suggested the plan of action, as Lucie had hoped she might, removing Lucie's biggest concern. Seeing Ann here now, Lucie felt relieved – happy she could finally admit that the glamorous-sounding life in Australia hadn't materialised.

"How are you?" Ann held her hand.

"Terrible. Shite. Awful. Horrendous," Lucie smirked.

"Any word from Hamish?"

"Nothing."

"Jesus." Ann gritted her teeth. "I'll kill him. I've never even met him, but I'll murder him all the same."

Lucie smiled at her level of protection. It was precisely how Lucie had felt when Ann had revealed that her own husband was cheating on her in Ireland. Back then, Lucie had gone into maternal mode at the flick of a switch and even though she was in Australia, she'd coached Ann through the difficult times over the phone.

It had taken Ann a while. She'd encountered a dubious set of speed bumps on the way to happiness – getting mixed up in that strange family from a rebound relationship before settling on Nathan O'Keefe, to whom she was now engaged.

"How is the wonderful Nathan?"

"He's great." Ann couldn't hide her grin. "He's holding the fort while I'm here. I have to be back by Saturday, which I know isn't ideal, but we're busy this time of year. It's all go. It'll be fine," Ann added when she saw Lucie's face. A round trip to Australia for a few days was a big ask.

Ann and Nathan ran a successful wedding venue out of the beautiful Knockmore House, which she'd bought after her divorce settlement. It had been the house in which her mother, Felicity, had grown up. Back then, it had been filled with unhappy memories from Felicity's childhood, but now, Ann had flipped it on its head, making it a joyful place.

"I still can't believe you did what you did with Knockmore House. I'm so proud of you. Your mam would be, too."

Ann smiled sadly. "Lu, you know only too well how bad things got for me before they got better. If it wasn't for you, I'd have given up. Now it's my turn to help you. It's going to be okay. There's nothing that can't be fixed. You said so yourself."

"Me and my darn positivity. Trouble is, sweet little Annie, I don't know what the hell it *is* I'm trying to fix."

"You'll figure it out. The most important thing is to get better first. That we can control." She stopped then, looking at her feet. "When I heard you were in the hospital . . ." Ann winced. "I thought it was happening again. I thought you were going to leave me, too. I couldn't bear to lose you, Lu. Not again."

"Oh, Ann," Lucie reached up and cupped her face. "I'm not going anywhere. The doctor is sure that I'm going to be okay. Physically, anyway."

"And I'll fix the rest." Ann hesitated then. "Lu? Just how bad is everything else? And I want you to be honest with me."

Lucie didn't know how to answer. How could she put it all into words? She could explain the immediate situation, sort of. Hamish had put them in dire financial trouble. From her hospital bed, Lucie had tried to look further into their accounts by calling the bank. She'd contacted Hamish's friend, Brent, the guy who'd been looking for him. Brent had been cagey with her, as she'd suspected he might be, reiterating that he really needed to speak to them both in person. When she'd explained that she'd be out of action for the coming weeks, Brent had asked for Hamish.

"Away," she'd said, losing patience. "With work. Just answer me this, Brent, please . . . are we going to lose the house?"

He'd paused for a few seconds too long. Long enough for Lucie to surmise that it wasn't going to be good news.

"Lucie, I've always liked you. Hell, Hamish and I go back a long way, but it's not looking good. My advice is to get him back here asap. Hamish was always very explicit that he didn't want you worried, but I can't keep this going for much longer . . ."

"Keep what going?" What on earth did he mean?

"How can I put this? In short, if Hamish doesn't make contact, and soon, then yes. You *are* going to lose the house."

"It's bad, Ann. I can do very little from here, but I made some calls." Lucie went on to explain what she'd been able to uncover. She put her hands to her face. "I had an inkling things weren't great, but not like this. The kids? What am I going to tell them? How am I going to manage? And where the hell is he?" When she thought about everything, it was hard not to get worked up.

"Shh, Lu. This isn't good for you right now. Not ahead of surgery. Listen, you *have* a home, in Ireland, if it comes to that. The house in the Estates in Knockmore is yours if you need it. I can give the tenants notice. Just say the word. It's *ours*, Lucie. I mean that."

Lucie nodded. Of course, it had already crossed her mind. A while back, when Ann had told her she'd bought Knockmore House, Lucie had panicked, thinking that Ann might now sell her parents' former house in the Estates. Perhaps Lucie had realised then that she and the kids might need to avail of it someday. Had Lucie been making a plan all along, pre-empting what was ahead? At the time it hadn't occurred to her, but maybe Lucie had had an inkling.

"The clues were there, Ann," Lucie conceded. "The bank cards not working . . . Hamish hiding things from me. He's been so distant. I thought that perhaps he was having an affair. But I don't think that's it. Anyway, I kept ignoring it. I didn't *want* to know, which makes me as much to blame. Then I lost my job."

"Dad would have loved the story about the compass and what you said to that little fecker who was bullying Declan." Ann bit her lip to stop herself from smiling.

"Wouldn't he just!" Lucie could just imagine Sammy punching the air and shouting, "Go on the Maguires!"

"Yep. And it was the right thing to do, Lu. It's what anyone would have done. Minus the weapon," Ann giggled before turning serious. "Everything will be fine. You'll see. Have you told Bella and Declan about the plan for the next few weeks? Are they excited?"

Lucie nodded. "Declan can't wait. Bella – not so much." She made a face.

"Leave her to me. They're going to love Ireland. A huge holiday while you recover. No school. Screw the school fees!" Ann exclaimed. "Where we're going, we don't need a big posh school. I can't wait to meet them. I can't wait to spoil them rotten, either. And as soon as you're better, I'll bring them back, or you can come to me . . . whichever comes first.

"You *can* do this, Lucie. You won't be left destitute." Then she stopped. "About Hamish . . . I don't mean to bash him. If you really love him, Lucie, you can figure this out together. Maybe he *is* in trouble. None of us is perfect. People mess up – all the time. But if Hamish knows that you have the house in Ireland, if he knows that you can fix this mess . . . if he's your person—"

Lucie was already shaking her head, staring straight ahead.

"Hamish was never my person."

Chapter nineteen

Lucie hadn't meant to confess so freely, but saying the words aloud came as a relief – her subconscious having finally forced the admission that had rested on the tip of her tongue so long.

"Okay," Ann had nodded slowly.

Once she'd acknowledged it, Lucie knew there was no way she could take it back, nor attempt to backtrack without explanation. Hamish had never been her person, that was the truth. And now that their marriage had stumbled, seriously, Lucie wasn't sure she wanted to go back. What would happen from here, Lucie had no idea, but she'd said it, spoken it aloud, creating a pivotal point – only time would tell in which direction it would swing.

Lucie wondered if Hamish felt the same. Did he also know, deep down, that their marriage, along with all of their other issues, needed urgent resuscitation? He must, of course he did – he'd said as much to her on the phone. But then, their marriage had been in tatters for years – the physical side of their relationship non-existent for longer than Lucie cared to remember. That side had passed away without ceremony. *Will we? Nah. Let's not bother.* Of course, Lucie had wondered a few times, without ever pressing him – why disturb what she didn't care to disrupt? — why he no longer seemed interested in her sexually.

Indeed, it had crossed her mind that Hamish might be having an affair, getting light relief elsewhere – he was a man, after all. Surely Hamish couldn't be satisfied with a wooden kiss upon returning from work each evening, the odd drunken fumble? Mind you, even *that* had ceased, replaced by a stillness that Lucie hadn't ever bothered to interrupt or question.

Through it all, though, Lucie had still never really considered leaving the marriage. Well, except that one time . . . There was always that old-fashioned belief instilled within her, she supposed – the idea of making her bed and having to lie in it.

"Martyr," Sammy might have said if she'd told him the reality of her marriage.

He was the only one who'd never minced his words. But it wasn't the idea of breaking up a marriage – it was more dissolving a family that frightened Lucie. And all that would come afterwards. That's why she'd stayed.

She'd grown too old for romantic notions anyway, or so she kept telling herself – hardly able to remember what it felt like to be part of a unit or to feel desired. That feeling of yearning had faded over time. Besides, it had been so long that she'd all but forgotten what intimacy felt like, learning to live without it.

"Life is busy. You have to make time for a marriage, for sex. It's important."

Lucie had heard it a thousand times over the years. It was what she, too, would advise someone in the same situation, but she'd never taken heed herself. Instead, letting her marriage dwindle.

But then, even more worryingly, so had Hamish. Perhaps Hamish had had enough, too. Maybe this disappearance was *his* way of beginning to distance himself. Years before, Hamish had stopped nuzzling into her on the sofa, putting his arm around her, holding her – not to mention their dead sex life. Without words, that said it all.

Ann hadn't pushed her further after Lucie had admitted it.

"He's not a bad person, you know." She made a half-hearted effort to explain. "He's a good father. The truth is, I'm just not sure we were *ever* right for each other. He was good to me, back then – when your mam died. Hamish was there . . ." Lucie had looked up at Ann for reassurance.

"It must have been hard for you, Lu. I suppose I never considered that you'd lost everyone, too – and being so far away."

How she'd wanted to tell Ann more, but the words weren't yet ready to form. It was still too painful. In a way, Hamish had saved her. In another, trapping her further into the wrong life – one that was now openly disintegrating.

"Anyway . . ." Lucie had shaken herself back to reality. "Thank you for coming. We'd better make a plan. I've only a few days before surgery. I wish I wasn't trapped in here. I've a million washes to do, the kids' clothes to pack. I've to contact the school, book the flights. Oh, God, it's so much. The house must be a mess . . ."

Ann had swatted her away. "Stop. Relax. I'm going to get a taxi to your house now. You said Nina would meet me there with the kids. We'll get the house sorted for you. And I already told you, I'm taking care of the flights and—"

Lucie had interrupted, putting her hands to her face. "It's too much, Ann. I can't expect you to cover the cost. I'm mortified."

"Lu. Please. We discussed this."

"I'll pay you back."

"I don't want it. All I want is for you to get better. Please. Let me do this for you."

There was no point in arguing. Ann could be just as stubborn as Lucie, if not more so. In the end, the only thing Lucie had had to do was make the phone call to Mr Downey at Woodfield Grammar. As always, he'd been understanding. Again, Lucie had felt relief flood through her upon making yet another admission.

"They won't be back next year, Mr Downey. Unfortunately, circumstances outside my control won't allow it and I don't want to be stringing you along further."

"I understand. You'll be missed, Lucie. I mean that. All of you. That business . . . my hands were tied. But know this – off the record, of course. You were victimised. I do know that. I just couldn't stop it. You should never have taken matters into your own hands, but I understood. He's your child and sometimes with your children, we act out of love. They're lucky to have you. I wish you all the best."

Lucie had hung up feeling content. It was enough to get some form of exoneration finally. The sudden realisation that she'd never see Amanda or any of them again, for that matter, was liberating. With another decision made and an interim period for Bella and Declan in Ireland, at least it would give them time to adjust while

Lucie made a plan for the future – one that may or may not involve her elusive husband.

"Where the hell are you?" Lucie spat into the phone.

She'd almost missed the call from the unknown number. Rushing out of the bathroom, she sat on the side of the hospital bed, pressing the phone against her ear to try to hear above the crackling line.

"I'm at the hotel. I've been flat out at the office. I'm only getting a chance to call now." Hamish sounded sheepish.

Lucie took a breath, vowing to remain calm – she needed answers.

"Have you any idea what mess you've left behind? I'm at the hospital, Hamish."

"Jesus. What's happened? Are the kids okay?" He sounded concerned.

"It's not the kids. It's me! Turns out I need a hysterectomy. It's happening on Friday."

"A hysterectomy?"

"Yes. After the little episode on Sunday with the car, which we'll talk about again, I collapsed. I haven't been feeling great for a long time, not that you've noticed."

"Are you going to be okay?"

"No. Yes. I'll be fine. It's everything else that's . . . Hamish? Can you hear me?"

The line cracked again and she could hear his voice breaking, going in and out.

"Yes, I'm here. Christ, Lucie, I'm sorry . . . I . . ."

"I spoke to Brent. The bank is talking about taking the house. Hamish, please. You've got to talk to me. What's going on?"

"It won't happen. Brent was always dramatic. We're a

bit behind is all. Did he say anything else?"

"He needs us to come in. He said that ignoring it isn't going to make it go away. You have to come back, Hamish. I had to call Ann. She's here, in Australia. She's taking the kids to Ireland for a while. I'm going to be off my feet for about six weeks."

"Good idea," he agreed.

Lucie hadn't expected that. She thought Hamish would be on the first flight back as soon as he heard she was unwell. "What do you mean, *good* idea?"

"Well, if you're going to be off your feet—"

"*Come home*!" she hissed.

"I can't, Lucie."

"Why not? Christ. What are you not telling me? You're acting like you're on the run. Hamish, I can handle whatever you tell me. I just need to know."

The line was silent for a moment.

"Is there something *you're* not telling me?" he asked then, turning it back round.

"What?" She shook her head in disbelief. "What does *that* mean?"

"It's a question. I have a right to ask, as well. Is there anything you need to tell me?"

Lucie's brow furrowed. "Hamish, if this is some sort of game, I'm not playing." She was having trouble keeping her voice down. "I don't understand."

"But I think you *do* understand, Lucie. I *really* think you do." His voice was peppered with bitterness.

"Is this about the school and my job again? Leave it out, will you! I'm going to give you one last chance to tell me why you can't come back, or I'll disappear to Ireland with the kids and you'll never see us again."

She could hear him exhaling loudly.

"And I'm going to give *you* one last chance . . ."

"Screw you, Hamish. I have no idea what you're talking about. I'll manage on my own. This has been a long time coming—"

"Yeah. It has. Hasn't it? You think I don't know that I've always been second best for you. And after all I did, taking you on—"

"Taking me on?"

"You know what I mean."

"Do I? You're an insecure arsehole. Come home and sort this out or like I said, we'll be gone, so help me God."

There was another pause, giving her time to gather herself. If she completely lost it now with Hamish, she ran the risk of him clamming up, and she needed to know the truth.

"But maybe that was your plan along . . ." he replied before the line went dead.

Lucie was left staring hopelessly at the hospital wall, wondering if her husband was more perceptive than he let on. Lucie felt more confused than ever.

With everything else, she'd all but forgotten the surgery ahead and how dreadful she was going to feel for weeks. The thought of not seeing Bella and Declan for six weeks was also making it difficult to breathe. And now Hamish was acting like a complete and utter prick. Knowing that Ann would be caring for the children was a huge comfort, but it didn't stop Lucie from feeling alone, especially when she saw how enamoured they'd become with Ann in just a few short days.

"Mum, Ann said we're going to be helping out at Knockmore House with the weddings. I'm chief door-opener and Bella is going to get to sit at reception," Declan explained the next day when they all came to visit.

"That's fab, Dec. I'm sure you'll make a marvellous door-opener. Have you everything ready to go?"

"Yep. Ann helped me to pack my bag and tidied the house and cleaned out the fridge. And everything is ready for you when you get out of hospital. Will you be lonely?" he asked innocently. "You can play my video games. I'm not taking mine. Ann said there's way too much to see in Knockmore. Is it huge?"

"Eh, not huge, but there's plenty to do." Lucie smiled at Ann, who was leaning against the windowsill flicking through a magazine. "Are you all set, Bells?"

"Like I have a choice?" Bella asked curtly, crossing her arms, from where she was sitting at the end of the bed sulkily. "I can't get through to Dad. When will he be back? I can fly back on my own when he gets back here. I'm missing all the end-of-year stuff at school."

"I know, Bells. I'm sorry. I spoke to Dad yesterday. He said he misses you so much and we'll all be together soon, but you can't fly back alone and he's working." Lucie caught Ann's eye and grimaced. "Besides, you're going to love Ireland. What an opportunity!"

"Yes, and I told Bella we're going to go to Dublin for a weekend on a major shopping spree." Ann leaned over to ruffle Bella's hair, who didn't react.

"Well, that's something, I suppose. When is your operation, Mum?" Bella looked worried despite her surly exterior.

"Tomorrow. I'm all set. I've asked for a boob job, a tummy tuck and great big lip fillers as well." Lucie tried to be light before turning serious. "You guys fly out tomorrow evening, so I won't get to see you after today." She smiled bravely.

She'd already discussed with Ann that it was best not

to bring the children to see her right after the operation. Nina would be there to keep an eye on her and she didn't want them to see her all groggy, and possibly weeping like a baby from the anaesthetic.

"So, I'm going to say goodbye to you shortly," she continued. "But I swear I'm going to be fine. *Everything* is going to be fine. I promise."

This was the part Lucie had been dreading – having to say goodbye for such a long time. She'd never been apart from Bella or Declan much over the years. In fact, being in Ireland a few years before, when Lucie had gone over to reunite with Ann, was the longest they'd been separated.

Holding Declan first, trying to capture his smell, the softness of his skin, was almost too much for Lucie to bear. The whole time she kept telling herself that this wasn't like before, it wasn't like it had been when saying goodbye to her family, not realising that she'd never see them again. She *would* be with Declan and Bella again, she knew that.

"Mum, I can't breathe."

"Sorry, Dec. Be good. Call me every single day. Won't you?"

"I will. Ann said Nathan's going to build me a treehouse." The excitement in his voice was comforting. "I can design it on the computer."

"I can't wait to see it. Come here, Bells." Lucie's voice caught in her throat as Bella rested her head on her mother's chest. "I'm going to miss you so much."

"Are you sure I can't stay, Mum? I could look after you here. You and me."

How Lucie wanted to say yes. Instead, she smoothed Bella's hair aside and swallowed her tears.

"Trust me, love. You'll be better off with Ann. Will you be okay?"

Bella looked up at her mother, registering her face. "She's cool, Mum. I like her. I'll be okay. I promise."

"That's my girl. I'll see you soon, okay? Go and wait outside while I tell Ann all the things you're not allowed to do," she winked, biting her lip to stop herself from crying as they padded towards the door, turned and waved. Lucie's heart splintered.

"I'll guard them with my life," Ann promised as the tears flooded down Lucie's cheeks. "And then I'll guard you. I'll be in touch every minute!"

"Ann?"

"Yes."

"There's so much I still need to tell you."

"I know. And you will, when you're ready – and if you want to, Lu. But I keep telling you, there's no need." Ann smiled encouragingly.

"I've been trying to piece it all together, but I can't seem to make sense of it all. I was so alone, too – back then, you know? All I wanted was a family. But somewhere in there, I vanished. I don't know who the hell I am any more."

"I won't let you vanish, ever. Take this time to figure it all out. Remember how I got myself together? I went all the way back to the start. Now, it's your turn. And accept help, Lu. Sometimes you have to let yourself be saved."

Chapter twenty

Doug

Doug's soft-soled shoes emitted a high-pitched squeal against the linoleum, making him jump. Looking up at the illuminated sign over the doorway, he stood back to let a trolley pass and then continued on tiptoe to prevent the sporadic sound of screeching rubber. The piercing shrill took him back to a time he didn't necessarily care to relive. The dull smell of disinfectant wasn't helping, either – nor the glaring artificial lights flickering and buzzing overhead, igniting his senses. Glancing left to right at the door numbers, he paused again.

Was this really the right thing to do? Knowing once he got involved it would be difficult to extract himself, to walk away unscathed – or worse still, come out looking anything less than virtuous. The thing is, he cared what she thought of him. That's what was causing such reluctance.

Perhaps he should leave. After all, was it really up to him to save her?

Mind you, Doug Offer couldn't have known, as he walked the corridor looking for room 212, that Lucie

Woods was at that same moment rehashing her niece's earlier advice. Or seconds before his head peered round the open door that Lucie had whispered Ann's parting words, "Let yourself be saved," into the silence of the hospital room.

From the look on her face as he materialised round the large white painted door, Doug could tell that his sudden appearance had surprised her. He stood unsurely, trying to read her features while awkwardly clutching a bunch of cheap flowers wrapped in crinkly cellophane in his hand. Of course, Doug could also never have guessed that Lucie's puzzled expression was partly because she felt her words may somehow have invoked the older man once more – precisely when she needed him most.

"And here you are again." Her face morphed into a wide smile. "We have to stop meeting like this."

"I hope you don't mind. I just wanted to make sure you were all right, give you these." He shook the bunch of flowers. Some of the petals broke free and landed by his feet. "Ah, maybe not," he grimaced, looking down. "I won't stay." He hadn't moved from the door.

"Come in, please." Lucie gestured at the armchair next to her bed. "Sit down. Excuse the state of me." She pulled her nightdress around her neck. "I wasn't expecting anyone, but I'm glad you came. I wanted to say thank you. I did mean to call. Let's just say it's been a bit of a whirlwind."

Doug made his way towards the bed and placed the flowers on the table then sat down. "You look a bit better. Brighter." He pointed at her cheeks. "There wasn't a drop of colour in your face when I saw you last."

"That's twice now you've come to my rescue, Doug. Is this a third time?" She asked, looking amused.

He didn't answer. Instead, he looked nervous – less

assured than he had been the other times – as he fidgeted, trying to remove his jacket. Lucie picked up a bag of boiled sweets from the table and offered him one.

"No, thanks." He put his hand up, pursed his lips.

Under the nylon zipped jacket, he was wearing a short-sleeved check shirt and a pair of cream trousers, in what Lucie imagined might be his daily uniform. Lucie grinned, showing her dimples.

"What?"

She shook her head. "Nothing."

"What?" He was smiling now, too.

"I knew you reminded me of someone. Did you ever watch *Home and Away*?"

Doug rolled his eyes. "That rubbish. I don't watch it, no. But if you say that I look like Alf Stewart, I'll leave." He pretended to pick up his jacket.

Lucie wrinkled her nose. "Not facially," she tried to defend. "It's the clothes or something." Her eyes lit up then. "When I left for Australia, my poor mother kept telling me that if I ever got into trouble that I was to seek out Alf Stewart, or someone like him, at least. It only came back to me a few days ago. It looks like I finally found my very own version," she smiled warmly.

"Look no further." Doug splayed his hands and then folded them on his lap. "Well, how are you? I really hope you don't mind me popping by. I was passing and I wondered if you were still here, so I took my chances and asked at reception to see you, and they directed me up."

"Ah, the cop in you! Quite the detective! Yes, here I am. Ta-dah. In all my glory."

"Are you . . . is it . . . will you be okay?" Doug asked uncertainly before checking himself. "Again, please don't feel you need to tell me anything. With my wife's history,

I suppose I feared the worst. It was all a little familiar."

Lucie smiled gently. "Of course. I never thought of that. Well, the good news is, I'm not going anywhere, yet. Healthwise, I'm not *too* bad," she said, filling him in on what the doctor had told her and of her upcoming surgery.

Doug looked relieved.

"It's everything else that's not great," she finished.

"How so?"

Lucie exhaled. "Oh, truth is, I'm not really sure. I suppose my life has come to a bit of a crossroads all at once. Being sick, needing this operation, well, if I'm honest, it's only the tip of the iceberg."

"Is this about that business at the school?"

Lucie gave a humourless laugh. "Nope. I took your advice on that and laid it to bed . . ." She trailed off. "Can I ask you something?"

"Yes."

"Do you ever wish you could do it all again?"

Doug looked confused.

"Life," Lucie laughed. "Sorry, me being stuck in here has me thinking about all sorts of queer things. I've turned all philosophical. What I mean is, start over, I suppose. Fix where you went wrong."

Doug shook his head. "Nope. I don't think I'd have the energy. The only thing I'd change is Rose dying, but then if it weren't her, it would be me. One of us had to go first and I suppose she was older," he admitted.

"Really?" Lucie cocked her head. "By much?"

"Ten years."

"Doug! You gigolo!" Lucie threw her head back and laughed when she saw his shocked expression.

"I've been called worse." Doug was laughing, too. "Would *you* like to start over?"

Her smile faded, a distinct shadow edging across her face.

"Maybe. I don't know. I wouldn't change my children, of course, but there are things I'd like to do again, perhaps. But then I wouldn't have them, so no." She wrinkled her nose again. "Not the way it works, is it?"

Doug tilted his head. "It's like that question if you could change just one little thing, isn't it? But it's the little things that often make the difference," he mused. "But you're young, Lucie. You *can* change your current life, if you want."

"I think I might have to." She turned to look out of the window for a moment before turning back to him. "My niece was here. The one I told you about from Ireland. She's taken the kids back there while I recover. They left an hour ago."

Doug tutted. "Ah, you'll miss them."

"I will," she nodded sadly. "Ann says I should take the time to think about my life while they're gone, decide my future . . ." she paused. "Sorry, Doug, you must think I'm half crazy. I'm not normally so forthcoming. It's your fault – you're far too easy to talk to," she teased. "*And*, since I've met you, everything has been going wrong. My husband . . . I don't even know how to explain it. There are things . . ."

Doug was wondering if she'd found out more since he'd last seen her. Perhaps she wasn't as in the dark as he'd first thought.

"Honestly, I don't know what's going on." Lucie threw her eyes upwards. "I'm not sure I ever have. But there's something. I'd love to say it's an affair, but that would be too easy." She was biting her lip.

"The other day, you said he was gone. What did you mean?" Doug asked.

"He left for Singapore. He says he's away working, but who knows?" She shrugged. "You know, that day you found me, the police had stopped me. They took the car."

"I know."

"You do?" Her brow furrowed.

"I saw it. I was coming off the slip road and I recognised your car. Then I rounded the corner and there you were. I assumed. The cop in me." He repeated her earlier words.

Lucie exhaled. "Hamish took his eye off the ball, never paid the registration and insurance. Or, as I've discovered since, the car loan, the school fees . . ." She was shaking her head in dismay. "Then this . . ." She gestured towards her stomach. "Can I ask you something else?"

Doug nodded slowly.

"Do you think you can live with someone, be married to them for as long as I've been, almost fourteen years, and not know them at all?"

"I think it's possible," he acknowledged. "But I think there's always an inkling there."

"Yes," she nodded back. "An inkling. The trouble is, I'm not sure I want to address the inkling. If I do, then my life as I know it is probably over. Ah!" She looked up at the ceiling. "I'm sorry. This is all very deep. I don't want to trouble you with all of my problems."

Doug looked at the ground, wondering should he just come out with it, like tearing off a plaster. Doug would end up as the bad guy. But in the long run, wasn't it better that she knew the facts? Then again, how could he land everything on her while she was lying in the hospital, awaiting intrusive surgery? Lucie made a snorting noise and he looked up to see tears in her eyes.

"Oh, God, sorry. I think I'm more nervous about this operation than I've been letting on."

Doug put his hand on hers. "Lucie, if I can say. I don't know you very well, but it seems to me like you have the world on your shoulders. If you'd like someone to talk to, I'd be happy to oblige," he smiled encouragingly. "You know, in my old line of work, I used to ask question after question, to which I'd often get monosyllabic responses. Eventually, though, people start to open up. As if all the little questions and their answers soon unlock the bigger ones. Do you know what I mean?"

She nodded, childlike. "I think so." She wiped her eyes with her sleeve. "Sorry, again."

"Stop apologising."

"It's an Irish thing, the constant apologising for nothing."

"Really?" he guffawed. "Rose must have missed that memo. You'd be hard-pressed to get an apology from her, ever. But then, in her own words, she was always right."

"Hah. See, for the first time in a long time, I'm all on my own again. Ann and the children are gone. Hamish is 'away' . . ." She made speech marks. "And my friend, Nina – you met her – well, she works full time and she has her own life."

Doug smiled. "I'm here. Alf Stewart to the rescue! I'm alone, too. We could chat. I could tell you about Rose. It might help you to figure it all out."

"Let yourself be saved," Lucie whispered to herself.

"What's that?"

"Ah, it was something my niece said. She said sometimes you have to let yourself be saved. That there are people who care, no matter how alone you think you are."

"Wise words. Your husband? Have you spoken to him? If you don't mind me asking, are you estranged?"

Lucie shrugged. "Not sure estranged is the word. Though, he's strange all right! Who knows? He knows

I'm here now. I spoke to him yesterday. It was odd. He sounded relieved that the kids were going to Ireland." Lucie didn't elaborate on Hamish's unnerving questions, or his accusatory statement before hanging up. "I keep thinking maybe he's messed up in some financial deal that's gone wrong.

"I wonder . . ." She glanced up quizzically. "Maybe . . . you might have connections . . . could you . . . ?" Then just as quick, she stopped and waved her hands. "Ignore that. I'll figure it out.

"Maybe you're right and I just need to talk it out. Funny," she grinned. "Lately, I've been thinking a lot about the past, my family. How I got to this point. Things like why I even left Ireland at all. I can't seem to remember now."

"Why did you leave?"

Chapter twenty-one

The bus journey home was, without doubt, Lucie's least favourite part of each week. She rotated her shoulder towards the window to look out enviously at the cars zooming past, peering into the mostly empty passenger seats, imagining the scent of pine coming from the air fresheners. What she wouldn't give to be sitting comfortably in a car, instead of here, pressed up against the glass, trying to breathe through her mouth.

The windows of the bus had steamed up by now. The occasional hissing of the swing door had ceased. Each time, she'd found herself lifting her head to see what poor sod had boarded the bus from Dublin for home this time. With no further stops before her destination, the bus was now crammed, heaving with passengers and their alcohol-laced Friday evening breath.

Lucie closed her eyes. If she managed to doze off for forty minutes, as she usually did when they hit the smooth stretch of motorway, she could make the journey go quicker. It was her only chance before the bus would swing left, journeying along the winding road to Knockmore, shaking her insides with the bumps and potholes along the country road.

The man beside her let out an enormous snore, one that caught in his throat and then gurgled on exit, like an engine failing to start. His head rolled slowly to the right before coming to a stop snugly on Lucie's shoulder. She shrugged sharply and his head bounced up, balancing on his inactive neck for a moment before lolling back to a resting position, *on her*. Typical. There'd be no nap for her now, not while this big gorilla snoozed away happily.

He'd grand big legs on him, that said. Lucie craned her neck to get a look at his face. *Not great* – the lips were a bit rubbery and he was now making a noise like a fish, blowing imaginary bubbles through his inflated lips. Why did the massive fellas always choose to pack themselves in beside her for the journey? It was invariably the same. Maybe it was her size – small enough to accommodate tree trunk thighs and enormous shoulders next to her.

"Honestly, not once in five years have I ever got someone other than the Incredible Hulk to sit next to," Lucie had complained recently after arriving home following a particularly arduous bus journey.

"Oh, but isn't Hulk lovely! Like, if anything went wrong with the bus: flat tyre, hostage situation . . . Hulk would be very convenient to be sitting next to. And I always think if he wasn't green, he'd be a catch. A fine head of hair on him, lovely and thick. And maybe a touch of lavender cream could tone his colouring."

Her mother had been waiting, kettle on, rashers sizzling in the pan. It didn't matter what day or what time

Lucie arrived home – Mam would always have the welcome home sandwich ready.

"Sorry, correct that," Lucie remembered, not paying attention. "I had a tiny wee nun once. Remember the one who looked at me like I'd just told her I'd lost all of my limbs in battle when I said I was still single. She said she'd say a novena that I'd meet a man soon. Apparently, she was going to get all the other sisters at the convent involved." Lucie had pursed her lips. "To be fair, on the return journey, I met a lovely lad."

"Oh, you never said."

"No, Mam. He was fine-looking, but he farted the whole way to Dublin. He didn't even try to hide it! Honest to God, every time the bus hit a bump, I could practically taste what Mammy had fed him before he left. My guess was Brussel sprouts." Lucie turned up her nose. "I had to cover my face with my jacket and hold my breath. I was dizzy getting off the bus. Then he asked me for my number!"

"And did you give it? He sounds grand."

"Mam! Did you not hear me? He had a foul bowel. I'm telling you. Toxic."

"Ah, Lu, maybe he was in a rush and he didn't have time to chew his sprouts properly. You should have given him a chance."

Lucie had shaken her head impatiently. Honest to God, if they'd had their way, her parents would have her paired up with a green beast with lavender cream on his face, or worse still, one that smelled like he'd shat himself before getting on the bus.

"Would you not buy yourself a car, girl?" her father had chimed in. "At least then you could roll down the window."

"It wasn't me farting, Dad! Anyway, where would I get the money to buy a car? I'm barely scraping in enough to survive up in Dublin. The room I have at the moment is horrible. Mushrooms growing out of the carpet and all. Sure, why do you think I come home every chance I get?"

"I'm sure Sammy could pick you up a little runaround. He gets some great little yokes in his garage. Isn't that right, Tess?"

"Oh yeah. And Sammy said the cars always come with a little bottle of holy water in the glove compartment and a sticker of Padre Pio to keep you safe," Tess agreed.

"I'll think about it."

Lucie wasn't going to think about it. There wasn't even any parking at St Vincent's Hospital, Dublin – not for the nurses, anyway. Besides, everything Lucie had spare she was saving. For what, she wasn't entirely sure, but she wasn't a child any more. At some point, she'd need to get her own place, or at least decide what the hell she was doing with her life.

Feeling exhausted, Lucie inched further towards the glass now, rolling up her jacket and resting it between her head and the window of the bus. In one way, she almost wished she had been working this weekend, so she wouldn't have to endure the journey home to escape the mushroom room in the house she shared in Stillorgan, Dublin. It was all right sleeping there during the week. Well, she could at least stomach it. She usually met friends most evenings after work, only going back to the house when it was absolutely necessary. She'd even taken up aerobics, which she absolutely hated, but at least the studio was warm and fungus-free.

In fact, she'd have done anything to avoid the damp four-bedroomed house that she'd moved into last year. It was icy-cold. So cold in places that Lucie was convinced there was a presence floating somewhere in the house. The ghost of breakfast foods, perhaps, guarding its fungi implicitly.

Of all the places she'd ever lived, she despised this one the most. Yet another of the friends Lucie had shared a flat with had got engaged and moved back home to save money for their wedding, forcing Lucie, once again, to find a room with a group of strangers in a house she could ill afford. One by one, her nursing friends were dropping like flies – moving in with boyfriends, buying apartments, going abroad to work. It was so different from the early days, working at the hospital and renting with the other nurses. Then, she'd adored Dublin – lately, not so much.

Lucie hated watching TV in the communal living room. Sitting bolt upright because she was too self-conscious to relax in front of strangers, or too afraid that she'd lie back on the filthy cream leather sofa and find herself luxuriating next to someone else's hardened snot. Being in the kitchen wasn't much better, looking at the dirty plates piling up in the sink, half-drank cans of beer strewn across the sticky pine table.

There was only so many times she could go out drinking at the weekends, ending up in Copper Face Jacks, the infamous nightclub where the nurses and the gardai of Dublin would gather to meet their future love interest. She hadn't had much luck there, anyway. Then having to spend Sunday alone, forced to tidy up where none of her other feckless housemates could be bothered, to stop them all from catching listeria. After which she'd be left wondering if she'd ever meet a man. It wasn't that Lucie was placing all of her future happiness on being part of a couple, but at this rate she was beginning to think it might never happen.

Lucie loved her job. At least she had that, she supposed. But nursing was a vocation as her father still warned – one where the salary, or lack thereof, made it difficult to survive on, especially in Dublin. There again, Dublin was the only place to advance her career in Ireland.

It was hopeless. There were times when she thought she should pack it all in and try her hand at something else. Some of the girls she'd trained with were working as medical reps, earning a fortune, with a brand-new car under their arse. But truth be told, when Lucie was at work, caring for patients, wearing her crisp, starched uniform, it was the only place she felt truly alive. It's what she'd trained for, after all. Talking to patients, joking with her colleagues who adored her, Lucie never tired of it.

"Why do you nurse?" she remembered one of the lecturers asking the class once.

"To save lives."

"To provide care."

"To make a patient's life easier," the other students had offered.

"Because I *am* a nurse." Lucie had been saying it more to herself, but the lecturer had raised an eyebrow and nodded appraisingly in her direction.

And nursing really was Lucie Maguire. It was everything else she struggled with.

"There has to be someone," Felicity, her sister-in-law, had said the week before.

Lucie had been sitting on the rug in the living room of Sammy and Felicity's little apartment on Saturday evening.

"Anyone," Felicity laughed. "Are you too fussy, maybe?" She squinted at Lucie, who was now lying back, staring at the ceiling.

"Fussy! Are you mad? Hah. I'd take anything at this stage, except anyone off the bus. And here was me thinking I'd have to leave Knockmore to meet a decent fella. Well, there's none in Dublin, either, I can tell you that for nothing. Bloody full of pompous rugby fellas.

"The only other guys I meet are doctors. No-thank-you. All jammed up their own arses. Or geriatrics in the hospital beds, who shout at me to hand them a bedpan, or wipe their arse. I'm over men, Fliss. Honest." Lucie sat up again, looking frustrated.

"Don't say that! Come on, now." Felicity looked up from where she was plaiting Ann's hair into two impressively neat French plaits. "You're gorgeous, Lu. There's someone for you, I know it." She tied her daughter's hair into the end of the second plait and pulled Ann onto her knee.

"No, Fliss. There's no one for me. We can't all have a perfect life like you, you know. I'm going to spend the rest of my life here at the weekends, as the third wheel to my brother's marriage. And then one day I'll be the creepy aunt at Ann's wedding with cobwebs in my hair, cerise pink lipstick all over my false teeth.

"I'll be one of those people who live until 104 years of age and who wears purple from head to toe." Lucie was on a roll now. She put on a whiny voice. "'Poor thing,' they'll say over the coffin, 'never met anyone. Very unlucky in love, but doesn't she look lovely laid out there in all the purple. Alone but regal.'"

Felicity burst out laughing. "Ah, Jesus. That's dismal. Besides, purple is shite on you! Well, you'll always have me. I'll hold your purple gloved hand until the very end."

"I know you will, and rub the lipstick off my teeth."

There was a tinge of bitterness to her voice. Lucie was

trying to be funny, but lately, she could feel it more and more. They *all* felt sorry for her and it was starting to irritate her.

"Amen. Anyway, Sammy's playing with the band next weekend in Lennon's. Tess said she'll take Ann for the night." Felicity made an excited face. "Why don't we go out? We can get dressed up – not in purple – and find you a fella, once and for all."

"Hah. A man in Lennon's? Sure, you'd have to be desperate to find someone there," Lucie snipped.

"Worked for me."

Felicity looked up as Sammy flung open the door, covered head to toe in oil from where he'd been working on one of the cars downstairs. She grinned hopelessly at her husband and Lucie inwardly groaned.

"Don't you two ever tire of each other?" Lucie rolled her eyes as Sammy bent to kiss Felicity and put his hand on Ann's head.

"Never," they both said in unison, while Lucie made a face.

"Right, next Saturday. One last attempt!" Felicity clapped.

"Ah, yeah." Sammy rubbed his hands together. "Next Saturday will be a big one. The drummer got engaged, so we're celebrating after the gig."

"The drummer!" Lucie moaned. "He was meant to my fallback guy if all else failed. Feck this, I'm emigrating."

Chapter twenty-two

"In here, Lu," Mam called from the kitchen. "How was the journey?"

Lucie dropped her weekend bag on the floor and closed the front door behind her. She could smell the bacon already.

"Marvellous," she shouted from the hallway. "A fine big, strapping, snoring baboon beside me this week. And before you ask—"

"Did you get his number?" Dad bellowed from the living room, where he'd be sitting in his armchair, watching the TV.

Lucie gritted her teeth. "Not quite that desperate, thank you, Father, dearest." She stuck her head round the door and waved. "But wonderful to see you have such faith in your only daughter."

"Married at your age, I was, with a mortgage." He didn't look up, continuing to stare at the quiz show he was watching. "Tick-tock. Tick-tock. Tick-tock."

"I'm twenty-three and this is the nineties, Dad. Not

everyone relies on marriage and babies to make them happy."

"Hah. Well, if you plan on being one of these bra burners, then you'll want to find a decent job and start making a bit of money, won't you? But you won't listen. Lucie knows best. Nursing was all you'd ever consider.

"Not your fault, of course. It's the government to blame. All those hours you work and what do you get? Minimum wage? And what's more . . ."

Lucie was already in the kitchen, trying to ignore the all-too-familiar lecture. No matter what she did, her father was perpetually judgmental on her choice of career.

"Hi, Mam."

Tess walked over and put her arms around her daughter. If Lucie was small, her mother was even more so. Lucie hugged her back, resting her head on her shoulder for a minute.

"Tired, love?"

"I am."

"I've the immersion on, so you can have a bath before we watch *The Late Late Show*. Here . . ."

Tess turned towards the worktop and handed her a plate with a bacon sandwich cut into four and a slice of Battenberg cake resting beside it. Lucie smiled at the beloved yellow-and-pink cake wrapped in sugary marzipan – the epitome of her youth.

"Get that into you."

Lucie plonked down wearily at the kitchen table and looked around. She loved being home, she really did, where everything was so familiar, homely, not to mention sparkling clean. Where you could walk around in your bare feet without worrying that you were going to step in someone else's wee. Not much had changed over the years in their house. Save a few coats of paint and some dreadful wallpaper in the living room, it was much the same. That, and the colourful kitchen accessories that Mam changed every few years to breathe a bit of new life into the kitchen. The current theme was red – red toaster, red kettle, red tea cosy, red tea towels, dotted here and there to brighten the brown melamine cupboards.

"Well, what's new?" Tess asked, leaning against the kitchen worktop and taking a sip from her mug of tea.

"Not much. You?" Lucie took a bite of her sandwich.

"Did you hear Ann's not well? Had a desperate temperature all day."

"Oh, should I pop over? I'll call Felicity now."

"No need. She took her to the doctor earlier. Another strep throat. That's the second this month. One more and they'll whip the tonsils out, I'd say. Anyway, Fliss said to tell you to call her in the morning. She won't be able to go to the gig tomorrow night, now. Poor thing."

"Really?" Lucie looked up, disappointed.

"Sure, she can't exactly leave Ann that way."

"Can't you mind Ann here? If she's on antibiotics, they should kick in by tomorrow. Ah, Fliss promised. I came all this way. I'd have stayed in Dublin."

Tess shook her head and raised her eyebrows. "Now, Lucie, don't be like that. Fliss is a marvellous mother – always puts Ann first. She can't be off galivanting whenever she wants to like you can. That's not how motherhood works."

"But she cancelled a few weeks ago, too. She was meant to come to Dublin, but Ann had some Irish dancing thing, so she said she couldn't come – at the last minute, as well. It took me weeks to find someone to cover my shift."

Tess tutted. "You'll understand if you ever choose to have kids that you can't just—"

"*Choose*?" Lucie interrupted. "I *will* have kids."

"Ah, I know. Someday, maybe."

"What does that mean?" Lucie jerked her head back. She was fed up with all the sly digs. "I'm twenty-three, for God's sake, not forty. It's not my feckin' fault Fliss went and got herself pregnant at seventeen. If she hadn't, then maybe you'd realise that *I'm* the normal one, not her, and you might stop putting pressure on me." Lucie pushed her sandwich away. "It's the bloody same every week."

"*Pressure*? Ah, Lu, we're doing no such thing, love." Tess softened and sat down beside Lucie, whose arms were now folded, sulking. "Look. I'm sorry. Maybe you're right. I suppose sometimes I forget Fliss is so young and of course you are, too. I suppose I expect both my girls to be at the same stage. Of course you'll meet someone."

"*Both* your girls?"

"Yes, you and Fliss. Both my daughters." Tess was starting to get flustered. "Ah, you know what I mean, Lucie. What's got into you?"

"But we're not *both* your girls. *I'm* your only daughter, Mam. Boring old Nurse Lucie, who everyone obviously thinks is going to end up a spinster. Maybe *I* should have got myself pregnant all those years ago, too. Maybe then everyone would drop everything like they've always done for Fliss or better still, leave me the hell alone. Sorry to be such a disappointment." Her face had turned bright red.

Tess frowned and leaned back. "Lucie! What on earth? You know exactly what I meant before. What do I need to do? Take my words out and read them before I say *anything*. If I didn't know better, I'd say you sound . . ." Tess paused and lifted her eyebrows slowly. "Jealous."

The word was like a slap across the face. Lucie was many things, but jealous, of *Fliss*?

"I'm not," Lucie huffed. "I'm just sick of feeling like I'm second best in this house. I went off to do nursing. I worked hard at it. And now it's constant criticism – awful career, no car, no house, no boyfriend, no prospects. I'm not the one who got herself into trouble at seventeen. I played by the rules. And now look at me!" Lucie stood up suddenly, made for the door and stopped to look back at her mother.

Tess was staring at her, her brows knitted together with concern. "You're tired, Lu."

"Yeah, I'm tired. That's all it is. I'm bloody tired!" she snapped. "I'll take a bath. Forget I said anything."

Sitting in the bath, Lucie replayed the outburst, unsure as to where it had come from. It had been out before she could stop herself. Felicity was Lucie's best friend in the entire world. Lucie loved her brother and she worshipped the ground Ann walked upon. Was she jealous? It wasn't an emotion that had ever run strong in her.

Then again, thinking of it now, it would be hard not to be a little envious. Felicity, Sammy and Ann were like this perfect family unit, utterly content with each other. Sammy was doing well working as a mechanic, moonlighting as a singer, and Felicity ran a little shop in the garage. Felicity had her own small car and they didn't want for anything. They were happy, satisfied with life – and Lucie was . . . miserable. There! She'd admitted it.

Perhaps it was something she'd been harbouring inside for years. After the shock of her friend's teenage pregnancy, for a long time it had *all* been about baby Ann. Then there was Sammy and Felicity's wedding a year later. Sammy taking over the garage, them getting their own place, Felicity running the shop. What seemed like success after success.

Of course, having baby Ann in the family had breathed life into them all, making every family occasion that bit more special. They all doted on Ann – and Lucie had been delighted, at first, to gain a sister in Felicity.

Maybe that was the problem. Lucie had never considered that she'd be losing her best friend in the process. Now, Lucie was unable to have a good moan about her family, peppered with all sorts of exaggerations to drive her point home, because Felicity was now family, too. Not only that, but she was also settled and married and motherly, flourishing in her life – everything Lucie wasn't.

When Lucie had first moved to Dublin, she'd barely had time to think about it all, nor feel left out. Back then, living at the hospital in her little room, studying, she'd inhaled the knowledge, acing her exams, living a life of freedom, spreading her wings. It had been fantastic.

In many ways, it was Felicity who Lucie had felt sorry for back then. As if it were Lucie who had life all figured out while her friend was back home, nursing a baby, trapped. Now, Lucie was the one feeling stuck – life no longer offering her anything other than existence. Working. Eating. Sleeping. Taking the bus to Knockmore beside farting, sleeping apes. Taking the bus back. Working. Eating. Sleeping. Repeat.

Lucie was sick to the teeth of them all passing comments, making her feel like a failure, questioning her life choices. Did they think she'd never considered it herself? Wonder why no one had come along to sweep her off her feet in Dublin? It was almost six years since she'd left Knockmore – six years of only ever a drunken snog here and there, the odd blind date, a fumble on the doorstep . . . and nothing more.

"Horny nurses." That's what she'd heard people say. Well, not her. Never having met anyone, she hadn't had the chance to see if it was true.

Lucie rested her head back against the green bath – another thing her mother had never got round to updating – and sighed. *Jealous.* For the first time in her life, she felt jealous, insanely so, of the one person who deserved all the happiness she got, after such a miserable childhood. Felicity now had everything Lucie wanted – love, a child, a family . . . *her family*! She got to stay in Knockmore with Mam and Dad, Sammy and Ann, while Lucie was in Dublin. Alone. Poor. Fed up. And now, jealous!

No. That wasn't who Lucie was. She wasn't going to allow herself to become bitter, slowly pushing everyone out of her life, one by one, especially not Felicity. If that's what Lucie was feeling, well then she had to do something – show them all that she, too, could be the vivacious person she'd once been, with the dream of a successful nursing career. It was all she'd ever wanted to do and if she couldn't make it work in Dublin, well then surely there was somewhere she could.

"I'll emigrate." Her jeering threat from the week before rang in her ears. Of course she'd been joking, being dramatic, but maybe there had been more to it. Perhaps leaving it all behind for a while, getting a change of scene and some perspective, would do her good. And she could always come back. It didn't have to be forever. But she was beginning to realise that unless she started living, and soon, maybe she *would* end up as the jealous old maid, wondering why the hell she hadn't decided to throw caution to the wind and dance.

Hugging her knees and looking up, Lucie peered dispiritedly at the watermarked ceiling of her childhood home. The she slipped down into the bath until she was immersed below the water, her hair billowing around her. Opening her mouth, she let the air float to the surface with great big exploding bubbles, carrying the word, "Australia."

Chapter twenty-three

"I've never told anyone that before," Lucie admitted now, looking down at her clasped hands resting on her lap.

Doug watched her speak, noticing how she was twisting her fingers as she did.

"It sounds so pathetic." She shook her head. "Some friend I was." Lucie reached over to get her phone from her bedside locker, unlocked it and scrolled through the screen. "Look." She handed the phone to Doug – it was a picture of a framed photograph. "I keep it beside my bed still. Have done for as long as I can remember. That's her."

"That's lovely."

Doug stared at the photo of the two girls in their early twenties, heads together, arms wrapped around each other. They couldn't have been more different – one with smooth fair hair, smiling happily, the other with her red curls thrown back, mouth open, laughing.

"Yin and yang, weren't we? She meant everything to me, you know. Sometimes I think more than my own family did, in a strange way, and I left her." She exhaled in despair. "I left them all. All because I was so caught up in feeling like I'd failed and she'd succeeded. Thinking my life hadn't turned out right. How could it? It hadn't even started yet. But I wouldn't listen.

"Sure, anything they said, I took it the wrong way. God, I'd love to go back and shake myself. I was just a kid, really, coming here. Headstrong, wanting to show them all that I could have this great life, too." Lucie shrugged. "I don't know. Looking back, I must have felt second fiddle to Felicity. I mean, look at her. She was stunning. But it wasn't just that. I was never *that* vain. It was more."

Lucie had stayed away from Felicity for the rest of the weekend.

"I must be coming down with something," she'd lied, remaining holed up in her room instead for the entire weekend.

"Rest, love." Her mother had sat on the edge of her bed. "I'm worried about you. Maybe you're working too hard, not eating right. I spoke to your father and we both agree, would you not come home for a while? See about getting a nursing post in one of the hospitals closer by.

"We'll get you a car if you're strapped for money and you could commute. It's only thirty minutes to St Patrick's with the new road. They're always looking for nurses. Sure, isn't there a shortage! Maybe Dublin is too big for you."

It made sense, even Lucie could see it, but by then she'd already started making notes in the notebook that was safely tucked under her pillow, a list of people to contact about her idea of Australia. There were other girls she'd trained with who'd already taken the plunge – someone would be able to advise her.

"No, Mam. I'll be fine. I must have a virus. I'll figure it out."

"But that house you're in . . . filthy, so it is. Is there nothing nicer you could afford?"

Lucie didn't want to reveal that she was already stretching herself far beyond her means to afford the dingy room with half a breakfast festering on the rust-coloured carpet.

"I'll be fine, Mam. Honest."

"Lu, if there's something else? You know you can tell me anything. Did you have a fight with Fliss?" Tess pressed. "It's just I noticed . . ." she hesitated. "Well, lately you seem a bit off with her. Ready to criticise at the first opportunity. It's not like you, love."

Lucie watched her carefully.

"Actually, I've noticed it for a while now. You know I love Fliss, but you're my little girl. You do know that, don't you?"

Lucie shook her head, trying to swallow the tears. "No, Mam. No fight. Did Fliss say something to you?" The thought of Felicity realising that Lucie was an envious cow was more than she could bear.

"No, she didn't. It was just something that I noticed."

Lucie wondered if she should tell her mother the depth of her feelings and how lost she was. After all, it wasn't like Lucie to mince her words. She was usually well able to express herself, but there was something shameful about admitting jealousy.

"I suppose I feel like my life hasn't started yet, Mam. I was so sure of nursing – I still am – but it's hard. Harder than I thought to make a go of it. I just wanted to make you all proud," she said instead.

Tess tutted. "Lucie, I *am* and always have been proud

of you. You and Sammy are my greatest achievements. And you're a wonderful nurse. How could you not be? With your heart as big as it is and your smile . . . Your life is going to be great." She leaned in to rub Lucie's cheek. "Trust me. It *hasn't* started yet. But when it does, you're going to go far."

The word stung. *Far.* Lucie was indeed going to go far – far away to start her life, farther than she'd ever been before.

For weeks afterwards, Lucie stayed up in Dublin. At the weekends, she used the internet café next to the hospital to email the girls who'd already made the trip – looking up pictures of blue skies, sandy beaches, the outdoor lifestyle, what she could expect to earn. What she discovered from the excited emails from friends, some living in Brisbane, some on the Gold Coast, was that she could earn more than she could ever expect to in Dublin. There were training opportunities, the accommodation looked bright – if not terribly luxurious. All Lucie could see as she flicked through image after image was the future – and she was sold.

Sydney. That's where she'd go. That's where adventure awaited.

Once the visa came through, Lucie knew there was no going back. It was time to tell them – listen to the opinions, the worries and concerns of her family – but nothing was going to change her mind. There, in Sydney, she was going to become the very best version of herself.

"It was Fliss I dreaded telling most. I'd thought a lot about her over the weeks of planning. I suppose once I started thinking about it, I became obsessed, questioning everything, thinking I was a burden to my family, wondering if I'd always had a problem with Fliss," Lucie explained to Doug. "We were like sisters, you see. My mam used to be the housekeeper where Fliss grew up. Her father was the reverend and her mother . . . well, that's a story for another day. But in a nutshell, Fliss was abused growing up. There were always unexplained bruises . . .

"She was this meek little thing and *I* was the strong one. I was the one who brought her out of her shell. And even though she had the big house and the life that seemed perfect, it was *me* who had it all – the family she craved . . ."

Lucie stopped and took a deep breath, smiled sadly. "Maybe I liked it that way. Maybe I liked that I had something she didn't." She laughed then. "Like, I knew all the cool songs, how to wear my hair, how to dress – and she was like something from the 1800s, dressed in little frocks and shiny shoes.

"I had the big dream of leaving Knockmore, becoming a nurse, and all Felicity wanted was a family. When she got pregnant, it all got worse for her for a while. So bad that she tried to kill herself. But then it all came out. How bad her parents really were.

"Of course, they scarpered and Mam took her in. And she became one of us – a Maguire." Lucie stopped and closed her eyes, almost wincing with anguish, then glanced towards the window. "God, I hate myself for saying this, but she seeped further into my life than I wanted her to.

"At first I didn't mind, but over the years, I found myself becoming snippy with her, belittling her life, her choices. Everything I thought my family were doing to me, I was actually doing to her." She put her head back, sighed. "I didn't know I was doing it at first until my mam said it to me that day.

"She was right. I *was* jealous. Fliss got everything she'd ever wanted and I hadn't. I even started thinking they preferred her to me. I mean, she was so lovely, soft, gentle. And I was this loud, booming, probably annoying yoke. Always saying what the hell I wanted, too honest to give a shit, wanting to shock everyone." Lucie shook her head in dismay. "Fliss loved me regardless. There wasn't a bad bone in her body. Fliss wasn't one of those ones who put on a big innocent act and then behind it, they're a dickhead. She was genuinely lovely."

Doug laughed at her unexpected choice of words.

"Beautiful inside and out. And I'd become ugly and dissatisfied – even distant. I didn't want to be like that. I thought if I could get away, have an adventure and then come home, then I wouldn't feel like that any more." She turned to look at Doug and raised her eyebrows. "Bitch, wasn't I?"

Doug tilted his head. "You were young – we all feel like that sometimes. I'm sure she didn't even realise how you felt."

Lucie shook her head. "I should have been honest with her. I should have just come out with it, told her how left behind I felt. If I'd moved home, like my parents told me to, spent time with them all, I think in time I'd have felt better. I needed to be seen by them and the only way I could think to do it was to disappear from sight."

"Jesus! you're in trouble with the law. Christ above, Paddy. Say something, will you?" Tess glared at Paddy, who was staring blankly at his daughter.

"Are you?" he asked.

Lucie groaned. "No, Dad. Mam, I just need a change. There are fantastic opportunities. You know, I can make more there in one year than I could here in three. Dad, you said so yourself – get a decent job. So I have. It's all sorted. The hospital there is amazing and there's the chance of a position in theatre, in time. Like I've always wanted . . ."

"But *Sydney*? *Australia*? What about England? Or Portlaoise?" Tess threw out the first town she could think of, clutching at straws and pacing up and down the kitchen. "Jesus, Mary and Joseph. Fliss, talk some sense into her, will you?"

Lucie glanced over at Felicity, who was eyeing her cautiously. Up until now, Lucie hadn't been able to bring herself to look at her friend.

"Lu?"

Lucie could tell what Felicity was thinking. "I'm sorry I didn't tell you, Fliss. I really am. I couldn't, not until it was planned." She reached over and placed her hand on Felicity's arm. "I . . . it's only for a year."

Tess broke the silence. "I can't look at you. I . . . I told you, didn't I, Paddy? I said she's up to something up in Dublin. Not coming home for weeks. Plotting your escape, so you were. *Australia*? Have you ever heard the likes? You've never even been on a plane . . .

"Jesus, you'll be taken in the night by a dingo. We saw that, didn't we, Paddy? In that movie. The next thing the poor woman is walking around calling for her baby and the dingo has it. It's a barren land out there and you'll burn something terrible in the heat. The Maguires aren't made for heat like that. Sure, look at us." Tess let out a little shriek. "I can't look at you," she repeated, storming from the room.

Paddy shrugged at Lucie and followed.

Sammy let out a laugh. He'd been watching the exchange with interest, munching on a digestive biscuit.

"Come on." He took little Ann's hand, whose eyes were out on stalks observing the rare outburst from her usually unflappable Nana Tess. "I'll talk to them," he said, turning to Lucie. "Sounds cool, little sis." He put his hand on her shoulder and left the room, leaving Felicity and Lucie alone.

"You're angry with me," Felicity said.

"I'm not."

"You are." Felicity didn't look up. "You have been for a while. I felt it."

Lucie stole a glance at her. Felicity's hands were clasped, resting on the kitchen table, in front of her, her head down.

"I know when you're lying. You're the worst liar in the world." Felicity finally lifted her face to look at Lucie.

"I'm not," Lucie sighed.

"Why didn't you tell me? I get you not telling Tess and Paddy, but *me*?"

"I couldn't. I was afraid you'd try to change my mind."

Felicity nodded. "Could I change your mind?"

"Nope."

"So you should have told me."

"I'm sorry. I . . . I don't know how to explain it. I feel . . ."

"Stuck?"

Lucie smiled. "You do know me well. Please don't be mad."

"I could never be mad at you – not for long, anyway."

Not like I am, Lucie wanted to say. *Not like I've been ignoring you.*

"I get it. I was stuck too once, remember?"

"Of course I remember." Lucie squeezed her arm. "And look at you now!"

Felicity smiled. "Sometimes I wonder . . . Do you ever

think . . . I mean, would you have preferred if I hadn't ended up with Sammy?"

Lucie closed her eyes to keep the tears from coming. Perhaps she hadn't hidden her feelings as well as she'd thought, but she couldn't admit it now, knowing it would crush her friend.

"You and Sammy were always going to be together, and I got a sister . . ."

"And lost a friend."

There it was. "No. You'll always be my friend. Remember that pact we made when we were kids? That day in the orchard in Knockmore House, that still stands. Blood sisters."

"I remember." Felicity looked crestfallen. "If I forgot to say it, thank you."

"For what?"

"*You* gave me this life. You're the reason I met Sammy. The reason I have Ann, a family. I'll never forget it. Of everyone, it was you who helped me the most."

Lucie's entire body broke into goose bumps. Beautiful Fliss. How could she have thought poorly of her? The guilt caught in her throat and for the first time, she started to doubt her decision.

"You would tell me, though?" Felicity continued. "I'd understand if you ever thought I'd moved in on your life, if you know what I mean."

It was exactly what she'd thought.

No. Moving away was the right thing to do. Felicity deserved *this* life, without having Lucie looking over her shoulder, resenting her. What they all needed was a chance to breathe, especially Lucie.

"It's just time for me to make my own life, Fliss. You'll look after them for me, won't you?"

"I will." Then Felicity leaned over and seized Lucie in a hug. "You're never coming back, are you? I have this feeling that you'll stay forever."

"So, she was right?" Doug asked.

"Yes. I did go back, though. Four times. Four funerals. Dad. Mam. Sammy. Fliss. After Sammy, I should have moved home for good. Fliss needed me, but by then, you see, I'd found a reason to stay." Lucie smiled, a faraway look on her face. "Sometimes what's more interesting than a person's reason to escape is their reason never to return."

They were interrupted by a gentle knock on the door behind. Doug glanced at Lucie's face, whose wistful smile suddenly morphed, making her appear like a deer caught in headlights.

"I'm sorry to interrupt," he said politely before looking nervously at Lucie. "Lucie," Max nodded once.

"Max," she answered evenly, brushing her hair from her face, blinking more than once.

"It seems there's been a staffing issue for surgery tomorrow. So, you've got me," Max grimaced as he approached. "I'll be the one knocking you out."

He attempted a laugh. It sounded more like a wheeze.

"Right." It was all Lucie could manage.

"I'll go," Doug said, standing suddenly, feeling the tension.

Max looked at Doug, recognising him and looking embarrassed. "No, please. I can come back. In say, half an hour? There are just some routine questions. And I *am* sorry, Lucie. If I could have avoided it . . ."

"It's fine." She sounded trite as Max edged away. "It's work. Anaesthesiologist," Lucie explained to Doug, who nodded, wondering if Lucie's reason to remain in Australia had just walked out of the door.

Chapter twenty-four

Max

The morning sun sat blindingly low, glistening off the water. With no barricade to stop it, the sweat poured freely from Max's almost hairless crown, travelling in streams down his face to his neck, like he was crying. Perhaps he was. The pain was undoubtedly excruciating enough. Then again, it was supposed to be, wasn't it? Relentless, unyielding agony in every single muscle.

Max had taken up running – if you could describe laboured plodding in that fashion. Trudging along the outer edge of Barangaroo Reserve by the harbour at 7 a.m. each morning had become his latest diversion. It was undoubtedly diverting something, he thought, feeling the excess flesh around his middle ripple with the movement.

Max felt sure at any minute his legs might detach and divert in the opposite direction back to one of the cafés in Walsh Bay, in an attempt to save themselves from carrying his expanding weight. And he'd been doing so well. He'd felt positively svelte – well, that was a push . . . slim, perhaps – before leaving Melbourne and arriving back in Sydney. "Straighter" at the very least. That was how his mother used to describe it whenever he managed to lose a few pounds. "Nice and straight."

As in less round.

Max grinned at the memory. It had been a constant battle, his weight. He'd always found that description amusing, as if his size had been fighting back, when in fact it had been very much a one-way struggle. It was odd to think how much he'd achieved in his career and yet he'd never managed to conquer the scales. Max didn't need a psychologist to understand that he was a comfort eater. What he would have liked a psychologist to divulge was why now, after all these years, he'd chosen to step outside his comfort zone by returning to Sydney – and straight to the start of the "all you can eat" buffet queue.

At his age, he should have known better. And now look at him! Running to negate the empty packets of Tim Tam biscuits stuffed in the drawer of his desk at the hospital. A medic should know better!

"Ouch."

He stopped to massage his knee and gaze longingly at the low brick wall by the water, where the ferries were buzzing in and out of the harbour. After righting himself, he kept going, despite the pain behind his knee radiating down his calf. Was it possible to shatter your tibia running on flat ground?

"Anything is possible. Anything at all," the voice issued evenly.

He'd started listening to podcasts as another way to focus his mind – a self-help series on how to relieve stress, become a better person, how not to harbour regrets . . . Max wondered if the calm male voice coming through his headphones carried any regrets. If he had, perhaps he wouldn't be able to talk about the process of living disappointment-free so comfortably. Then again, was there anyone who *actually* lived entirely in the present without *ever* looking back?

Max would love to able to say after he'd left Sydney for Melbourne years before that he hadn't dwelled on all that had happened. Back then, he'd tried to limit his thoughts to day by day. Since returning and dipping his toe in the past, Max could already see his reflection begin to ripple. Or was that his belly? What might happen if he decided to plunge feet first into all of his issues? A tidal wave?

"Repeat after me," the voice interrupted. "When the past comes knocking, don't answer. Inhale the future. Exhale the past. Say it with me."

Max stopped suddenly and placed his hands on his knees to catch his breath. Christ, he was unfit. He'd barely been moving, for pity's sake.

"Inhale the future, say it. Come on. Shout it." The thundering voice was relentless.

Right then, Max was having trouble inhaling anything, let alone shouting about it at the same time. He took a deep breath, attempting to suck the future up his nostrils before blowing the past out through his mouth.

What was the point? Max Woods felt utterly out of place here, in among the beautiful people, effortlessly striding like gazelles – how were they doing it? –brimming with endorphins. One or two smiled encouragingly at his stationary form as they passed. At least he thought they were smiling – the sweat was now stinging his eyes so much it was hard to tell.

What wasn't hard to decipher was the reason Max had come back to Sydney in the first place and why he was now trying to remove a decade of comfort eating from his body in one outing. The past *had* come knocking. Not only had Max answered, but he'd also invited it in, no matter how much he tried to tell himself otherwise.

Max straightened and started walking, wiping the sweat from his face with the back of his arm as he went. Some people just weren't built for running. Clearly, he was one of them. Too big and cumbersome, his knees would never survive it – and he was far too busy with his new job to take the time to recover from a double knee replacement. He'd eat a salad for lunch instead. That would do. Besides, he'd been this way most of his life: six foot four inches and "Built like a brick shithouse," his father would say. "Would have made a sweet lock if you'd stuck at the rugby, son. That's one position where size matters."

He hadn't been bad at rugby, either. But instead, he'd followed his heart, or at least his brains. Quiet, intelligent, with a fondness for cake, he'd chosen to study medicine before going on to specialise in anaesthesiology.

"You get the brains from me," his mother would say, infinitely proud of her only son.

"And the shape," his father would add, winking.

"Don't mind him, love. Big is beautiful! Besides, it's what's inside that counts."

Hah! For as long as Max could remember, it had never been about what was inside, not really. For much of his life, he'd felt utterly out of place in his oversized body, noticing the stares, the nudges as people passed – even still.

"Size of him!"

"How's the weather up there?"

"Give us a hand with the gutters!"

He'd been listening to it since he was a boy. At first tall and gangly before growing into himself – and then, well, he'd just kept on growing. He wasn't precisely obese.

Max was just a big guy – an enormous presence, with broad shoulders, big legs, hands like shovels.

He'd often wished that he'd had the personality to match. People expected that – for the big guy to crack all the jokes, be the life and soul of the party. That wasn't Max. He wasn't bad-looking, either. He'd often heard people say he had lovely eyes, good straight teeth, a pleasant smile. Perhaps he could have used those assets to appear more confident. But he was the laid-back one, calm under pressure, kind to a fault. Perhaps too kind.

It was why anaesthesiology suited him. He was happy to fade into the background where he could. Of course, he knew his worth at work. Without him, there was little that could be accomplished in the hospital theatre. And he'd worked hard to get where he now was. Head of Anaesthesiology. There was now nowhere else to go. Career-wise, he was at the peak of his game. Shame his personal life had never caught up.

"The past is a place of learning. Not living," the voice continued.

"Oh, piss off, mate!" Max ripped the headphones from his ears, rolled them in a ball and stuffed them in his pocket.

The past was the *only* place Max wanted to be, painful as it was. Reliving those days was the one thing that helped him to escape his present. Wondering how it had all turned out as it had . . . Now that was the torturous part.

Being back in Sydney General Hospital, after almost fourteen years away, he'd honestly believed it had been time enough. At first, he'd tried to ignore the scouting emails. Living in Melbourne had suited him, but he'd reached a glass ceiling in the hospital there. After all, his career, his work, it was all he had.

"You'd be a fool not to take it," his mentor in Melbourne advised. "This is the final step in your career."

So he'd taken it – gone back to go forwards. Enough time had passed, surely it was all water under the Sydney Harbour Bridge . . .

"Max? Holy shit! There's a blast from the past." Nina had almost walked straight into him that first morning.

"Nina!" He'd nearly had to kneel to hug her. "You're still tiny."

"And you still give me whiplash!" she'd giggled, craning her neck to look up at him.

"I didn't expect to see many familiar faces. It's been so long. I've got a new job here."

"Yes, I heard on the grapevine. Congrats."

"You still in theatre? Will I have the pleasure of your company?"

"Nah, mate. I'm in outpatients now. I left years ago. Right after Lu . . ."

"How is she?" It was out before he could stop himself.

Nina looked at the ground before straining to meet his eyes. "She's good."

"Good?"

"Yeah, good." Nina smiled awkwardly this time.

Max shuffled from foot to foot. "I'd better get on. I'll see you about."

His heart had been racing as he walked away, his palms already sweating. Right then he'd known it had been a mistake to come back. Fourteen years. It would never be long enough to make him forget, or wish that he could rewind it all, right back to the very first moment where he'd set eyes on Lucie Maguire.

* * *

Max had never seen anything like it – a mixture between a dust devil and a leprechaun. A small crowd had gathered at the nurses' station to cheer for whatever it was, dancing up and down the corridor. Max watched, mesmerised, at its legs flying out in front, wobbling side to side on its toes and then taking off again in a flurry of high kicks. Red hair bouncing everywhere, its face shining from the apparent attention.

Grabbing one of the doctors by the arm, it linked him and they skipped around in a circle before it dropped him suddenly and grabbed hold of someone else. It wore a garland of shiny green shamrocks around its neck, a headband with green, white and gold streamers. Just when Max was convinced it was going to lift off the ground and fly away, it stopped, tilted its head to the side and then curiously broke into what appeared to be a series of robot dance moves. Was it having a fit? Then it threw its head back as the crowd applauded and took a bow.

"Happy St Patrick's Day, everyone," it shouted before plonking back down in a swivel chair.

"Who's that?" Max grabbed the arm of one of the doctors who'd been included in the performance.

He stopped to smirk at Max. "See something you like, buddy? That's Lucie. The Irish girl. Great nurse – been here maybe four years. Sharp as a tack and as you can see, a real firecracker. Single, too." He raised his eyebrows.

Max glanced back at Lucie, whose head was now diligently stuck in the computer, her lunatic dancing already forgotten.

"I see."

"I'm sure you do, mate." He jabbed Max in the stomach.

"And the other one?" Max gestured at the girl beside Lucie with the smooth dark hair before turning away.

"That's Nina. That pair are like peas in a pod. Where one goes, the other is right there."

"Right. I see," Max repeated, not noticing the doctor throw his eyes up as he moved away.

Max looked over his shoulder and flinched. This time Lucie was staring straight at him. The other girl, Nina, who was standing beside her, followed Lucie's line of vision. Then bent to whisper something in Lucie's ear before they both broke into peals of giggles.

Lucie looked up again, beamed and lifted her hand in a wave as enthused as her dancing. Max frowned, turned and walked away before she was able to clock an identical grin spreading across his face.

After that, Max saw her everywhere. They'd pass each other in the corridor. She'd stand back, bow her head once in mock reverence, flash a smile. For weeks it was like a game – one in which he wasn't entirely sure if he was a player or spectator.

She was beautiful. Not traditionally so – pale-skinned, freckly faced, mop of red hair that changed colour in the light, flecks of gold shimmering through. Her features were as delicate as she was, but she had an enormous presence – as if being in the hospital was exactly where she wanted to be. Was he imagining it? Was she this friendly with everyone?

And then there it was. The opportunity – standing at the stainless steel sink outside theatre, scrubbing in beside her.

"So, is it true what they say?" she'd asked eventually, turning to him, her eyes dancing.

"What's that?"

His heart had been hammering. It was probably going to be some gibe about his height. It always was. At least he'd be prepared. After years of ribbing, he now had an answer for every wisecrack.

"That you're all as boring as sin?"

Here we go . . .

"Who?"

"Anaesthesiologists."

Oh!

"That you could put people to sleep without drugs?" She raised her eyebrows. "That's what they say, you know. Not what I say, mind. I'd never judge a book by its cover."

"That would mean I *look* boring. Do I?" Max didn't smile, and she looked momentarily perturbed.

"Well, I suppose it would," Lucie mused, pursing her lips. "I hope you're not sensitive, but I didn't mean it that way."

"How did you mean it?"

She bit her lip. "Eh, as I said it. I asked were you boring."

"Strange question to ask someone you've never met."

She tilted her head. "I suppose it is. Sorry. My mam says I've a big mouth. It's my tragic flaw. Far too open. Always putting my foot in it."

Max looked down at her feet. "You've small feet. Better than *me* putting my foot in it." He lifted his foot and shook it. "Could be dangerous."

She laughed. "See. I knew you weren't boring. Nina said you might be, but I'm an excellent judge of character."

"I've mostly found that people who claim that are often the worst judge of character. It's the ones who say nothing who judge best."

"Is that right? And how would you judge me?" She sucked in her lips, trying not laugh.

How would he judge her? "I'd say you have a big mouth."

"Hah! So you *are* a good judge of character. I know that much now. I also know you have big feet, that you're not *too* boring . . . I feel we've achieved something here, don't you? Great chat."

Max smiled at last. "I'm Max. Max Woods."

"That sounds very much like a detective."

"Not a very good one. You've found out more about me than I have about you. All I know is that you've a big mouth."

"Ah, come on. You know more than that. You also know I have small feet. Good for dancing," she winked. "You dance?"

"Never. It would be a health risk."

"I could teach you. How does that sound?"

"Terrible."

"Ah, go on. People will think you're boring."

"Maybe I am."

"We'll soon see. Now, will you be using drugs today, or just talking the patient to sleep?" she asked, another smile spreading across her face. "You've nice eyes, by the way. Honest-looking. If I could be so bold as to offer some advice, I'd use drugs today. We've been talking for at least two minutes and I'm still wide awake. Could be a risky move."

"Sometimes it takes longer." Max glanced over his shoulder to make sure no one was listening before lowering his voice. "Perhaps I could try over a drink?" He could feel his face flushing as he said it.

Max looked down at his feet before meeting her stare. Was she blushing, too?

"Maybe." Her smile had changed. "By the way, that's a good chat-up line, in a slight stalker-cum-murderer way. You should write that down. Could come in handy for another time."

There would be no other time – not for Max, anyway.

Max glanced at his watch. He had to be at the hospital soon, where all he could feel was Lucie's presence. He'd voluntarily put his name on the board to scrub in for her surgery, not that he'd admitted that to Lucie. But regardless of the past, he wasn't going to let her be in theatre alone, especially with Hamish away. It was Nina who'd confirmed that much, with a somewhat hesitant look.

After all that time away, it had taken Max only a matter of days to uncover that he still felt as strongly for Lucie Woods as he always had. Christ, he was pathetic. It had *never* gone away. He'd been fooling himself to think he could ever erase her.

Max put his headphones back in and pressed Play on his phone.

"Never regret anything that's happened in your life," the voice picked up where it had left off. "It cannot be changed, undone or forgotten. So take it as a lesson learned and move on."

"Bullshit," he muttered back.

Over the years he'd accepted his fate, but regardless of the encouraging voices in his ear, he *would* spend the rest of his life regretting it. Imagine, at last, Lucie shared his name, but she'd picked the wrong Woods. It should have been him.

Chapter twenty-five

Doug

Doug had stopped at a diner on the way home. He couldn't remember the last time he'd felt so ravenous – not even one of Irene's overloaded plates could have satisfied him. His mind had indeed been suffused earlier at the hospital, but it had only left him hungry for more. Sitting alone, he pushed away the now empty plate, took a sip from his lukewarm coffee and rested his head back against the red leather of the dining booth.

He had been right about one thing – asking Lucie the right questions had certainly been enough to open the flood gates. Listening to her stories about home, it was evident that she'd adored her family. It was just as clear to Doug that they'd loved her, too, but it was as though she'd become blind to it. *Guilt*. That's what he'd been able to establish. It was written clearly on her face, laced through her words. Lucie was carrying unrelenting regret for having left, for finding a life away that had excited her and for not wanting to return to Ireland.

* * *

"It was always *here* I felt most at home," Lucie had gestured after Max had left them alone again.

Her entire demeanour had changed as soon as the doctor had materialised at the door, becoming instantly fidgety, restless, adjusting herself, fixing the rigid white sheets of the hospital bed. Afterwards, Doug had glanced quickly at his watch to see how much time they had left before Max returned and Doug would have to go.

"At the hospital," she continued. "I really loved it. Without sounding crazy . . . I was born for it."

"And him?" Doug signalled towards the now empty door, delving right in. "Is he a relative? I noticed his name badge. Also Woods."

Lucie smiled crookedly. "Does nothing slip by you?!" Then her nose started to twitch. "I suppose we are sort of related. By marriage. He's my husband's cousin."

"Oh. And you don't get on?"

She grimaced this time. "That obvious? We did once." She shrugged. "Not any more. Ancient history."

He detected an abrupt hint of causticity in her voice. It was something he hadn't witnessed there before, even with everything else she'd already told him.

"Go on."

"I think that's a story for another day, one that would more than likely involve copious amounts of wine, and I'm not allowed that in here. Although . . ." Her eyes were dancing. "Perhaps you could smuggle some in."

"I'm a man of rules, I'm afraid," he tutted.

"Ah, come on. Rules are meant to be broken, aren't they?"

"You sound like my Rose." One corner of his mouth lifted as he rolled his eyes.

"Tell me about her. Why did she leave Ireland?"

Doug leaned back, crossed his arms. "Her mother

died. She had one sister there, but they didn't see eye to eye. And there was a man . . ."

"Isn't there always."

The first time Rose had spoken about it, Doug had been shocked, somehow spoiling his inflated opinion of her.

"He was married," she'd revealed honestly. "I didn't know at first. Of course, you never know, do you? But once I found out, it didn't stop me. It should have, but it didn't, and then . . ."

Rose – like Lucie, Doug supposed now – had always known what she'd wanted to do with her life. Listening to Lucie talk about nursing, it reminded him of how passionately Rose once spoke of photography and taking pictures underwater.

"But back then," Doug explained to Lucie, "there was no place in Ireland for women divers, not really. So, when she finally found someone willing to teach her, she grasped at the chance. She used to tell me she'd sit at the side of the pier back in Wexford, watching them all load their diving gear onto the boats. There were a huge number of wrecks off the coast of Wexford. Plenty to explore.

"Rose would sit there all day until they returned. It was her dream to take pictures of the forgotten life underwater. She was fascinated by it all. The divers, well, they were more interested in salvaging what they could from the wrecks – ships' wheels, portholes, anchors, plates, anything, really."

Lucie sat back against the pillows of the bed, listening with interest.

"I soon plucked up the courage to ask them to take me out with them on the boat. At first, they laughed. A slip of a thing like me wanting to join in with the lads," Rose had told him. "They used to jeer me, saying that soon as I put the tanks on my back, I'd topple over from the weight. I was blue in the face telling them I was stronger than I looked."

Only one of them had been willing to teach her. At last giving Rose an opportunity to use the underwater photography equipment that she'd saved for for years by taking family portraits and photos of children on their communion day in white dresses with missing teeth.

"Patrick Meagher." Rose had said his name with a faraway look. "He took me under his wing. Before I knew it, I was spending more and more time with the men from Dublin. They'd descend from Dublin every Friday evening to spend the weekend diving."

It wasn't long before Rose had headed to Dublin, on Patrick's advice, to do the appropriate courses, to come back waving her certificates triumphantly.

"My sister thought I was mad. My mother was thrilled. In her eighties by then, she thought it was all terribly exciting. Living with her, I was able to save the money I needed to do what I wanted. I took care of her, all those years after my father died. My sister was off having babies and I was there for my mother.

"All Mam wanted was for me to be happy. And I was, more than I'd ever been. I was in love with the sea . . . and him. In hindsight, I think I was more in love with what we were doing, but it had all begun to mesh together. Until . . ."

"What happened?" Lucie asked, intrigued.

"Well, they got involved romantically. Tangled up in each other, diving, living the high life. Rose became a part of this team of rich blokes from Dublin. 'Looking for thrills,' she used to say.

"They were doing these dives at the weekend, dangerous ones, pushing themselves beyond what they should, going to depths they shouldn't. Well, it always ends badly, doesn't it?

"By then, Rose had discovered that her man had a wife and children in Dublin." Doug shrugged. "Rose had him at the weekends. Staying in B&Bs together. She said it was enough. You get the picture."

"I was hooked," Rose had told Doug. "It was like a drug. It was exciting. It was dangerous. The dives got more treacherous. I was seven years at it by then. I was working on a book – photographs of all the wrecks off Ireland. That's when we discovered the location of the *Carlo*, a cargo ship carrying lead bars, torpedoed by a German U-boat in 1917 – sixty-five metres down."

Even then, you could see the adrenaline pulsing in her eyes.

"There were very few going to those depths, but we knew we could do it. Hell, I would have made some name for myself." Rose shook her head and exhaled. "I was forty by then, with nothing to lose – no kids – and Patrick, well, he wanted the adventures, the history . . . me."

Telling Lucie the next part, Doug watched her eyes widen in the same way his own had when Rose first told him.

"So, they went for it," Doug continued. "Sixty-five metres to the bottom, on mixed gases. Do you know what that means?"

Lucie shook her head.

"A mixture of helium and oxygen, not the usual compressed air in tanks – not for the faint-hearted, believe me. In all my years as a police diver, we never did anything like that. This was technical diving.

"Once they got down there, they'd only have had about fifteen minutes tops before they'd have had to come back up. The journey back up would take about forty-five minutes with decompression stops."

"Wow!" Lucie's mouth was in an O. "That sounds terrifying. She was hardcore."

"She sure was. Anyway, three of them went down that day – two were left on the boat."

"I should have called it," Rose had said. "I had this feeling all that morning. I wasn't sure if it was nerves or dread, but I should have pulled the plug. But then, I wanted those photos – and Patrick, he wanted those lead bars," she'd told Doug, shaking her head. "Once we got down, well, I was nervous. It was dark. Even the strobe light made it impossible to see and I stupidly did what I'd always been warned not to."

"So, she went one way, the two men went another. It's breaking the number one rule of diving, never to leave your buddies," Doug disclosed. "By the time she circled back, she could see Patrick was in trouble. The buckle of his fin was caught in a monofilament net."

"What's that?" Lucie was leaning towards him now, engrossed.

"A really fine fishing net, almost invisible. The other guy was trying to cut him free and Patrick was starting to panic."

"Did they free him?" Her eyes were huge.

Doug shook his head, sucked his mouth in. "No. They were running out of time and at those depths, well, you're on your own. If someone gets in trouble, you can try to help, but you have minutes, literally. If they'd stayed, they'd all have died. If not there then on the way back up if they didn't leave enough time to go back up the line and decompress. If you ascend too quickly, it forms a build-up of bubbles in your bloodstream. It can kill you."

"Yes, I've heard that. Oh my God." Lucie put her hand on her heart. "They left him?"

Doug nodded slowly. "They made a decision. Like I said before, hesitating . . ."

". . . can get you killed." Lucie finished the mantra and shivered.

"There wasn't time. He was panicking, grabbing at us." Rose's voice had been a whisper. "The more he fought, the more tangled he became in the net. And then, just like that, he stopped. Froze. It was like it had dawned on him that it was over.

"Patrick grabbed at me one last time and then, with everything he had left, he pushed me away. I . . . God . . . I don't know how I did it, how I left, but the other guy pulled me away . . ." she'd paused. "Of course, we'd had the conversation. You know it, too, if someone is in trouble. You aren't all going to lose your lives.

"We knew what we were doing was dangerous. It was an agreement. A pact." She'd squeezed her eyes shut and then opened them, looking into his. "It's different when you're faced with it. The whole way back up that line, I wanted to go back. If the other guy hadn't been below me, I might have, but I'd have been endangering him, too. All the time I was hoping, at the last minute, that Patrick would appear, that he'd freed himself . . ."

Lucie gasped. "He never came back up, did he? Oh my

God, poor Rose. Poor him. I have goose bumps. I can't even imagine."

"No. He never came back up. They radioed for help, but it was too late by then. The coastguards were called . . . they could do nothing until the next day."

"It felt like a dream or a nightmare. I kept trying to imagine what he'd been thinking down there, alone, waiting to die. I've never stopped thinking about it," Rose had revealed. "Afterwards, I met his wife, his children. God, it was only when I saw them that I realised . . . I had no right to mourn him. Our egos, our stupid egos, had robbed them of a father and I'd robbed her of a husband. We'd been living in a selfish pocket of fantasy."

"Shortly afterwards, her mother died, so she left Ireland behind," Doug finished.

"Did she never go back?" Lucie asked.

"Not once. Not ever."

"But her sister?"

Doug shook his head. "She never spoke to her again. In fact, she hardly spoke of her."

"But she kept diving?"

"She did. But shallow stuff here in Australia. She never got over it, not really. Something like that stays with you forever." Doug exhaled. "She was always banging on about helping people if you ever get the chance. I think it was because she felt so helpless then."

"Wow," Lucie breathed out. "That's enormous. What a decision to have to make."

"Rose always used to say that life boils down to one or two big decisions. Afterwards, she left Ireland and never looked back. Although I sometimes wondered, maybe I still do, if there was a part of her that longed to return. As if she'd left something of herself there."

Lucie nodded knowingly. "It's true. Leaving your country behind, where you were born, your family. It's not an easy thing to do. By severing that tie, you lose something of yourself. I wonder . . ." Lucie paused and then shook her head.

"What?"

"I suppose it seems strange that she never went back, not once. It's so final. Is her sister still alive?"

"I have no idea."

It had been something he'd thought about a lot lately, too. In truth, it was something he'd like to know now. All those years it had just been Rose and him. He supposed, selfishly, he'd liked it that way, not really caring what had come before. All he knew was what she'd chosen to share from her past.

"It's funny," Doug admitted. "In a way, I was jealous of that other man, Patrick, the one who came before me. But Rose always told me that he was just one part of her story and I was the ending. Sounds stupid."

"Sounds lovely," Lucie smiled. "Sounds like she found real happiness with you. It was what I always hoped for."

"And did you find it?"

Lucie glanced at the door where Max had reappeared, indicating that their time was up. Doug picked up his jacket off the back of the chair and leaned over to pat her hand.

"Are you nervous about tomorrow?"

"A little." Her voice had become meek. "But it has to be done. At least I'm in safe hands." She'd gestured with her eyes towards Max. "Or maybe he'll drug me and I'll never wake up."

"To be continued," Doug had winked. "Can I come

back? In a few days, when you're brighter."

"I'd like that. And, Doug . . . thank you."

Thank you. What had Doug done? Only let Lucie speak. It was him who should be thanking her for allowing him to glimpse the other side of her story, the background to the chapter he already knew. What he'd learned today was that the woman sitting in that hospital bed was all heart. Lucie Woods was one of those bright souls, somewhat tarnished by life. Doug just hoped he could make Lucie realise in time that she deserved more than the life she'd fallen into.

He was eager to hear more now, sure the next part of Lucie's story might involve the "ancient history" to which she'd referred earlier. By the look on Max Woods' face when he'd looked at Lucie, Doug could tell that history was not a term the doctor might use. Observing the tense looks, how the energy had changed in the room, Doug was confident that there was some unfinished business between Lucie and Max. He supposed he'd have to wait to find out what that was. Doug knew what Rose would be saying.

"Tell them to fix it before it's too late. Everything can be mended, but there isn't always time."

It struck Doug then how often his wife would say that everything could be so easily welded back together. Then why had she chosen never to mend her relationship with her sister? He wished he'd asked more. Now, it was too late. Perhaps there was something that Rose had failed to divulge.

Doug rooted in his pocket, pulled out a twenty and left it on the table of the diner before standing up to go. He could barely wait to see Lucie again. There was something so real, raw, almost mundane about her story.

Quite the opposite to Rose's, but he was drawn to it.

"Rose used to say we all have two lives. And the second one starts as soon as you realise you only have one," he'd told Lucie earlier.

Lucie had looked at him with such sadness.

"I'm not sure I'm brave enough to start a second life. I've made so many mistakes. Too many to count, almost."

For the first time, Doug felt sure now he'd done the right thing in going to see Lucie again, glad he'd listened to Rose's message from beyond. Rose was still with him and maybe, just maybe, through Lucie, she was trying to tell him something more. For once, he was all ears.

Chapter twenty-six

She didn't want to wake up. Lucie could feel reality pulling, tugging at her to open her eyes, haul her forwards, but she wanted to stay where she was, trapped in her memories, locked in the past.

"Tell me everything," Felicity had squealed down the phone.

It wasn't often Lucie got to speak to her. It was costly enough to call her parents every week.

"Oh my God, Fliss, it's unbelievable. Like something off the TV. The beaches, the sea, the city, the harbour, the Opera House! I love it. And the hospital is so modern compared to back home. Well, there's this beautiful old building at the front and then a massive newer building. That's where I am.

"Everyone is so nice and so bloody laid-back! Must be the outdoor lifestyle and all the sunshine. Jesus, I burnt the shite out of myself the first day on the beach. Lobster red! I couldn't move for a week. Now, I'm covered in sunscreen all the time. Factor 50. Even going for a walk."

"Stop! Factor 50! I didn't even know they made that. My God, it must be sweltering. How's your hair?" Felicity chuckled.

"Dreadful. Frizz central. Like a bush fire on my head. Oh, Fliss, you'd love it here. How's Ann? How's Sammy? Are Mam and Dad okay?"

"All great, I promise. Don't be worrying. Have you made friends? What's the apartment like?"

"Shite. Tiny, but at least it's clean. I'm sharing with this girl Nina from the Philippines. She's a laugh a minute. She's not long in Australia, either. And another girl – not mad on her. But Nina and myself are having a blast."

"I'm so glad. Send me photos. I need a visual."

"I will. I'll get some developed and stick them in the post. Did you get my letter?"

"I read it a hundred times. Sammy said he's going to set me up on email. I can't be waiting weeks for letters. The postman is driven demented with me running up the road after him. God, I hope I'll be able to use the computer. I'm going to do a course in the community centre so we can chat online. Anytime we want. Imagine!"

"Did Ann get the kangaroo teddy I posted?"

"She did, thank you. She hasn't let it out of her sight."

"And Mam? I miss her so much."

"Ah, look, she still cries whenever I mention your name, but she'll be fine, Lu. Sure, the months are flying by already. You'll be home before she realises."

"Yeah, it is flying by. I'm so happy, Fliss. Before I left, I was—"

"I know. You needed a change. I can hear it in you. It's like having the old Lucie back, only you're miles away. I miss you."

"I miss you, too."

"You'll call next month?"

"I will. I promise."

"I didn't call. I should have called . . ."

"What's that, Lucie? You're all right, love. You're just waking up from the anaesthetic." The nurse leaned over as Lucie opened her eyes groggily, feeling disoriented. "Good girl. It's all over now. You've had the operation and you're doing great. Good girl." The nurse patted her hand and smiled down at her.

Lucie tested her eyes, moving them from left to right of the recovery room before looking back at the nurse.

"I'm alive."

"You are. Slowly wake up there and we'll take you back to your room. No rush. Nice and slow."

"Max? Where's Max?" Lucie's words were slurred. "Can I see Max?"

"What's that, love? Max? Is that your husband?"

"No, sorry. I think I'm still asleep."

Lucie was sort of enjoying the spaced-out sensation. She tried to shake her head as a blurred memory hit. Oh, God. She frowned, trying to remember. Had she said what she thought she had earlier, or was that a dream, too? She couldn't tell.

"Is Nina here? Can you call Nina?"

"I'm sure Nina's here, dear. Don't worry. You're a bit confused from the medication. You'll come round now." The nurse rubbed Lucie's hair. "I'll be back in one second, love. You doze away there. Nice and slow. Good girl."

"I'm a nurse, too," Lucie slurred after her, still talking gibberish. "I was a great nurse. Better than you. Everyone said so."

"I'm sure you were, love. There's a good girl."

Lucie closed her eyes again, another memory piercing.

"The tripe that guy down the end is talking . . ." Nina looked over at Lucie and rolled her eyes. "I wish I could record him. He's just asked me for a Chinese massage. He said he won't tell. It'll be between me and him."

"Dirty thing. Did you do it?" Lucie laughed, flicking over the page of her clipboard.

"Ah, yeah. Said his wife gave him permission." Nina stuck out her tongue.

"I just got a kick in the stomach from bed two. He's one of those aggressive yokes. I'd say he's the same at home. You can always tell what they're like in real life by the way they are when they wake up from the anaesthetic."

It was one of their popular conversations, sharing the funny things people would say after a dose of relaxation medication given before or after surgery.

"*In vino veritas* and in pre-med even more so," Max used to laugh when they'd tell him about it. "The things I've been asked! One woman asked me to marry her, right before I asked her to count back from ten."

"And what about that one last week?" Nina chimed in. "The one who said you can look, but don't touch!"

"Oh, sweet Jesus," Lucie giggled. "You're grand, thanks."

"It all comes out when you're vulnerable," Max added. "Someday I might have you on the operating table. I'd be very interested to see what you'd tell me," Max joked, grinning at Lucie.

"Yes!" Nina added. "I'd give anything to be there for that. I wonder what she'd own up to. Those innocent Irish eyes don't fool me." Nina slung her arm around Lucie's neck.

"Actually, I'm not sure we'd get anything out of Lucie.

Nothing we don't already know. We can all read her like a book. Subtle, she isn't," Max added.

"Hah. I'd like to see you try."

Flicking her eyes open briefly, Lucie closed them just as quick. She wasn't sure how long she'd fallen asleep for again, but she could now feel a dragging sensation in her stomach and realised that the drugs were probably wearing off. Now for the not-so-fun part of recovering.

Hearing a cough, she looked up.

"How are you feeling?"

It was Max, still dressed in his scrubs, the blue making his eyes look crystal clear. She'd always liked him dressed this way.

"I'll be heading off soon. I just wanted to check on you."

"Okay," she grimaced. "Starting to hurt a little."

"Right, we'll get you hooked up to pain relief. You know how it works. Press the button if you're uncomfortable. You did well. It all went good."

"Do I have a lovely womb?" Lucie tried to smile. "I hope you got a good look. It isn't often you get to see the internals of someone you know. Was my blood blue?"

Max grinned. "Practically navy. Very regal, indeed – and your womb is beautiful. I must say, I've never seen one like it."

"I'm planning on having it bronzed. Make it a feature," Lucie joked and then winced all of a sudden. "Whoa."

"Hey, take it easy." He moved closer. "There'll be plenty of time for your epic one-liners in time. Just get better, okay? I'll knock in on you tomorrow."

"Thanks . . . For being here. I . . . I'm glad you were."

He patted her arm gently, comfortably resting his hand

there for longer than necessary. The familiarity of it made her eyes well.

"Oh, God, here we go." She wiped at the tears. "Sorry. I don't know where that came from."

"It's just the anaesthetic," he reassured. "Making you emotional."

"Is it?"

Max didn't answer. Instead, he turned to leave.

"Max?"

"Lucie." He turned back, more serious.

"Did I say anything weird? You know? With all the medication . . . ?"

He shook his head, smiling. "I'm afraid not. Not this time. Nina will be very disappointed with your lack of divulgence. I had the camera ready to capture it. I'm terribly let down," he mused, pulling the blue surgical cap from his head and scrunching it in a ball.

After Doug had left the day before, Max had sat on the recently vacated chair and routinely asked the pre-anaesthetic questions.

"You already know the answers to these," Lucie had said, growing impatient.

"Still, I have to ask," he'd replied, ticking the page in front of him, making notes as he went. "Besides, it's been almost fourteen years since I've seen you. Things change. People change." He'd paused to look up at her, his expression unreadable.

"I haven't changed that much."

"No. I suppose not. Still stubborn."

Her eyes flashed. "Have *you* changed?"

It was out before she could stop herself. The medical questions now veering into other areas. Max rested his clipboard on his knees and held her gaze.

"I mean, you don't look all that different."

To Lucie, he was the same old Max, perhaps with a few extra kilos here and there, but he looked well, relaxed in himself, obviously content.

"I'm older, obviously. Fifty next year," Max groaned.

"Jesus! you can't be." Lucie feigned shock. "That's very, very, very old."

"Hah. Less of that! You're not that far behind me."

"Don't remind me." Lucie pursed her lips. "Shocking, isn't it? How did it happen? Feels like yesterday we were working here, thinking that we had all the time in the world to . . ." Lucie stopped, not knowing what she'd been about to say.

"To what?"

"Live?"

"Is that a question?" Max noted the brief look of terror in her eyes. "Hey, you're not done living yet. How are the kids?"

"Great."

"And Hamish?"

Lucie bristled. "Good."

"Nina said he's away."

"Yes. Singapore. For a few months." She looked towards the window.

"Who's minding the children?"

Lucie glanced back unsurely before saying the name. "Ann."

His eyes met hers, a look of confusion in them. "Your niece? She lives here?"

Lucie shook her head. "No. She's still in Ireland. She took them back with her for a holiday. Their first time. They were weak with excitement. They've never been."

Max nodded, hesitated slightly. Lucie could see he wanted to ask more but was adamantly avoiding it.

"She got in contact. A few years back," Lucie explained anyway. "Well, she found me, through some nurses-living-abroad website. I went to see her in Ireland. All grown up. Married. At least she was – she'd just separated. She's thirty-one now."

"Wow. So all those years, you weren't in contact?" He sounded shocked.

"No. I never went back again after . . . well, you know why."

She couldn't meet his eyes. The air in the room had changed, suddenly feeling as suffocating as it had years before over a similar discussion.

"Was she okay? *Is* she okay?"

"She was. Is. She's better now." Lucie exhaled, not knowing if she should bring it up. "I should have . . ." She stopped again. "Let's not go there."

"I'm glad she's in your life again. Was it hard being back in Ireland?"

She smiled wistfully. "It was, but it was also great." Then she said it anyway. "I should have gone years ago. After Felicity died, I suppose I was in a bad place." She looked at her hands. "I had a lot of healing to do, but then, you already know that, don't you?" She didn't wait for him to answer. "It helped me to remember all the great times."

"I'm glad. Really, Lulu."

Hearing him call her that made an unexpected pang shoot through her chest.

"What about you? You never married?" she asked suddenly.

"You know I didn't."

"Why not?"

He shrugged and laughed. "No one would have me."

"That's not true. A doctor is always a catch, so they say." She'd been about to say, "I would have," but she stopped herself in time.

"Anyway . . ." He'd stood and picked up his notes. "The past is the past, so they say. I'd better go. I'll see you tomorrow in surgery. Rest." He'd made for the door and then turned. "Are you happy, Lucie?"

She hadn't been expecting that. It was unlike him to be so forward. She smiled woodenly.

"Good enough for me," he'd muttered when she'd answered.

Lucie looked up at Max now, hovering beside her bed uncertainly. There was so much more she'd wanted to tell him the day before – all that she should have years ago. After he'd left her alone, she'd ached to call him back, order him to sit down and shut up, so she could report every real detail of her life. But she hadn't. Instead, she'd lied, as she once had before.

"Very," she'd said when he'd asked if she was happy.

Had he believed her? Lucie had a feeling this wouldn't be their last conversation on the subject. She could feel it inching towards her, finally catching up, ready to erupt.

"Life boils down to one or two big decisions."

Lucie had been repeating it over and over since Doug had said it the day before. She wondered could she pinpoint what her big decisions had been. It certainly felt like there had been more than just one or two – not life or death, like Rose had faced, but big enough to alter her life.

Possibly, right now, Lucie was facing another significant decision as she looked into the face of the man who still cradled her heart in his enormous hands. One thing was for sure, Max was back in her life. In what form, Lucie had yet to see, but the truth she'd hidden throughout every second of her marriage would eventually surface. And she was petrified.

"I'll see you tomorrow, Lucie."

Max had touched her arm again before walking away, trying not to dwell on her earlier words in the operating theatre. They'd been barely a whisper, but he'd seen the air that carried them fog in her oxygen mask and he'd heard them. Lying there, defenceless, a surgical cap on, face scrubbed clean, she'd held his eyes. Her inebriated truth had felt like a punch in the gut, a shot straight to his heart.

"He's a shit. But then you warned me," she'd slurred. "I didn't listen . . . it should have been you, Max, it was always . . ."

Max had pressed the button, administering the anaesthetic to quieten the painful truth. And as Lucie had drifted off to sleep, at last, he felt as though he'd woken from the nightmare of having lost her all those years before.

Chapter twenty-seven

Lucie was pleased to see Doug, grateful for the distraction from recovering from surgery and wanting to talk – scratch the itch that had been disturbed. It was three days now since the operation. Aside from Nina having visited when she could, and a few rushed but excited phone calls from the children in Ireland, she'd been alone, with herself and her thoughts.

"All looking superb," Professor Stone had told her that morning on his rounds. "We were right about that fruit basket. Quite the selection. You must have been in a lot of pain, Lucie," he scolded. "Next time, don't leave it so long. "And the good news . . . no cancerous cells. You're all clean. Once you're over the surgery, you'll be ready for that second life."

Those words again. Was every person reading off the same script? Everyone except her.

"Are you up to a visit?" Doug asked from the door. "How was the surgery?"

"It went well. The doc was here this morning and gave me a clean bill of health. I'm sore but getting there. Come in, please." She winced as she attempted to haul herself upright.

"Here, let me." He walked over and let her use his arm for support before placing a punnet of strawberries on her table and sitting down.

"Thank you. You know," she began, jumping right in where they'd left off, "I've been thinking a lot about your Rose, that story. It made me think if she could overcome something so terrible and move on, well, it gives me hope, if that's the right word, that this blip in my life will pass, too."

"She'd have liked that," Doug agreed. "Funny, I've been thinking a lot about you and your story – also, why you left Ireland. I hope I didn't make you feel silly following it with Rose's tale. Her story is a bit more unique."

"Not at all." Lucie waved her hand. "It was a reality check, if I'm honest."

"Can I say something?"

"Of course," she nodded.

"It's just, this Felicity, your friend, she sounded like a nice girl and I suppose – actually, I know – she wouldn't want you feeling guilty for going off to live your life. Similar to that incident at the school," he looked at her pointedly, "I think you need to park that regret."

Lucie watched him shrug.

"You left Ireland. Big deal. Sometimes life sweeps you away in different directions. Like you said, it was your calling." He put his palms up. "So, you were a little jealous of Felicity. She was like a sister, that's normal. It doesn't mean you let her down."

Lucie nodded slowly, letting his opinion sink in.

"Maybe you're right."

"I'm going to stay on a little longer in Australia." Lucie was picking at her nail when she said it.

Felicity and Lucie were sitting on her old bed upstairs, trying to escape the crowds who'd come to pay their respects following her dad's funeral.

"I know."

"You do?" Lucie looked up.

It was heartbreaking being back in Knockmore under such circumstances. At least she had another week to spend with them all, especially Mam, before she was due to fly back. It would ease the guilt of telling her she was planning on extending her visa.

"You love it there, don't you? Whenever I'm talking to you on the phone, you sound so happy. *I'm* happy for you."

"I wish I was as happy now." Lucie grabbed Felicity's hand suddenly, feeling another wave of grief take hold. Over the past few days, there had been a few times that she'd forgotten, for just a second. "Can you believe he's gone?"

Felicity shook her head. "No. It feels like a dream."

"I should have come sooner." Lucie let out a pained sob.

"Hey. Stop that. It was so sudden in the end, Lu. None of us knew it would be so fast."

After getting the phone call at work, Lucie's legs had almost gone from under her on hearing the news that her father had died. Felicity had had to repeat it four times before Lucie understood the words. Dad had been unwell of late, but it had all sounded reasonable enough – a head cold, lousy flu, followed by a chest infection that had finally forced him to go and see the doctor.

"Riddled." Mam's voice had broken down the phone when she'd first called to tell Lucie the terrible news. "Riddled with cancer."

The doctors at the hospital had said months. Mam had brought him home straightaway, and Lucie had booked flights to go back and see him. She'd had to rebook them following the phone call at work from Felicity, just two short weeks after the diagnosis. Lucie hadn't got to say goodbye, not in person. In fact, she hadn't seen her father in person since the day she'd first left for Australia – and now she never would again.

"He gave up," Felicity said finally. "Sammy said he was too tired to fight."

"Well, he always loved a good rest." Lucie attempted to smile through her tears. "I never thought the next time I'd get to see him he'd be in a coffin, though." The words choked her.

"He was *so* proud of you, Lu. He talked about you non-stop, you know. Sammy was forever telling him to zip it. He used to say that he was glad you got the hell out of this god-forsaken country run by a shower of feckin' eejits." Felicity mimicked his voice.

Lucie smiled sadly. It was the same thing he'd told her almost every time they'd spoken over the phone. The Irish economy had been booming, but Paddy Maguire hadn't been falling for it.

"Jaysus, you won't believe what the houses are going for now, Lucie. Hovels up the road selling for close to a million. You'd never afford anything here. Stay where you are, girl, do you hear me? I keep telling Sammy and Fliss, get out while you can. The country has gone mad.

"The feckin' banks are responsible. Mark my words, the arse is going to fall out of it and we'll all be up shit creek. Jaysus, I hope I'm not here to see it. Ah, you did the right thing. Are you listening to me? If I was young enough, I'd follow you."

"I'll miss him forever, the narky old thing," Lucie managed. "But then, Mam said he'd had one foot in the grave for ages. Always giving out. Nothing was bringing him any joy any more – except for Annie! The size of her, Fliss. Can you believe she's a teenager?"

"I can! She's all attitude. A good kid, though. She's so happy you're here."

"I miss her. I miss you all." Lucie squeezed Felicity's hand. "But I want to stay on," she was quick to reaffirm.

Even Mam in her state of shock had taken her aside and hugged her fiercely, reiterating Paddy's words.

"He was so proud of you, Lucie. And he made me promise that I wouldn't make you move home after he went. It was one of the last things he said before . . . 'Let her live her life,' he said. So I'm telling you now, don't go getting any notions about coming home to take care of me. Jesus, I miss you every day of my life, little one, but I'll be okay," Tess had sniffed. "We all will."

Felicity smacked at Lucie's leg playfully. "Anyway, Lu. It's been five years since you left. We're used to it now. I knew you'd never come back."

"I will, though. Someday. Just not yet. Will you look after Mam for me?"

"Always. We're going to move back in here."

"Really?"

Felicity nodded. "Sammy doesn't want Tess here alone – and before you say it, we don't mind. No guilt, okay? Life is too darned short."

"There's so much I'd forgotten." Lucie turned to Doug. "Talking about it again, with you, it's brought back so many conversations. I think you're right. Felicity did want me to be happy. Mam and Dad, too," she paused. "But then, none of us knew what was coming next. That's the part I still struggle with."

"I wondered was there more," Doug admitted. "Do you think you can tell me?"

"I wouldn't even know where to start."

"Allow me," Doug smirked. "What happened after your dad died?"

Lucie took a breath.

That first taste of unexpected grief, the sudden understanding of the brevity of existence, curiously affected Lucie, almost gifting her with a lease of life. Everything felt different on returning to Australia. Sometimes Lucie felt like she was seeing everything for the very first time, experiencing it all over again. It made her feel braver than she ever had before, affirmed in her life choices.

Her father had approved of her. It was a strange thing to admit to herself that she'd spent much of her life seeking his praise, waiting for him to tell her that he was proud of her. What was even stranger was how he'd withheld what she now considered liberating knowledge. But in his passing, her father had awarded her the longed-for self-assurance.

When she'd first left Ireland, Lucie had genuinely believed that she'd been a burden to her family. That it was Lucie who'd become "the one". Every family has one – the one they all worry about, the one who hasn't quite got it all figured out, the one they rely on to make themselves look better. But on her return to Australia after her father's funeral, she began to see herself differently. At night, she grieved, with Nina wiping her tears, but in the day, Lucie swore to live, for her dad – to make him even prouder than he'd already been.

***

"That's when I met Max. Or at least, threw myself at him," Lucie laughed. "Thankfully, he caught me. I practically coerced him into asking me out. I'd been giving him the eye for weeks. I remember it so well, scrubbing in for surgery beside him, flirting like mad.

"Then he asked me for a drink. 'Maybe,' I said, all coy. Maybe, my eye! We went out that very night. After that, we were always together.

"I often think it was a parting gift from Dad. He gave me the courage to finally go after what I wanted. I'd *never* had any luck with men." She paused and rolled her eyes. "I suppose I didn't have as much confidence as you might imagine comes with this face," she teased, and Doug laughed.

"But Max was different. He was quiet. I was wild, like his total opposite, but finally, *finally*," she emphasised, "I began to understand what Felicity had felt for Sammy.

"I was thirty by then. Christ, we moved in with each other after a few months. In many ways, after losing Dad, it was the best and the worst of times," she paused. "Then came the next call."

This time it was different, much darker than before. Then again, everyone says it, don't they? How a daughter losing her mother is *the* most defining moment. But then you don't understand it until it happens to you.

It was almost a year to the day since Lucie's father had died. Felicity had sworn before Lucie left for Australia again that if Mam got sick, or needed her in any way, that Felicity would summon Lucie on time. Once again, there hadn't been enough time. Tess Maguire passed away in her sleep.

"I'll come with you to Ireland," Max had told her. "I'll just tell them I have to take time off."

"You can't. You're too busy. I'll be okay. I'm going to need you when I'm back." She'd sank into the safety of his arms.

The heavy guilt descended once more, this time making it difficult to breathe. All of a sudden, Lucie understood why her mother had always taught them to be strong, because she'd known that this day would come and they'd need every bit of strength to weather it.

"She couldn't live without my dad," Lucie whispered into Max's chest.

"Like I'll never be able to live without you," he confided back. "You'll come back? Promise."

"I will. This time, I have you to come back for."

"I remember it so well." Lucie exhaled and glanced at Doug before staring ahead again and glancing up at the flickering lights above. "Standing at the front door at home in Ireland, saying goodbye to Fliss after the funeral. You know what she said? She told me to go home and marry that doctor. To live my life."

"But you didn't marry him?" Doug asked.

She shook her head. "No. Not that I didn't want to. It never seemed important. He was busy. I was busy. After Mam, it was Max who put me back together. I wouldn't have got through it without him." She put her head back, closed her eyes.

"But?"

"I was doomed. Everyone just kept dying." Lucie released an acidic sob. "My brother, Sammy, was next. A car accident. Drunk driver."

Doug closed his eyes and shook his head. He was beginning to wonder how this poor girl was still here to tell the tale.

"I went back for the funeral, *again*, then came back to Australia – and that time I did consider moving home to be with Fliss."

Felicity wouldn't hear of it. By that time they'd been able to talk on FaceTime. Seeing Felicity's face helped, made her feel more like she was with her in person. Lucie had suggested they come to Australia, to live with her, but again Felicity had been adamant.

"My life is here. Ann's life is here. All of my memories with Sammy. Lucie, please. Don't let me ruin your life. I'll be okay. I have Ann – and I'm going to make another life for her."

"But—"

"No."

It was final. Lucie would stay. She had Max, her job, a future in Australia.

"I've said it before, time doesn't heal you. All time does is dampen the screaming in your head, allow you to get on with what's left. And then . . ." Lucie swallowed. "And then, Felicity."

It came as an even greater shock than the others, if that's possible, just when life was finally getting back to some sort of normality. Lucie stayed in close contact with Felicity. It was the reason why when *that* phone call came, it hit Lucie harder than anything before.

"Lu, I've something to tell you." Felicity's voice sounded strange.

"FaceTime me, now," Lucie demanded, hanging up the phone. It had been months since they'd spoken online, Felicity always making up some excuse about Ann using the laptop.

"Oh, Fliss." It was all she could manage as her own face crumpled.

Felicity was a different person, ravaged. So much so that Lucie knew immediately what was coming, even before Felicity opened her mouth. This time, it was too much to bear.

"Why? Why didn't you tell me? Oh, God, why didn't you tell me?"

"I never forgave her for that," Lucie admitted now. "It was breast cancer. She hid it from me the entire time." She shook her head in disbelief. "I still don't understand why. I never will."

Doug watched as Lucie's hands grabbed the sheets on the bed and twisted them in her hands.

"Instead, she gave me another horrific surprise, and I was furious – maybe I still am. By the time I spoke to her that day, it was too late. She was being nursed at home. She'd already made arrangements for Ann to go and live with a woman in Dublin, in digs. Felicity didn't want Ann to be there at the end. She didn't want anyone there, not even me, and it broke my heart."

Doug listened quietly as Lucie explained the part about Felicity's deranged mother threatening to take custody of Ann after Felicity's death.

"Felicity was terrified. I could see it on her face. That woman, her mother – not that she was deserving of the title – was pure evil – cracked! Like, you have no idea. It would take me an age to tell you all of it . . . Another day . . ." She raised her eyebrows at Doug. "But for some reason, Felicity went to see her before she died – after no contact for seventeen years.

"I don't know why she did it. I suppose she wanted to

settle things before she died, ask the questions she'd never had a chance to." Lucie shrugged. "But all that woman did was threaten to take Ann away. It frightened her, so much so that she made arrangements for Ann to leave straightaway. Fliss could be stubborn and she wouldn't hear of me coming back."

"I'm coming," Lucie had said.

"There isn't time," Felicity wheezed. "I need to tell you . . . Ann, I've sent her to Dublin. It's all set. There's a woman there. She's going to take care of Ann until she finds her feet."

"Fliss, she's a child! She's only seventeen. What are you thinking? I'll come back."

"*No.* I've thought about this, Lu. A single woman living abroad won't be allowed to take Ann and I can't risk Mother getting her hands on her. Please. I know Ann will find you when she's ready. But leave it, please. It's all I want for Ann now – freedom. Promise me."

The next part rushed from Lucie's mouth, the frenzied memories evident in her words.

"She wasn't making sense. None of it made sense. And I was so bloody far away. I booked flights and left the next day. By the time I got there, she was dead and I . . . I crumbled.

"I tried to find Ann. But no one knew where she was, so I went to Dublin – for what, I don't know." She put her palms up and then squeezed her hands into fists. "It was like trying to find a needle in a haystack. I couldn't call the police. If I had, then maybe Felicity's mother would have got custody of Ann. It would only have been until she turned eighteen, but I would have been going against

Felicity's dying wish. So instead, I came back to Australia." She smiled sadly at Doug before finishing, "I came back on a mission to destroy myself."

Chapter twenty-eight

Max

Max couldn't sleep – thoughts of Lucie permeating his mind. Lucie was different. Regardless of her saying that she hadn't changed that much, something had. She was less bubbly, more sober, her expression altered somehow as if her eyes could no longer open as wide as they once had, her cheeks no longer able to lift into that full-toothed grin. Yes, Lucie looked older – they all did.

Over the years, his own offering of hair had slipped completely off the back of his head, a ladder of lines now permanently visible on his forehead – but that wasn't it. It was like she'd become older – something the original Lucie had planned never to be. He hoped it was still in there somewhere, that natural effervescence, the twinkle that had once drawn him to her flashing eyes like a moth to a flame.

"I fell for you as soon as I saw your smile – one that could light the up the Sydney Opera House," he used to tease. "And dance moves that could shut it down just as fast."

Lucie had always managed to bring out his fun side,

the part that Max once feared didn't exist, making him feel lighter than he'd ever felt in his outsized frame.

"For me, it was this . . ." She'd fold herself against him, squeezing him tightly, nestling her head against his chest. "You make me feel safe."

And for the first time, Max imagined that he'd been uniquely designed especially with her in mind – no longer feeling like a cumbersome, plodding giant who might accidentally knock down buildings or trample on cars in his wake. Lucie shrank him to a place of comfort – rarely mentioning his height except to praise it.

"I always knew I'd end up with someone who could plough Wicklow with their bare hands, crack coconuts with their thighs and lift a burning bus full of school children, stopping them from falling off the edge of the Sydney to Melbourne coast road," she'd laugh. "Then again, the tall fellas always liked me, Max. I've figured out why now. So I'm like half a person, and you're one and a half. See. Perfect."

Little Lucie Maguire and mammoth Max Woods fit together like the missing piece of the other for five happy, yet sometimes pain-filled, years. That first day, standing at the sinks outside theatre when they'd officially met, had been shortly after Lucie's father had died. Max still remembered her telling him about it over a drink after work. That drink had turned into dinner, followed by another drink, Max thirsty to learn more.

He'd been surprised by how openly she was able to discuss her feelings. There was more to Lucie than the perky persona she conveyed, far more. Over the months, he'd discovered that she was incredibly compassionate and wonderfully honest to the point of transparency. Lucie *felt* things, far more deeply than most with her enormous heart, even if she was the worst overthinker in the world.

"Or the best," she'd respond boastfully.

Max would often shake his head at some of the impossible scenarios she'd invent – her imagination charging into overdrive at times. Lucie wasn't perfect, but then neither was he. And he quickly accepted that gloomy lows for her were often followed by staggering highs. But she was pure. Sometimes he thought she was the most genuine person he'd ever met.

"Never?" he'd asked when she confessed that she'd never before slept with anyone.

"Never." She'd been as mortified as he'd been shocked. "I've never told anyone that, not even Nina. There must be nuns less virtuous than me. It's not by choice, believe me. I just . . . I never . . . I don't know. I never met anyone decent and . . . Oh, God, do you want me to go? I'll go.

"I suppose I got it into my head that I was lucky in other ways and that a relationship might never happen for me. Then the older I got, I thought the romance, the love story – it was for other people."

By people, she'd meant her friend, Felicity, he soon discovered. There was this deep connection between the two women that fascinated Max. It was more than friendship, perhaps even more than sisterhood. It was a reflection of Lucie, he reckoned, impossibly loyal.

"Come here." He'd picked her up and carried her to his bedroom. "Let's see what we can do to rectify your virtue. Unless, of course, I send you to sleep first."

People gravitated towards Lucie, especially men. She was beautiful, sexy, fun. Scratch that, she was downright hilarious. But Lucie couldn't see it, or perhaps she'd never felt brave enough to look. That she'd selected him, well, Max felt like the luckiest man alive.

"Good things come to those who wait," she'd said afterwards. "Now, tell if I'm pure shite at it, won't you? I can read a book or something. Do a bit of research . . ."

"No need. But I think we should definitely practise more. You know I'm a perfectionist!"

After her mother died, a year later, Max had held Lucie through the nights of tears. Then came her brother's turn. That time, Max had wondered if Lucie would come back to Australia at all. But she had, crushed and broken, once again to be healed – as only he could, she used to say. Two years after that . . . well, Max had tried, he really had.

Max had planned to catch up on sleep that afternoon, being his day off, but instead, he was staring at the ceiling, replaying her words.

"It should have been you, Max, it was always . . ."

He hadn't been to visit Lucie since, not trusting that everything he wanted to tell her wouldn't come tumbling out.

"Speak now or forever hold your peace," he whispered to himself. Would he have spoken up at the time if he'd been given a chance?

"Swear we'll always tell each other the truth, Max. I want us to be honest, always. No matter what."

He wondered did Lucie still mean what she'd once declared. Or were the words now defunct? Perhaps when you say the word always, you don't *always* mean it.

Max grabbed another pillow from the vacant space beside him on the bed and put it behind his head. He'd temporarily rented the harbour-front apartment until he'd settled back in Sydney and was sure that he was going to stay. Now that he was back, it hadn't taken him long to realise why he was here. Why, after all this time, why now? He couldn't put his finger on it, but he felt as though something had drawn him back – and he wasn't sure if he could resist finding out why.

"It should have been you . . ."

That Lucie had been drugged to her eyeballs when she'd said the words was inconsequential – a side note – one that Lucie might have laughed at if the situation weren't so delicate. There was indeed the tiny problem that Lucie was married, but where was Hamish now? Surely . . . No, Max was sure – if there weren't enormous weeds in the marital garden, even Hamish, his self-centred cousin, would be present while his wife underwent a hysterectomy.

Max had genuinely been pleased to hear that Lucie and Ann were back in contact, since it was the death of Felicity that had damaged Lucie most. He'd seen it as soon as she'd returned from spending that week in Ireland. Straightaway, he'd felt as though a stranger had walked through the arrival gates to stare woodenly through him. It wasn't like before when her other family died. Then, he'd been able to see glimpses of Lucie shining through, here and there, confident that *his* Lucie would eventually return to him in some form.

This had been different.

"What?" Lucie had looked up defensively before Max even had a chance to speak.

There had been a vacant expression on her face as if she were asleep but with her eyes open. He'd come home to find her sitting on the sofa of their then rented apartment, still in her pyjamas, the place a mess. It had been that way for weeks.

Max had suggested she take a leave of absence from work and for once, she'd agreed. The hospital had allowed it – after all, turning up late for work, still smelling of the night before, was something that hadn't gone entirely unnoticed. Lucie's mind was elsewhere and when it was people's lives they were dealing with, well there wasn't room for sloppiness. And that's precisely what Lucie had been lately – sloppy.

"Nothing." He took off his coat, hanging it on the hook near the door and pretending not to notice the empty bottle of wine in front of her, nor the smoke-tinged air in the apartment. "Have you eaten?"

"Yes," she lied, not looking up as he went into the kitchen and opened the barren fridge, shutting it just as quickly. "Come on, get dressed. We'll go to the Italian. Can I tempt the lady with a pizza? I'm starving."

"I'm not hungry."

"Lulu, please." He made his way over to her, sitting down and taking her hands.

She glanced up briefly then looked away. It took her eyes a moment too long, moving in unfocused slow motion to reach their destination, before settling on the floor in front of her.

"Come on, get dressed. It'll do you good. There's nothing a big feed won't fix."

Her eyes shot up quicker this time, an ugly grimace thwarting her features.

"Is that right?" she slurred. "I'm not sure a pizza will bring *them* back. Will it? Will a pizza help find my niece? Will a pizza bring back Felicity?" she snorted before standing up, losing her balance and plonking back down on the sofa.

"How much did you drink?"

Lucie tutted. "Now now, Max. You're not my father. He's dead too, remember? All gone. Bye-bye." She waved at the air dismissively in front of her.

"For fuck's sake, Lucie. Please." He tried to grab her hands again, but she slapped him away.

"Leave me alone." She curled herself into a ball and closed her eyes.

"No." He stood over her. "You stink. Come on. You're having a shower."

Reaching down, he then scooped her effortlessly into his arms and walked towards the bathroom, ignoring her jerking limbs, her violent words. Placing her in the bath, he reached up and ran the shower over her fully clothed form before she could protest.

"You shit," she hissed. "Go fuck yourself. You have no idea." Her wailing sobs turned to silent thrusts, shoving him away. "You have no idea."

Not knowing what else to do, Max climbed in beside her, the water drenching his clothes. At first, she hit out, pounding his chest, over and over, until she gave in, allowing him to hold her.

"I know I don't, Lulu, I really don't, but I'm here. You're alive. I won't let you disappear. We're going to do this together, just like before. Step by step."

Sobbing into his chest with the water gushing over her, Max tried to shield her face.

"You're going to drown me," she objected.

Her sobs had slowly morphed until she was laughing and crying simultaneously, but she'd smiled for the first time in months. That had to mean something.

Max shook his head now at the memory, adjusted the pillow behind him and rested his head back once more.

He honestly thought he'd broken through that time. Afterwards, they'd gone to the restaurant and she'd spoken more than she had in weeks. Her words, though, her thoughts, they were disturbing – her grief manifesting itself differently from before. It was destructive, as if she didn't care any more what happened to her.

When she went out, which was rare, she'd carelessly go to step out in front of traffic without looking, drive faster than she ever had before, drink until she couldn't speak. She was smoking, hiding it poorly, tucking empty cigarette packets in the rubbish, leaving scrunched-up butts on the balcony of their apartment. She was taking sleeping pills, not eating. The list was endless. But it was her words that concerned him most – her immense lack of reason. Unlike the times when she'd reveal her illogical endearing thoughts and he'd smile, these were *not* pleasant thoughts.

"You know what the worst part is? I think Felicity wanted to die." Lucie was leaning forwards, thumping the table with her finger for emphasis. "That's why she didn't tell me she was sick, because *I* could have stopped it and she didn't want me to. I bet she couldn't wait to be with Sammy. Stupid bloody Sammy. She picked him over me *again*." She sat back and crossed her arms.

Max had frowned at her nonsense. "I don't think that's true, Lulu. I don't think you ever *want* to get cancer and I don't think you could have stopped it. I think she may have kept it from you because she didn't want you to worry. I think she loved you that much."

"Hah!" Lucie spat. "Or maybe the 'holier than thou' was all an act. You didn't even know her, Max. No one is *that* perfect. You know, I think she was doing it to punish me. Maybe she was back in Ireland cursing me for not having come home for good after Sammy died.

"Or maybe she *was* angry with me for having left in the first place." Lucie's eyes were wild, moving from side to side as she spoke. "Or maybe she was happy for me to emigrate back then, so she could have *my* family *all* to herself."

Max listened as Lucie madly tried to rationalise.

"And the final insult, to rub salt in the wound . . . Felicity didn't trust me to take care of Ann. My own niece!"

"No." Max shook his head. "No, Lu. I don't think that's true, either. I think Felicity was dying and she was frightened. It was the last thing that she could control. I'm sure Ann is safe. I'm sure, in time, you'll—"

"What? Find each other, like a big happy ever after. This isn't a movie, Max. Ann should be with *me*, here. She's my only family." Lucie put on a whining voice, leaned forwards again to reveal her conspiracy. "'They'd never let you take her,' Felicity kept bloody saying. And you know why not?

"I keep going over and over it. I think *they* wouldn't let me take her, because you and me, we're not even married. That's why." She opened her eyes wide and nodded once. "That's what Felicity *really* meant. 'A single woman living abroad wouldn't be allowed to take her niece,'" Lucie finished with the same moany voice.

Max had exhaled, trying to keep his cool. "No, Lu. I think Felicity had a gun to her head, that's what forced her decision, not us *not* being married. I believe she was doing what she could with what little time she had left."

Nothing Max had said could make her see sense. Even Nina had been at a loss as to how to help her.

"Maybe she should go back to Ireland, try to find Ann. That might put her mind at ease," Nina had suggested when Max begged her for help.

"She's out of control, Nina. Jesus, what should I do?"

"Find Ann! I think it's the only thing that will bring Lucie back. She told me that she never got a chance to tell any of them how much she loved them before they died. She *adored* them. Even though she was far away, they were her world. It's tragic. I can't even begin to imagine how she's feeling."

Max nodded in agreement.

"Look, I'm going out with her later. At least she's agreed to that. That's progress. I'll try to talk to her again," Nina assured.

"Keep an eye on her, will you? She's . . . well, she's drinking more than she normally does. I don't think she has a problem or anything, I just . . ."

"You're a good man, Max." Nina had patted his arm. "She'll come round."

Max thought about Nina's words all that evening. The next morning, he'd dressed for work and crept from the room, leaving Lucie asleep. She'd been drunk when she arrived home after her night out with Nina, but she'd been happy drunk, at least. Seeing Lucie's blue diary on the table in the kitchen, he'd opened it then flicked to that day before writing a note and smiling, hoping that that evening they'd be veering towards the path of recovery.

Max threw back the covers now, got out of bed and padded to the bathroom to run the shower. To this day, he still couldn't make sense of what had happened next.

Chapter twenty-nine

"Max was there for me, same as always, but it was like I couldn't see him. I was so *angry*." Lucie clenched her fists and gritted her teeth. "At everyone and everything. At Felicity, mostly. I *hated* her. Isn't that terrible?" Lucie glanced at Doug for a reaction.

He said nothing.

"I *hated* her for dying. And what came next . . . I blamed her. If she'd just let me go to her when she needed me, if she'd given me the chance to be with Ann, then what happened next may never have happened."

Lucie had woken with her mouth like sand, her bottom lip stuck to the pillow with dry saliva. Reaching for the sheet, she'd dragged it over her naked body, rolled onto her back. Max must have left for work already – she noted the vacant space beside her. Lucie ran her fingers through her hair, tried to moisten her lips, and frowned. Now, how had she got home? She felt utterly muddled.

After meeting Nina from work, they'd gone for food.

Nina had been full of energy, trying to perk Lucie up, gently offering advice. She was good at that. It never sounded like a lecture, not how it sometimes did with Max. By the time they'd finished dinner, they'd already drank a bottle of wine each. Well, that is, they'd ordered two. Lucie couldn't be sure of the exact distribution. Nina said she'd better get home, but all of a sudden, Lucie had felt this great liberation, as if a weight had left her shoulders.

"Please, Nina. Come on. I haven't felt this good in ages. Let's go dancing, like old times."

"Just this once, Lu. Please tell me you heard what I said tonight. You've got to get yourself back on track. Think about getting back to work and taking care of yourself. Max is worried. *I'm* worried."

"I swear," Lucie promised as they made their way to some high-flying club Lucie had heard someone talk about once.

She could remember feeling irritated, for some reason, whenever Nina mentioned Max, which was more than usual. It was apparent that they'd been discussing her behind her back. Max had probably said Lucie was drinking, not looking after herself. Recently, he was suffocating her – always on at her. Eat. Sleep. Shower. Talk. Rest. Nag, nag, nag.

It had been his idea that she take a break from work – and now that wasn't good enough, either. He just didn't get it. Sure, Max had lost his parents years before, but this was different. *Her* family had been obliterated. Lucie hated the thought of Max telling Nina that Lucie was losing it, even if she was. Worse still, she didn't want them thinking of her as a burden. She'd already felt like that years ago in Ireland. No, she'd show Nina that she could still be "fun" Lucie.

Nina had mentioned that she'd "bumped" into Max and that he'd had a brainwave for Lucie. She wouldn't say what it was, which had annoyed Lucie. He probably wanted to put her into therapy. Perhaps it wasn't a bad idea, but she'd already decided what she was going to do. She'd spent the day thinking about everything and at last, she'd reached a decision. She was going back to Ireland to find Ann. If she couldn't take Ann to Australia, then Lucie would move home. So what if she and Max weren't married like Felicity had said. She could still be with her niece.

It was another thing that Lucie had recently started to obsess over. Why the hell *hadn't* she and Max got married? Maybe there was a reason. Perhaps he wasn't sure. At any rate, it was a good thing now. It meant she was free to move home if that's what was needed. She did love Max. Of course she did. But look at what happened to everyone she loved – eventually, they left her. Maybe it was only a matter of time before he did, too.

Standing in the nightclub now, swaying, Lucie closed her eyes and relaxed her shoulders. It felt good to dance, to let loose, to know that she could still feel something other than agony. Nina was doing all sorts of crazy dance moves beside her on the dance floor. They were pissed – and it felt great.

"Look!" Nina grabbed Lucie's shoulder and swivelled her towards the bar. "Isn't that Max's hot cousin?"

Lucie glanced towards the bar, where sure enough, Hamish was leaning against it, surveying the dance floor. Noticing her, he smiled and lifted his hand in acknowledgement. She waved back, and he pointed at his drink and beckoned her with his finger.

"Twat," she shouted at Nina over the music, then

quickly changed her mind. "We'll let him buy us a drink."

She'd never really warmed to Hamish, probably because Max despised him, but Hamish had always been friendly enough towards her at any of the rare family get-togethers. She supposed Max's disinterest stemmed from the fact that Hamish was *that* cousin – "the one" whom Max had been pitted against when they were growing up because they were the same age.

"He was forever staying with us," Max had complained to Lucie years before. "His mother was all about her stupid gallery. Vera's just as selfish as him. The apple doesn't fall far from the tree. He never knew his dad – I doubt Vera knew who he was, either. So Mum always felt sorry for him. But there was no need. Hamish is well able to handle himself."

Lucie had been surprised by the strength of Max's feelings.

"He spent five years in school slagging the crap out of me, trying to make himself look better. See, he was the one with the girls hanging out with him – loads of friends. And I was . . . Well, I was this . . ." Max had gestured down his body. "This prick. He couldn't cope when I got into med school. He had the looks, but now *I* had something over him."

"Good to see you, Lucie." Hamish bent to kiss her on both cheeks.

Lucie could imagine Max rolling his eyes at his cousin's affectation.

"How's that loser cousin of mine? Still can't believe he bagged someone like you." He shook his head in disbelief before turning serious. "Hey, I was sorry to hear about your friend dying. My mum told me. She ran into Max. Drink?"

He ordered shots. Lifting his glass, he stared into her eyes, nodded once reverently and said, "To your friend," before sinking the clear liquid.

"To Fliss." Lucie followed suit. It burned.

Hamish turned back to the barman, circled his finger around the empty glasses, and Lucie watched, impressed, as three more shots appeared. They chatted easily over the music until Nina turned a vile shade of mint green and had to dash to the bathroom, leaving Lucie alone with him. Hamish was entertaining, telling her stories about his job at the bank, his hectic social life.

"I'm here nearly every night of the week. Mind you, I'm getting a bit long in the tooth for it all. We all are. Might be time to settle down." Hamish eyed her.

Lucie was finding it difficult to keep her own eyes from straying towards his perfectly ironed white shirt, which was open, revealing a smooth, tanned chest.

"Hah! I've been thinking the same thing lately. Mind you, I'll probably end up a spinster. My family used to joke about it." Lucie didn't elaborate that it had been her fear and not her family's.

Hamish stared intently at her then laughed. His impossibly white teeth looked fluorescent under the neon lights of the nightclub – his exaggeratedly pointed incisors almost menacing yet terribly appealing.

"What?" Lucie was laughing now, too, unsure as to why.

"Ah, I'd better not say. Max wouldn't like it."

Hamish stared at her like he had the power to melt her with his brown eyes. How was he doing that? Lucie glanced at the ground for a few seconds to avoid complete liquefaction, then straight back to his gaze.

"Go on. I won't tell." Was she flirting? Oh, God, she was.

Hamish raised one manicured eyebrow, looked away for a moment, bit his lip, then met her eyes again. "You won't find what you're looking for with Max. Didn't he tell you he'd sworn never to marry?"

Lucie tilted her head. "Did he now?" She tried to act cool. It was like Hamish had read her earlier thoughts. "Whatever. I'm moving home, back to Ireland, anyway." Lucie shrugged it off.

"Wow." Hamish jerked his head back, raising both threaded eyebrows this time and pursing his lips.

Christ, the lips. Lucie hadn't noticed them before – pouty but not full, the perfect Cupid's bow. Jesus! was he wearing lip liner? No, he couldn't be. Her thoughts echoed his earlier response. Wow was right.

"And what does Cousin Max think about that?"

That stare again.

"I haven't told him yet." She was acting bolshie, hurt by the revelation of Max's vow never to marry, perplexed by Hamish's appeal.

"So, did you break up?"

"No. Not really. It's something I need to do."

The way she'd said it, it was unclear as to whether she was referring to breaking up with Max or returning to Ireland. Perhaps that was the reason why Hamish lifted her phone from the bar, gestured for her to unlock it and then tapped in his number.

"It was good to see you, Lucie."

He stood back and looked her up and down appraisingly. Then he put one hand on her shoulder, brushed her hair aside and brought his mouth close to her ear.

Mother of Jesus, he smelled amazing.

"If you ever need anything, Lucie."

Did he just lick his lips saying her name?

"And I mean, anything. Call me. I'm always here for you."

An unexpected delicious shiver ran up her spine and she opened her mouth slightly as Hamish reached over and moved his fingers along her cheek until they were near her lips. Then Nina grabbed her from behind.

"I've puked everywhere. We need to go, *now*."

Lucie remembered glancing over her shoulder, to see Hamish watching her leave. In her hazy reality, she'd wanted to kiss him. That was the last thing she could remember. Everything after that was gone. Right, that was it. Max was right – she was out of control. Lucie needed to stop drinking. Flirting with her boyfriend's cousin and having blackouts was a clear warning if ever there was one.

By the time Max arrived home that evening, Lucie had tidied up and showered. She'd spent the day going over the night before, still wondering if she'd missed something. Nina had texted to say she was at home with her head stuck down the toilet and to call her later. Nina didn't mention Hamish, thankfully. At least that was something. Still, she couldn't shake the uneasy feeling she'd had while talking to Hamish and what that must mean.

She had no idea what telling Max that she was going to Ireland was going to do to them as a couple. Coupled with a crippling hangover and an intense feeling of paranoia, it was making her nervous. In fact, all day she'd felt odd. There was something about the previous night that she couldn't put her finger on. Earlier, Hamish's words about Max vowing never to marry had flooded back to her. Max and she had spoken about marriage before, hadn't they?

Ugh, why was she so confused? It was almost like her entire life up until now had been some sort of weird jumbled dream. Anyway, what did it matter now if Max never wanted to marry? But it did matter, as Lucie soon discovered. Perhaps more than she'd ever realised.

"If you asked me to tell you now, how it got *so* heated *so* fast, I couldn't." Lucie stopped talking for a moment to try to jog her memory.

"That happens sometimes," Doug assured. "There were times Rose and I would argue and afterwards, I couldn't remember what we'd said or what we'd even been fighting about. Arguments often take on a life of their own."

"This certainly took on a life of its own." Lucie swallowed and sighed. "It started with me telling Max that I wanted to go back to Ireland to find Ann. And just as quickly it turned into me screaming at Max for never having married me. I didn't even think I cared that much about marriage, but I must have. Otherwise, I wouldn't have said what I did."

"No intention, ever, did you? You never bloody wanted to marry me. Happy to have me here and keep your bit of freedom. Felicity must have realised it, too," Lucie had shouted.

"What? How the hell would *Felicity* have known my intentions?" Max threw his hands up. She'd accosted him as soon as he'd walked through the door. "We talked about it before, Lu, remember?"

"Not really," she hissed. "We never *really* talked about it."

They had.

Max sighed impatiently. "We did. You seem to be

experiencing selective memory loss. You were never bothered about marriage. We were always too busy. You said so yourself. But I've *always* been fully committed to you. You know that. Come on. This is us." He walked towards her, but she edged back.

"Why didn't you offer to come to Ireland with me this time?" she continued. "Busy. *You* were too fucking busy, that's why." The tears were spilling through the accusations.

"I should have come with you this time, Lulu. I'm sorry. I don't know," Max shrugged, looking exhausted. "You told me not to. You always seemed so brave. I . . . I don't know."

"But I'm not the brave one. That was *Fliss*. Fliss was the brave one. It was never me. Oh, God, it was never me." Her legs appeared to buckle for a moment, but she grabbed the worktop.

"But you are brave," he reassured. "Look at what you've been through. I understand if you need to go to Ireland. I wanted to talk to you about it. I wanted to say you should go—"

"So he *was* right," she barged in, not letting him finish. "You don't care if I go." Her eyes were dangerously narrow. "I'm nothing to you, am I?"

"Lucie, you're everything to me. Let me finish—"

"We don't even have sex any more. It's been months. I worked it out. At least five. Things have changed, you have to see that." She turned to stomp away.

Max glared at her. "Wow." The word rang in the silence.

Lucie turned back, her features twisted, suddenly lost for words.

"Now I've heard it all," Max snorted.

He looked furious.

"What the fuck does that mean?" She walked towards

him as if about to lash out, then stopped to look him up and down in disdain. "He's right. I *am* too good for you."

"Who the hell are you talking about?" Max frowned.

"Hamish." She said the name slowly, allowing it to hit.

"My cousin?"

"The very one." She was acting cocky now. "I ran into him last night. He told me *all* about your vow never to marry."

Max let out a sharp, humourless laugh. "Is that right? And what the fuck would that shit-stirrer know? That you're too good for me? Is that what he said, or is that what *you* think? Funny, Lucie, lately I've thought *I'm* the one who's too good for you." Then he'd grabbed his keys off the worktop and stormed past her. "I can't do this any more. I can't. Go to Ireland." He slammed the door behind him.

"And that was it," Lucie said now. "The fight to end all fights. The end."

Doug leaned back and squinted. "But you must have talked after that?"

Lucie's mouth was set in a thin line as she shook her head.

"So you went to Ireland?"

"No. I packed my bags there and then, and I left." She looked down at her hands. "I didn't want to call Nina. I was angry with her, too, I suppose. I thought she'd take Max's side. I just wanted to disappear. So . . ."

Lucie's shoulders bounced. Doug wondered was she about to sob, but the next part sounded acidic.

"I called him."

"Him?"

"Hamish." Lucie screwed her eyes shut. "I just needed something different. I needed *not* to feel. And he took me in."

"Wait. I'm confused." Doug narrowed his eyes, and Lucie laughed.

"Yes, clearly – I was, too. Like I said, I was a mess. I needed somewhere to stay. I still didn't feel strong enough to go to Ireland on my own, so Hamish convinced me to wait a couple of months. Have a last big holiday in Oz before I left for good.

"I couldn't face Nina, but I texted her to tell her I was safe and where I was staying. I didn't want to see Max. I just couldn't face him, despite him calling my phone non-stop. When he heard where I was, he stopped . . . and then, as they say, the rest is history.

"Hamish was kind to me and for some reason, being around him, I started to feel normal again. At least, I started to feel something other than intense pain. He didn't push me to get better like I thought Max had been doing. He just accepted me for who I was at that time.

"We were just friends – for about a week, anyway." She threw her eyes up. "Hamish was hard to resist and I thought . . . oh, God, well, I thought what was the harm in having a little fun before I left. And then . . ."

Doug wasn't sure where else the story could possibly go. He was almost cringing listening to it.

"I got pregnant." Lucie caught Doug's surprised face. "I was happy, though. Finding out I was pregnant with Bella – it stopped me wanting to sabotage myself. It gave me a focus. Hamish was thrilled. I've never seen someone so happy."

"You can't have been together long?"

"No. It was funny. It was almost as quick as it happened for Felicity and Sammy. Maybe I thought it was a sign. Sammy was always saying that the unexpected things in life were the greatest. So, I went with it. Hamish asked me to marry him. I accepted." She rubbed her hand down her face. "Then I couldn't go back to Ireland, could I? I was getting my very own neatly manufactured family," she guffawed. "I packed my emotional baggage away and tied a bow around it.

"I reconnected with Nina. She was shocked. More than shocked, in fact. But we were friends – she'd have supported me whatever. And what was she supposed to do? Tell me that I'd screwed up? She knew I already knew that.

"It was Nina who told Max. She couldn't have avoided it for long. She saw him almost every day at work. A few weeks later, he left Sydney. Then Bella was born and we got married shortly afterwards. I went back to work. And that brings us to present day . . . The end?" She said the words like a question and made jazz hands.

"Except it's not the end, is it?"

Chapter thirty

Doug

Listening to Lucie's story, hearing her confide something that she'd never admitted to another living soul, had almost broken Doug's heart. Of every single person in the world, she'd chosen him – a stranger. Then again, perhaps he'd been the first person to ask in all sincerity. He'd always found that no matter how open a person is, even the most forthcoming sometimes need a little encouragement, a spark of interest, a chance to tell their side. It had certainly worked with Lucie – and Doug's intrigue hadn't been an act.

He'd genuinely wanted to understand her background, the choices that had made her who she is, and now, he did. It was simple, he'd asked and she'd told. It was easy to understand how Lucie had arrived at where she was now – a few bad decisions, a large dollop of bad luck. But it only cemented the idea in his mind that somehow he'd been selected, if that was the right word, to help her.

There was so much he'd wanted to say as she spoke, at times wanting to stop her to ask was she sure she wanted to continue, because once she'd revealed it all, it would be out. He wasn't going to use the information – he'd never break her trust like that – but in the past, he'd found that once something is said aloud, well, it's no longer a secret. It can take on a power of its own, and then there's no going back.

"The worst thing you can ever do is kick someone when they're down," his mother used to say.

"Better to be cruel to be kind," Rose would have argued. "In the long run, it's kinder."

When Lucie had answered his final question – "Except it's not the end, is it?" – Doug had winced. The whole way through her story, he'd never have guessed what she'd say next. He'd closed his eyes for a moment, sucked in his lips and sighed upon hearing the revelation. The poor girl. What was he supposed to do now? Doug knew that the time was fast approaching where he'd be forced to deliver Lucie another truth, and he had no idea how to do it.

Lucie was at home now. She'd been discharged from the hospital the day after she'd brought her tale to the present day, almost a week ago.

"And now for the hard part," she'd sighed before he'd left her that evening. "Now it's out, I can't really put it away again, can I?" There was a look of terror on her face.

"Well, you could," he admitted. "But no. Now, it's time to deal with the future."

Throughout her story, Lucie had mentioned other seemingly inconsequential things here and there. He had to hand it to her – she'd honestly tried to make a go of it all. In the evenings, at home, he'd taken out his file and cross-referenced what she'd unconsciously told him about her life. The time Hamish had arrived home with a new car for her. The expensive holiday they'd gone on another time, the diamond ring for her fortieth birthday. It all made sense.

"Hamish is impulsive," Lucie had said. "At first, it was exciting. Really. I didn't know month to month what he'd do next." She threw her eyes to heaven. "Until it became not knowing day to day what was happening. He's a whirlwind, full of energy. It's funny, I suppose, how in many ways Hamish and I are more alike than Max and I. But then, I suppose two wrongs don't make a right, do they?"

"That's what they say. Opposites attract," he'd agreed.

"What about you? What was your marriage like?" Lucie asked.

Doug smiled and thought for a moment. "Like home," he said at last. "That's the only way I can think to describe it. Every time I was with her, I felt like I was home. She was wild, but then she was so incredibly calm. Kind. Mind you, she had a temper, too."

"Oh, the Irish always do," Lucie grinned.

"Certainly sounds that way!"

Lucie looked out of the window briefly, pushed her hair aside, tilted her chin.

"A year or so ago my niece, Ann, was going through a hard time in Ireland. Her marriage had broken up and she'd moved back to Knockmore, where we're from.

"Anyway, she was going out with this guy, Mark. He seemed perfect. Good-looking, loads of dosh, nice, and I kept encouraging her to give it a go. Then right in the middle of it all, she met this other guy, Nathan. Let's just say, on paper – not so great. In the end, though, Nathan turned out to be fantastic, but it took a lot of toing and froing to get to that point. They're engaged now."

"That's nice."

"Yeah, it is. I remember saying to Ann when she was having doubts that if she was even *questioning* her relationship with Mark, that *that* was her answer. If she was sure, she wouldn't have been having doubts. I mean, I know doubts are normal, once or twice – but not all the time."

"When you know, you know," Doug added.

"I'm very good at giving advice," Lucie laughed. "Just not great at listening to it. Did you ever doubt Rose? Whether she was the right person for you."

"Once. Just once. She was older, like I said. There was a lot of chat about her not being able to give me children. For about a week, I thought about nothing else. You always think you'll have children someday, don't you? But, in the end, I knew that if I couldn't have them with her, well, it just wasn't on the cards for us," he finished.

"You'd have been a good dad," she smiled.

"And you? Did you have doubts?"

Lucie raised an eyebrow. "About which one?"

"Hamish?"

She nodded. "All the time. Another truth, Doug! You're like a walking lie detector." She tried to make light before turning serious and admitting it again. "All the bloody time. But then when you have kids, it's different. It's not all about you and what you want. It's about them."

"And with Max?" He already knew how she'd answer.

"Just that one time. It was enough to end it, though. That has to mean something."

"Maybe, but then, grief does funny things to people, drives them to make strange decisions."

Doug lifted the copy of his file from the table next to his armchair. What he really wanted to do was go out down to the beach, light a bonfire and destroy that thick brown envelope containing the blueprint for Lucie's life with Hamish. He flicked through it blindly then tossed it back on the table before standing to commence his customary pacing.

"Where there's one, there's always another," his buddies on the force would often say. "Nine times out of ten, the wife knows something."

On this occasion, he felt that Lucie was the one who knew nothing of how Hamish had operated his life till now. There was always the possibility that Lucie was just a good liar, but to Doug, she didn't seem like the kind who was motivated by wealth or greed. What drove Lucie Woods was family, that was plain to see. He walked towards the window and looked out at the waves.

"And you know what else?" the lads from work would be saying. "Most of the time, the wife doesn't want to know. She's happy to bury her head."

He wondered would Lucie want to hear what he was now compelled to tell her. Because he *had* to tell her. It was time. Lucie had already admitted far too much from the confines of her hospital bed to have the stamina to figure out the rest alone, as he'd hoped she might. The story, *her* story, had taken an unexpected twist.

Honestly, he'd imagined that by going to visit Lucie, by asking the right questions and prompting her to talk, she might somehow deduce the reason for Hamish's recent Houdini act. He'd naïvely believed that Lucie might piece it all together for herself. Selfishly, he'd hoped she might. Then he could disappear off into the sunset, like some sort of old-age pensioner superhero.

Only now he couldn't. And more telling still – he didn't want to.

How could he have known that Lucie's truth would end up being the divulging of her soul, her struggles, her mistakes? More than once, he'd wondered if Lucie was just one of those "unlucky" people you often hear about – the ones who for some reason are forced to shoulder more than most. Sadly, the unlucky ones were usually those who never expected much more from life than happiness, yet somehow the world keeps bearing down on them. In retrospect, Lucie had made mistakes, errors of judgment, even black-and-white Doug could see that. But who didn't make mistakes? To him, they'd been unconscious, driven by grief. Not like Hamish. No. His were conscious errors. Surely, Lucie would be able to see it, in time . . .

The unexpected phone call that morning had irked him. By all accounts, Lucie was doing well health-wise. The hospital had let her go home, but she was still weak and tired, and he was hesitant to hinder her recovery. He thought he'd have more time.

"Afternoon, Doug. I know you said you were done with the case, but we've run into some difficulties. It seems the husband has hoofed it out of the country. And here's the thing. The cops were on to me yesterday and since the wife also signed the papers, well . . ."

Understanding what he meant, he'd felt his stomach flip.

"I can assure you, she has nothing to do with it. This is all him. I have all the evidence, you've seen it."

"It'll be a way to tease him out of hiding. And you know as well as I do, nine times out of ten . . ."

"Yes. Yes." He didn't need to hear it again.

"True, though. People can't go round signing things willy-nilly. You put your name to it, it's on you, too, simple as."

"It could be forged. And even if it isn't, half the time, they don't know what they're signing, or what the implications are," he tried to argue.

"She should have thought of that. He's a scumbag. I still can't get over all the other stuff you dug up, Doug. Pardon the pun," he guffawed.

Doug exhaled loudly. "Can you buy me a little time? I'll find him. I know the wife has been in the hospital for major surgery."

"Jeez, you really don't leave any stone unturned. How d'you know that?"

"Ask the right questions, people tell you more than they intend." He pretended to laugh. "Look, give me a week. I'll find the arsehole. Deal? Get another prick behind bars." Doug was playing the hard man to appease him.

"Now you're talking, mate. I like the sound of that."

Doug had hung up feeling utterly deflated. His initial plan hadn't worked.

"Don't look at me like that." Doug walked back into the living room and stopped in front of the urn. "I told you I'd help, and I'm helping. It's just not as simple as I first thought." Then he rolled his eyes, knowing that Rose would have been grinning, saying I told you so. "She's a good girl, Rose. You'd like her."

He shook his head, reprimanding himself once again for talking to a vase, but continued anyway.

"Made a heap of mistakes. Christ, she's a disaster zone, but she means well. All heart." He adjusted his hair neatly to the side, pursed his lips and rolled his jaw from side to side. "Actually, listening to some of her stories has me thinking. You know what she said, Rose? She said, 'Sometimes what's more interesting than a person's reason to leave a place is why they never go back.'"

He reached out and twisted the vase, moving it so the pattern on the front was facing out.

"Was there a reason you never went back, Rose? I'm

racking my brain, but I can't think of anything. Your sister? You said you didn't see eye to eye, but I've just seen how important family is to you Irish. I wondered . . ." He stopped and stuffed his hands in his pockets. "I wondered should I find out." He paused, leaned towards the vase as if it were about to whisper a reply.

"Feel free to send me a sign, Rose. Anything at all will do."

He waited with his eyebrows raised and then laughed at his own stupidity. Then the phone rang.

Doug turned to grab it off the table, looked at the screen. It was Lucie. He glanced back at the vase, titled his head and narrowed his eyes.

"That'll do, Rose," he smiled before answering the call.

Chapter thirty-one

Lucie had preferred being in the hospital than at home. The familiar smell of disinfectant had felt comforting, making everything seem cleaner, more manageable than it was now. There, she'd felt untouchable, shrouded in a temporary pocket of warmth and the mundane routine of hospital life. Hearing the tea trolley rolling down the corridor at the same time every day, the nurses coming to wake her each morning, continually checking on her to make sure she was up and trying to move about, it had felt secure. Lucie had spent so much of her life caring for other people in the hospital, minding Bella and Declan, and then the children at Woodfield Grammar in her old job, that she'd relished being on the receiving end, for once.

She was sore from where she'd been opened during surgery, still finding it difficult to stand up straight, terrified her stitches might tear open, even though she knew that wouldn't happen. No. Instead, it was the past that had torn apart during her convalescence: the past.

Doug had listened patiently while she told her story

during his visits. It was his unassuming demeanour, his emotional detachment from it, that had finally allowed Lucie to come clean, lay it all bare, so to speak. He hadn't judged. Even when she'd told him the part that was now making her feel so very uneasy, he'd barely flinched. Well, there had been a wince, but what had she expected?

Had Lucie known that she was going to tell him *everything*? Not really. After all, she'd sworn never to reveal it, even though she'd always feared that at some point the truth might catch up. She supposed she was now at that point.

"I guess, finding Ann after all those years, reconnecting with her . . . I knew it was only a matter of time before I'd have to tell her the real reason I never came back. I remember when I got that first email from her after she finally tracked me down, I was so happy," Lucie had told Doug. "But then there was this part of me that thought, oh crap, here we go. That it was going to be the start of it all. I still haven't told her."

"Ann won't care," Doug had reassured. "That isn't *her* part of the story, it's *yours*."

"I never looked at it that way before."

"I'm sure all that matters to Ann is that she has you in her life again."

"But all those horrible thoughts I had about Felicity? I honestly blamed her for ruining my life."

"You were grieving, Lucie. You know what *I* get from all that? It's that Felicity loved you so much that she didn't want to ruin your life. She wanted to stand alone, so she didn't infringe on your happiness."

Lucie exhaled. "Max said the same thing. I couldn't see it then. It was still too raw."

"Well, Max sounds like a clever man," he grinned. "You have nothing to feel guilty about with regard to Felicity. Really. Felicity said that Ann would find you when she was ready?"

Lucie nodded.

"And she did, didn't she? She went off, made her own mistakes and then found you."

She nodded again. "I helped her through them."

"And she'll help you, too. That's what families do."

She smiled and placed her hand on his. "You've helped me too, Doug. A great deal. I can't thank you enough."

He'd batted the air. "It's nothing. The question is, what are you going to do now?"

What *was* she going to do now? She'd been home for almost a week now. Almost as soon as Nina had dropped her off and instructed her to rest, Lucie had gone straight upstairs to Hamish's office. Rooting through drawers, pulling out unopened notices from the bank about overdue mortgage payments and such. It was all there, tucked at the back, waiting to be found. They were up to their eyes in debt. Of course, she'd already guessed as much, but seeing it there on paper had startled her.

Physically she was feeling more robust, the previous agony she'd been experiencing now replaced with a dull post-surgery ache that would hopefully soon pass. Nina had brought her a ton of ready meals and Ann had left the house spotless. Lucie had nothing to do but think, decide what she was going to do – but as yet, she still had no idea.

Wandering into Bella's for once tidy room, Lucie took an empty notebook and pen from Bella's desk before hobbling back to her own bedroom to sit on the bed.

Writing everything down, trying to weigh up the pros and cons of each scenario, did nothing but make her even more confused. Instead, she drew daisy chains around her words, spiralling until they were almost covered, the reality once again concealed.

Max hadn't come to see her again at the hospital like he'd promised that day in recovery where she'd been half-cut on all the medication. Secretly, she'd been hoping he might, but she could hardly blame him. He must still despise her after everything.

All those years ago, when the dust had settled, she'd been able to see how irrationally she'd acted, how poorly she'd treated him when all he'd been doing was trying to help. It was the *worst* thing she could have done, freezing Max out back then, shacking up with his cousin.

If the roles were reversed, she'd never have been able to forgive him. Her only excuse, and it was weak, is that she'd been incarcerated in a fog so dense that the only light she'd been able to see was Hamish. It made no sense, but she'd wanted to vanish, and Hamish had offered refuge. By the time she'd realised her mistake, it had been too late. And now here she was once more, immersed in darkness.

The only difference this time is she now had Ann, who would always have her back – and Doug, she supposed, in an odd way. She had Nina, too. And her own children – she'd always have them. Lucie held up her hand and counted the names on her fingers – five fingers for the only five people in the entire world on whom she could rely. Was five enough? Well, there was Stacy, the secretary from the school. Could she add her as a sixth? Probably not. Lucie was fond of Stacy, but it was a friendship confined to work and they no longer worked together.

The other mothers at the school? Definitely not! They'd

shown their true colours. Besides, Bella and Declan wouldn't be returning to Woodfield. Lucie blanched at the idea that she had yet to tell the children that piece of news. Hamish's friends? No. Not them, either. She couldn't add Max to the list, no matter how much she might have liked to. And Hamish? Yet to be confirmed.

It was hard to believe that at almost forty-eight years of age, having lived on two continents, all she'd amassed was five names. Let's face it, even Doug was on there at a push – she hardly knew him – although he'd proved to be a lifesaver in many ways.

Lucie had phoned him the day before.

"I think you should tell the truth," he'd encouraged down the phone. "Tear off the plaster. It might help you to move forwards, Lucie."

She'd thought about it all that evening. It was the right thing to do – of course it was – but now, lying on her bed, looking at all the photographs on the wall of Bella, Declan, Hamish and her, she felt unsure. Admitting it would be as good as taking a shotgun and aiming it through their lives. Even though Hamish had his fair share of explaining to do, how could she act all pious about his errors of judgment when she'd made so many herself?

And then the thought struck her suddenly. She held up her left hand again, palm towards her, splaying her fingers out. With her right hand, she folded down the little finger of her left hand. What if afterwards, she was left with not five people but four? What if one of the people who she loved more than anything else in the world wouldn't forgive her? She whispered the name as her eyes filled with tears.

"Oh, Jesus. What *have* I done?"

Sitting here now, Lucie felt the sensation of the air

exiting her lungs, the same way it had that day, many years before, when she'd picked up that little insignificant blue diary. At the time, she'd been searching for it for months. Before Lucie had lost the plot after Felicity's death, she habitually used to write everything down. Her mind had often been far too busy to remember anything past the hour. After Bella had been born, she'd started doing it again. This time the diary had been pink.

Pink for a girl, Bella Woods was their pride and joy. Both Hamish and Lucie adored their baby daughter. It was Bella who'd eventually healed Lucie, finally bringing Lucie back to herself. Lucie had never realised before how much she'd craved being a mother, but as soon as Bella was born, the very moment Lucie saw the shot of familiar red hair, she'd never loved anything as much.

It had taken becoming a mother for her to finally understand how Felicity had felt about her own daughter, Ann. Felicity's ultimate decision of sending Ann away had *not* been to punish Lucie, after all. It had been about protecting Ann. Holding Bella in her arms, Lucie had understood – and with a focus again, a family of her own, she was happy. That was until she'd opened that blasted blue diary.

"Honestly, bin it all," she'd told Nina over the phone when her friend had called to say she'd had the box of her things for months. "If I haven't missed it by now, I don't need it."

"Look, I'll bring it over. Bin it yourself! Anyway, it'll give me a nice excuse to squeeze Bella's chubby cheeks again."

Lucie hadn't bothered to root through the box while Nina had been there. Instead, they'd talked about baby Bella, almost six months, and Nina's pregnancy. Nina had married by then and was expecting herself. After Nina had left, Lucie had put Bella down for a nap before ambling into her own bedroom to sit on the bed.

Looking at the box that Max had given to Nina to pass on to Lucie months before, Lucie was half-tempted to throw it straight in the bin. She didn't need any reminders of the past. Regardless, she opened the lid and peered in at a couple of old T-shirts, a sweater, a few books . . . the missing diary perched on top.

She picked it up and flicked through, noticing the clean pages, blank from where she'd felt so empty during that time. Seeing the unfamiliar black writing jump out, she stopped, leaped off the bed and stood frozen, staring at Max's words written the day before she'd left him. Then everything had started to spin.

She read it a thousand times, holding it in her shaking hands before it made sense. It was only then that a clouded memory raced at her. The night she'd gone out with Nina and bumped into Hamish in that sleazy nightclub. There had always been something about it that had bothered Lucie. Some memory that had been there but not quite there – and all of a sudden she remembered.

Waking to the sound of Lucie banging around the apartment after the night with Nina hadn't surprised Max, certainly not lately, but looking up to see her standing in the doorway naked had. It had been months since they'd slept together – not since she'd returned from Ireland. Max had missed the connection, the feeling of them being together. She was drunk. He could tell by the way she was swaying, resting her hand on the doorframe, giggling.

"Good night? How was Nina?" He sat up and rubbed his eyes, glancing at the clock beside his bed. It was 3 a.m.

"Let's not talk," Lucie grinned, wobbling towards him, her face somewhat menacing in the half-light.

She was on top of him then. He could taste drink and cigarette smoke on her breath, but he didn't fight it. She seemed like a stranger, snaking her way under the covers, taking him in her mouth, slurring words at him that he couldn't understand. He pulled her towards him, attempting to caress her, but she had other ideas.

Mounting him, she let her head roll back, grinding fiercely against him, moaning. He gave in, offering her what she needed until he came, when she rolled off him onto the bed. She was snoring even before he'd wrapped his body protectively around her, placing little kisses on her shoulder.

"Come back to me, Lulu, please," he'd whispered into her hair before closing his eyes, hoping that tomorrow when they spoke, she might.

The flashback was disjointed, but Lucie had been able to recall parts of it. Worse still, in her inebriated state, she could remember wishing it had been Hamish.

The next day, before her argument with Max, Lucie hadn't been able to piece together the night before, nor where the strange suspicion that she'd slept with Hamish had come from. Travelling back to the argument, Lucie could picture Max's face, looking at her as if she had ten heads when she'd shouted that they didn't even have sex any more. It hadn't registered at the time, but it did now.

Rushing to Bella's bedroom, Lucie stared down at her sleeping daughter as if seeing her for the first time. How had she not seen before now? It wasn't Hamish who Bella looked like, it was Max. Christ! it was Max.

Lucie turned slowly and on trembling legs, walked back to her room and picked up the diary from where she'd dropped it. Making her way to the kitchen, she opened a drawer then took out a roll of black bags before staring at the words one last time:

Last night was great. It felt so good to be with you again after so long. I've missed it. I've missed us. Let's talk tonight. Let's make love again. Let's go to Ireland. We can fix this. I'll do anything to make you happy again.
Max

Snapping the diary shut, Lucie held it against her heart for a moment. Then, mechanically, she stuffed the blue book inside three refuge bags before throwing it in the bin. Staring blankly ahead, she almost reached in to take it back out, but Bella had cried out.

Lucie had gone to her, picking her up to soothe her while her own tears slid down her face.

"It's okay, little one. All that matters is you. You have a mammy and a daddy who love you very much, and that's all that matters."

Shaking herself back to present, Lucie closed her eyes tightly, picturing Max's face. If he hated her for having left him and for marrying his cousin, how would he feel about *this*? And Hamish? He'd never forgive her. He adored Bella. And Bella? Lucie couldn't even go there. What would this do to her?

It was unforgivable. Doug was right. Lucie should tell the truth that she'd carried around with her for many years, but how could she? Surely it wouldn't play out like it had several times in her mind:

Max would shake his head in denial as the truth dawned

on him. Lucie's hair would be swishing in slow motion, like it does in the movies. Then he'd take her in his arms, dip her back before pulling her up quickly, looking into her eyes and kissing her. His mouth would be moving on top of hers like he was chewing a lump of fatty steak. Then he'd look in her eyes and say, "She's mine. Bella is mine?"

Lucie would nod slowly. "Yes, Max. Oh, yes. I've waited so long to tell you. Can you ever forgive me?"

"All that matters now is us, and my beautiful daughter."

Then they'd all hug. Hamish and Max would shake hands. What a silly misunderstanding!

The end.

Cue lights.

B'bye now, the best of luck in the future.

Except this was no movie. In real life there would be shouting, screaming, fists flying, all with Lucie at the centre, trying to explain.

"Okay. Everyone get comfortable. It's sort of funny. You see, what happened was, I was off the rails. I was pissed as a fart, like blackout drunk – kids, don't try that at home. So, Cousin Max and I used to be together and we had sex. But silly Mummy couldn't remember. Then there was this huge big row. I left him. Fell into the arms of his cousin, your now daddy.

"I got pregnant, or so I thought, but I was actually already pregnant. Got married to the wrong man. Then Nina, you remember her? Little friend from the hospital? She came over with a box of my things from my old apartment. I went through the box. Found my diary.

"Plot twist! Wait for it . . . There was a note to remind me that Max and I *had* actually had sex.

"But by that stage, sure, I'd already given birth, was already married. And well, it would have been a massive upheaval. So I just said nothing.

"Anyone else need the loo? I'll be right back."

Perhaps Lucie *had* taken the easy way out, guided by trying to do what was right in providing a stable home for Bella. Over the years, Bella had ended up looking mostly like Lucie, but the truth was always there lurking in the background. *Max* is Bella's father.

Lucie could see it in her mannerisms, her smile, her laid-back attitude. But Bella worshipped Hamish – he'd become her father. How could Lucie take that away?

As life had moved on and Declan was born, Lucie had mostly been able to forget. Until Ann had shown up again in Lucie's life, disturbing her past demons, and then Max had suddenly reappeared.

Lucie had wiped Max from her life back then, but his presence would *always* be there. Lucie would always love him until the day she died, she would. But she'd destroyed her chance with him *and* denied him his child. And aside from all that, there was someone who she loved more than Max.

Lucie lifted her little finger back up again and looked at her hand – five people. She couldn't risk losing Bella, not now, not ever.

This time, she looked straight ahead and let the word "Knockmore" drift into the emptiness.

Part Three

Future Truth

Chapter thirty-two

Hamish answered straightaway as if he'd anxiously been waiting with the phone in his hand. Her call? Lucie wasn't sure. She'd been avoiding him for weeks after their last cryptic phone confrontation – that day she'd spoken to him in the hospital. Besides, she hadn't wanted to talk to Hamish again, not until she'd finished what she'd now come to consider her "therapy" sessions with Doug. Now, it was time.

At this point, whether Hamish agreed or not to what she'd decided was of little relevance. Deep down, there was one small part of Lucie that secretly hoped he might not. Either way, she was going to plough ahead with her decision – this time, nothing would stop her. Curious to gauge his reaction, Lucie began. The atmosphere was glacial between them as she sorted the housekeeping, evenly bringing him up to date on her health, telling him about the children in Ireland before getting straight to the point.

"I know everything, Hamish."

He didn't reply. The only break in the silence was his ragged breathing down the line.

"I've found the letters from the bank. I've seen how much in arrears we are."

Again, silence.

"Are you there?" Her voice was growing impatient.

"I'm here."

"Hamish." She placed one foot on the floor to steady herself, from where she was balancing near the edge on the bed, and took a breath. She had to get this right. "Look, I don't want to fight. If you start, I'm hanging up. I'm too tired . . . I'm bloody exhausted, actually, but we have to face this – my way, now. Understand?" Her tone was level.

There was another pause before, "I'm listening."

He sounded as if he was lying on the hotel bed, stretched out. She could picture him with one hand behind his head, legs crossed, shoes off.

For once, Hamish was prepared to listen. So much so that afterwards, she wondered if distance had finally helped her flighty husband to gain some much-needed perspective. It had certainly benefited her – that and finally admitting the truth to herself. There was only one way she could imagine life moving forwards again and being able to salvage some sort of decent life for the children.

"Whatever's happened is in the past. I want to draw a line in the sand now, with everything." She didn't elaborate that she was also referring to her own blunders. "Start over," she persisted. "Wipe the slate clean. It's not going to easy, but I think there's a way.

"Our life in Australia, as we knew it, is more or less over, as far as I can see. I assume you agree." She didn't wait for a response. "We're too far in debt to be able to crawl our way back out. What we need is stability for Bella and Declan, and to simplify. To seriously simplify." She paused to let it sink in.

"Okay. How?"

Hamish was quick. He sounded more alert, perhaps sitting up now, running his hand through his hair.

"Ireland."

The word was out almost before he'd finished the question.

"It's the only option, Hamish. The house is there for us in Knockmore. Ann's already told me as much. We hand this house back to the bank, cut our losses and we leave. The kids already love it there and if we do it now, being the ages they are, it'll be an easy transition."

Lucie braced herself for an objection, ready to play dirty if it came to that.

"What about money?" he asked calmly.

"Well, there's no mortgage on the house in Knockmore. There'll be no school fees. And there's still that money you said was coming. What's the story with that?"

She could hear him taking a drink, then coughing loudly, saying something she couldn't catch.

"What?"

"I said I don't know . . . I'm not sure we can rely on that," he said, recovering.

Lucie held the phone away for a second and frowned. "Why not?"

He started spluttering again. "Sorry. Something went down the wrong way."

"Forget it," she shouted over another coughing fit. "I'm sick of waiting for things to happen. All we need is money to get there. I can find a job straightaway. I know I can." She sounded excited now. "And—"

"I hate to be the bearer of bad news." Hamish had caught his breath, but his voice was meek. "I don't even know if there's enough money to get us there . . ."

She'd been expecting that, too.

"I might have a way," she answered quickly and continued talking so he wouldn't ask how. "I can enrol the kids in school and there's a hospital not too far. I'm sure there's an equivalent back-to-nursing course, and I originally trained in Ireland. Ann can help with the kids. It's perfect. It's a different lifestyle, but it's not *bad*. It's a nice place to grow up."

"Okay. So, say we get there. What am *I* supposed to do?"

"Work, Hamish! Work! Do anything. Now is not the time for pride. Work in a shop, work as a labourer, just work!"

"A labourer?" He sounded offended.

She rolled her eyes, blowing out a breath slowly. "Don't you dare, Hamish! You're lucky I'm even giving you this opportunity to come with us and be with your kids again. After the past few months, I'd be well within my rights to tell you to piss off. Losing the house? Bleeding my bank account dry? I'm sure there's plenty more I don't know about, too.

"If you want me to go looking, I can. And whatever the hell you're up to in Singapore, disappearing like some sort of fugitive . . . Pathetic. What is it again . . . A contract? With whom? You've told me nothing," she scoffed.

She knew she sounded like a hypocrite, but she didn't care.

"I'm working, like you keep telling me to. It's a tech company. I told you," Hamish spat then tutted. "If you want me to be honest, the contract hasn't exactly worked out."

"Surprise, surprise." She was starting to lose it, then took a deep breath, remembering her goal, and composed herself. "Look, you always said that family is what matters to you. Well, we have a family. What difference does it make how we feed them? Currently, we're on our knees and Ann's offering us *free* accommodation. The children love it there. Bella has made friends. Declan is having a ball.

"It *will* be a change, but a good one. It's where I grew up. We have support. And right now, there's nothing keeping us here. If we stay, well, then the past, all of our mistakes, will keep coming at us. We'll always be trying to keep up with the Joneses.

"I don't want that any more. Just come home and let's make a plan." She stopped, running out of breath. "Please, Hamish. I've never asked anything of you before. I've always gone along with what you've wanted."

"And if I don't?" he interrupted.

Here it was. Lucie could be free if she chose to be.

"I'm going anyway. Bella and Declan come first. That's all there is to it."

Hamish said nothing.

Was he thinking? Was he going to explode with rage?

"I miss them," he said finally. And then, "I miss you."

"I know." She closed her eyes, feeling the same longing for Bella and Declan that only Hamish would understand. "I miss them, too."

"Okay," he agreed.

"Okay?"

"Yes."

Lucie could hear him smiling.

"But I'll have to meet you there."

"What?" Oh, for fuck's sake. "Why? There are things we need to do here first. I can't just—"

"Listen, Lucie." It was Hamish's turn now. "You said we weren't going to fight. You said so yourself, the house is going to be repossessed. Call Brent at the bank. He'll help you. Just say I've left you and you don't know where I am. People do it all the time."

"What?" She couldn't believe her ears. "Hamish, is there something you're not telling me? If there is, now is the time, while we're calm. I can take it, please."

"No, Lu," he tutted then scoffed.

Was he laughing?

"Stop being so cynical. It's nothing like that. You're right. I just want to draw a line in the sand, too. I have to see this contract out, much as I'd like to ditch it. It shouldn't be too much longer. *And* we need the money. You wrap up everything there. Sell what you can—"

"Sell? There isn't much left to sell."

"Exactly." He sounded suddenly elated. "So it shouldn't be hard. It'll be an adventure. Remember when we got together . . . Those days, they were . . . Ah! they were the best. We didn't think, we just did. We had Bella. Remember going up the coast and getting married, the two of us, and Bella? It'll be like that again. A fresh start.

"You're right, Lucie, about all of it. I made mistakes. I was too focused on having a high life. Now, all I want is you and the kids. Let's do it."

Despite herself, Lucie was smiling. Was she relieved that he'd agreed, or that she was about to run away once more? Leave her troubles far behind as she once had before.

It was only Doug who knew the truth about Max being Bella's father. Hamish didn't need to know and nor did Bella. Doug would understand her decision to return to Ireland and if he didn't, what did she care? She'd probably never see him again after she left. And Max? Maybe it was a good thing he hadn't come to see her again. Now, she wouldn't have to face him. Hamish was a good father. She couldn't deny him that because of her own stupidity. Perhaps this *was* the second chance that everyone kept harping on about.

"Book your flights, Lu. Don't bother bringing the kids back to Australia first. It shouldn't take you long to wrap everything up there. I'll be finished in less than a month and I'll meet you all there. The kids are going to be stoked. You're right. No past worries, just the future."

Lucie had hung up feeling as if a weight had been lifted from her shoulders. At last, she was going home, back to Knockmore, to where it was safe. Wasn't that what Ann had meant? Go back to the start. Okay, so their marriage had been rocky, but surely with all the financial pressures out of the way, they could give things another go.

"Secrets . . ." Lucie could hear her mother clicking her tongue as if she were sitting next to her on the bed. "What on earth are you doing, love?"

"Don't, Mam, please. Not now." Lucie closed her eyes to block it out.

"But you have to tell the truth. You're only hurting yourself. Can't you see that?"

Lucie could picture them all then, staring at her disapprovingly – Mam, Dad, Sammy, Felicity, Ann. But it was something Felicity had said to her once that flooded back to her now.

"Always be the fun one, Lu. That's who you are. That's your gift. You're the one who brightens the day."

It was what Felicity had said to her years before when Lucie was leaving Knockmore after her mam's funeral. Why did she remember it now? *The fun one.* She hadn't felt like that person in so long. Would she ever again? Certainly not here, not trapped in this mess. Back in Knockmore, she *had* been the life and soul in a room, the smile waiting to happen, the joke that could have them all rolling about clutching their stomachs. If she had to keep a secret to become that person again, so be it. Let the secret damage *her*, but she wouldn't let it hurt anyone else.

Opening her eyes, Lucie picked up the notebook again, lifted the pen and wrote the word Ireland at the top of a clean page. She could do this. Pack bags, talk to the bank, close off their current lives. This wouldn't be the biggest challenge. The greatest obstacle would be closing her mind to the past again. She'd opened Pandora's box, but she could close it just as quickly, for the sake of Bella and Declan.

She got off the bed and opened her wardrobe door. Bending as best she could, while supporting her bruised stomach, she opened the box tucked right at the back of the wardrobe. It was the one containing all of the children's baby keepsakes.

She rooted around until her hand touched the object. Clutching it in her hand, she squeezed it, feeling the contents, and then put it back in the box, replacing the lid. Satisfied that it was still there, she stood, took a breath and blew it out slowly. In a month, she'd be safe in Knockmore. It was the very reason she'd kept this smaller secret all to herself. Now, it would be the ticket to her future. There had been a reason all along.

Lost in her thoughts, she almost didn't hear the doorbell. Pulling her dressing gown on, she made her way slowly downstairs, leaning on the curved bannister for support. She couldn't make out who it was behind the frosted glass window, and was about to turn and make her way back upstairs, choosing to ignore it, when she remembered Doug had said he might drop by.

For the first time since meeting him, she didn't want to see him, anxious that his calm voice would once again tease the truth from her. Once again, that she was about to run away.

Chapter thirty-three

Max

Driving along the coast, Max could still picture her sitting next to him as if it were yesterday – an enormous smile on her face, one arm resting on the open window frame, hair blowing in the wind, the other hand on the gear-stick tucked under his. It was what they'd done most weekends, jumping in the car and heading off to see the sights, bag packed in the boot to stop for a swim if the mood took them. Max would be demonstrating his vast geographical knowledge, while Lucie would feign boredom.

"Ah, go away. Sure, all countries are the same," she'd brushed him off. "Once you've seen one beach, you've seen them all. What is it about you Aussies? You think you're the only continent with sand, sea, blah-blah. There are huge beaches in Ireland, you know. Right the way round." She nodded deliberately. "Sorry to disappoint."

Max laughed. "Yes, Lucie, unless a country is landlocked, there's always a coastline right the way round."

She tutted. "Ah, you know what I mean. Honestly, the only thing you have here that we don't is koalas and roos and . . ." She stopped to think. "Dingos. But who wants them, anyway! Shameful creatures. And maybe that drive to Melbourne along that road on stilts. But we both know how I feel about that. Danger!"

Lucie had almost passed out the first time they'd driven it, covering her eyes, terrified they were going to fall off the edge, despite the incredible views.

"Everything else, pfff . . ." She threw her free hand up dismissively. "All the same."

"Is that right?"

"Absolutely." She was nodding again. "In fact . . ." She stopped for a moment, tilting her head to the side, holding up her hand. "We have better tea bags and butter in Ireland. Oh! and crisps. I'll get Fliss to post some more packets of Tayto crisps and I'll let you taste them this time. Or at least a few. Jesus, I'd murder a packet now.

"Other than that, and aside from the weather, we could be on our way to Brittas Bay in Wicklow. That's our equivalent of Bondi." She was on a roll. "Now, we don't surf, but only because the chill of the sea would turn your organs inside out, but we could if we wanted to. And . . ."

Max could see she was desperately trying to think of another Irish asset to boast about.

Lucie clapped her hands together. "*And* we drive on the proper side of the road."

Max rolled his eyes. "We drive on the left here, too. Look. Same as Ireland."

"Well, I never drove in Ireland – I can't remember. Okay. Forget that one. Right, I have another. We drink from glasses, not tinnies. And . . ." She was running out of steam. "As a nation, we're just more intelligent-ier."

"That's not even a word."

"Brainier, then. Because there's less of us, on the whole, we're cleverer."

"Fewer of us," he corrected, then glanced over to where she was smiling back broadly, showing her teeth. "You're full of it."

"Well, there's that, too. Irish have the gift of the gab. Anyway, where are we off to today on our mystery tour, Maximus?"

"Double Bay."

"What? That's a bleedin' stupid name. Is it full of twins or something?" She put on her thickest Irish accent. "The land of the doppelgänger, Double Bay. Ah, you made that up." She swatted the air.

"I didn't. It's a real place. Great beach. Loads of cafés. Shopper's paradise. It's where all the rich folk live. Perfect suburbia."

"You mean boob jobs and dickheads?"

Max spluttered. "Such a way with words, my beautiful lady." He reached over to rub her cheek and she rested her face against his hand.

"Jesus, would you look at them? Notions!" She lifted her head and pointed at a row of large houses. "Wouldn't fancy cleaning the floors in them. Litres and litres of bleach you'd need. No, thanks."

"You wouldn't like a house like that someday?"

"Christ, no. Slippery floors and zero craic? You're grand, thanks. Swear to me, Max, we'll never live in something like that. I want cosy, easy to clean, a teeny garden, maybe a swing chair. But no swinging balls!"

Max raised his eyebrows and she started giggling.

"Did you not see the poor lad who came into the hospital last week who'd got the ball in the side of the head? You know, that game where the ball is attached to a string and it flings round in a circle? Poor fecker! I said to the mother, go home and bin that thing. Dangerous sport. A ball on a string, flying at you . . . come on."

"Right, no swinging balls," he promised. "No slippery floors, no big house."

"Settled." Then she looked over at him. "We *should* probably buy something someday. Where would you like to live?"

"Anywhere, as long as I'm with you. We'll look soon."

"Deal. Jesus, would you look at the head on yer man?"

Max glanced out of the window at the man standing near the beach, hands proudly on his hips, wearing a minuscule pair of swimming trunks almost concealed by a colossal pot belly.

"Christ, no one, and I mean *no one* should wear budgie smugglers. Bless him, the sea wouldn't give him a wave. What a tool!"

Max laughed again. "I swear, Lucie, sometimes I have no idea what you're talking about. All these crazy Irishisms. What was the one yesterday? Oh, yes, that fella could peel an orange in his pocket. What does that even mean?"

Lucie grimaced. "That he's tight. You know, a stingy fecker."

Max looked lost.

"Wouldn't spend Christmas. Wouldn't give you the steam off his piss. No? Have I lost you?" Her shoulders were shaking with laughter as she blurted out saying after saying in the hope of confusing him further. "Okay, I'll stop. Fair go, mate." She did her best Aussie accent. "Struth, it's hot! Time to go walkabout. Feelin' pumped!"

He burst out laughing again. "Now you're talking my language. Come on." He pulled the car into a parking space. "Let's go and explore the place where we'll never live."

* * *

Driving through this same place, Max searched for the house. Pulling in on the opposite side of the road, he switched off the engine and kept his hands on the steering wheel. He was wondering how Lucie would react to seeing him here and if the conversation, once again, would be peppered with uncomfortable pregnant pauses.

Not for the first time, he longed to rewind time, right back to that day he'd been thinking of – one like any other where they'd been so relaxed in each other's company. Back then, there would never have been an expanse of silence floating between them. She had always managed to fill any lull, often with a unique jumble of words with no specific meaning, yet replete with life and energy.

Whatever was going to be said today would undoubtedly be filled with meaning. It was the energy that he was more worried about. If nothing else, he wanted to apologise – tell Lucie that he was sorry for never having gone to Ireland with her. Perhaps he hadn't taken her grief seriously enough . . . Selfishly, Max was hoping that an apology might set him free, finally allow him to move on. He'd wrestled for days over what to do. Whether or not he should try to discover if she'd meant what she didn't even know she'd said, that day on the operating table.

Lord knows, he'd wasted enough of his life. A lot of what had happened was Lucie's fault, but there were two sides to every story. Maybe he'd missed something. Was he hoping for more? Of course he was. What? He didn't know. He ran his hands down his face, suddenly nervous that his surprise visit was only going to serve to make things worse.

Taking a deep breath, he got out of the car anyway. He was here now – and some things needed to be said, once and for all.

Max glanced across at the house. It was nice. Not *as* big as some of the homes in Double Bay, but impressive nonetheless. Knowing Hamish, it had probably been bought as much for the address as the house itself. Hamish had always had a chip on his shoulder growing up, living in the studio apartment with a curtain separating his bed from his mother's.

For years, he'd told the other kids that he lived full time with Max's family, that his mother was an actress working abroad. It had sounded exotic. Better than the truth that his mother used to drop Hamish off at their house whenever she had a date with some wannabe artist and the curtain separating their beds would undoubtedly be drawn back.

Lucie had been right about one thing. Double Bay obviously was where all the people with "notions" about themselves, as she used to describe it, came to roost. Crossing the road, he noticed there were no cars in the driveway. He wondered if she was even at home, although she still wasn't meant to be driving so soon after surgery. In one way, he wished that Lucie would be there. In another, he was hoping to knock on the door and hastily escape when it was unanswered.

Heading up the driveway, he looked to his right at the broken swing chair on the veranda. One side of it was sitting on the ground, the other still suspended from the spring attached to the frame. There were pots with wilted plants either side of the front door. Little signs of neglect next to the otherwise perfect family home – weeds growing up through the patio, paint chipping off the windowsills.

When he got to the front door, he rang the doorbell

and stood back, feeling as if his heart had dislodged and was sitting in his neck. He was about to leave, when the door swung open – and the smile slipped from her face.

"Max?"

She looked older all of a sudden, standing there, crouching forwards slightly. Her hair was thrown back off her face, her dressing gown hanging open to reveal spotty, almost childlike pyjamas. Lucie pulled the dressing gown tighter, stuffed her hands into the pockets and stood back.

"What are you doing here?" Her eyes were on his feet.

"I was passing."

"Who passes Double Bay?" Her eyes flashed up and she smiled.

"Home of the doppelgänger," he grinned, feeling as though her eyes had just pierced his heart.

Her smile faded again. "Actually, it's a great place to raise kids." She sounded defensive.

"I'm sorry . . . I didn't mean. I was just remembering . . ."

"Do you want to come in?" She took her hand out of her pocket and opened the door further. "Sorry I'm not dressed."

"Thanks." He stepped inside. "I'm glad you're not dressed."

Her brow furrowed.

"I mean, you *should* be resting. I'm glad you are."

"Can you give me a few minutes to throw on some clothes? Somehow, clown-like pyjamas don't seem right." She gestured towards Max, who was wearing khaki shorts and an ironed white shirt, sleeves rolled up casually.

"Sure," he nodded.

"I'll be right back." She turned and ambled up the stairs, holding on to the bannisters for support. "I'm like a granny," she called over her shoulder.

"Take your time."

Chapter thirty-four

Max looked down at the slippery floors. It was hard seeing it all with his own eyes, how Lucie had lived all these years without him. He'd often tried to picture her new life with Hamish, thinking it might help him somehow, as if it might displease him. Seeing it now, it didn't. Instead, he felt like an intruder, seeing her "grown-up" existence. For a moment he thought about leaving, opening the front door and fleeing before she returned. But he knew he wouldn't.

Glancing to his left, he walked towards the archway and peered into the living room at the large sofas, taking in the bare walls. He could see where pictures had been removed, leaving behind a lighter shade of paint underneath. He counted them: seven. The room had a stark quality to it, as if it was about to be redecorated or they were in the process of moving.

Dipping his head to walk under the arch, Max made his way towards a table positioned behind the sofa. It contained mostly framed pictures of the children, aside from one of Hamish and Lucie together, clearly taken years before. Max lifted it. The face staring back was that of the girl he'd known so well, the one who should have been next to him in that photo. Did she look happy? It was hard to tell. On the other hand, Hamish wore what Max could only describe as a smug grin. All Hamish was lacking was a speech bubble coming from his mouth, saying, "I won."

"Prick," Max muttered to himself, putting it back down.

Max lifted another frame. It was a school photo of Bella and Declan. Bella was so like Lucie, it almost took his breath away. The boy was Hamish, through and through. Putting it back, he went back out to the hall to wait for Lucie. There was a loose tile next to the first step of the stairs. He pushed it with his foot, slotting it back in its place. Yes, it was a lovely house. Was it a home? He wasn't sure.

There were giveaway signs that he couldn't help but notice. It was his job, after all, to see things, to be ever watchful, quick at making decisions. Shame he hadn't been so fast at making decisions in his personal life. Still, from what he could see, this looked like somewhere that may at one time have been a happier place than it now seemed.

"Sorry about that." She reappeared at the top of the stairs.

"Here, let me help." He bounded up the stairs and linked her arm to help her back down.

"I really am a granny!"

"Not for long – you'll be right as rain soon."

They reached the last step.

"I just wanted to see if you needed anything. Painkillers? Food? Anything?" he lied.

"I'm good, thanks." Her face was severe. "Is that really why you're here, Max?"

"No." He shook his head. "Not really, but if you *do* need anything. Anything at all . . ."

Lucie closed her eyes and let out a breathy laugh. "Someone else said that to me once. If you need anything, anything at all . . ." She trailed off on seeing his confused expression. "Sorry, ignore that. Will we sit outside?"

"Sure."

She led him through the kitchen at the end of the hall, which looked a little more lived-in.

"The kids are big." He pointed up at a huge canvas print on the wall.

Lucie smiled. "Yeah. Aren't they? Taller than me!"

"It's like seeing a ghost."

She jerked her head. "How so?" Again, she was defensive.

"She looks so like you. A mini Lulu."

"Yes, she does, I suppose. Come on." She pushed open the back doors and they made their way outside to sit on the sofa in the shade.

"This is nice." He patted the chair.

"Max, please. Spit it out. What is it you want to say?"

Max needn't have worried about pregnant pauses. Once Lucie said the words, it came spilling out altogether as if he'd waited all these years to be asked. She stared at him, a startled expression on her face as he, at last, got the chance to tell her all he needed to say.

Her hands were clasped on her lap, her knuckles whitening while he spoke. It went all the way back to the first time he'd set eyes on her, dancing in the corridor of the hospital, then weaved its way through their entire relationship. How he'd felt when she was so low after losing her family, how all he'd wanted was to make her better.

"That evening. The last evening," he continued, barely

drawing breath, rubbing his now bald head as he spoke. "I never got to say what I wanted." At last, he paused, searching her face. "You used to say that you never got the opportunity to tell your family how much you loved them and how that left a space in your heart that could never be filled."

She swallowed and glanced up briefly at the memory, the tears now evident in her eyes, before looking down again.

"*All* I wanted to do was to fill that space. And all I want to do now is tell you what I never got to say." He reached for her hand and she let him take it. "What I wanted to tell you then, what I'd already decided, was that you couldn't go back to get Ann *alone*. I wanted to go with you.

"I was going to ask you to marry me that night." He rooted in his pocket and pulled out a small red box, placing it on the table in front of her. "I've had this since then. I'd bought it that day. I thought we might have a better chance of bringing Ann back to Australia if we were married, like you said. It was what I wanted anyway, all those years. Argh," he growled suddenly, looking frustrated. "I was so stupid. I didn't think it was important. But it is. I should have married you years before that."

Lucie was staring at the box on the table and had taken her hand away from his.

"And I would have stayed in Ireland with you, if that's what you'd wanted. I would have done anything."

He stopped when he saw her face. Then he put both hands to his face and exhaled through them before looking back at her.

"That night, when we fought and I stormed out, I came back to the apartment late. I'd gone for a walk, a beer. I just needed some space to think. It wasn't exactly how I'd imagined the proposal going," he smirked. "I was hurt by some of the things you'd said. I thought . . . when you mentioned Hamish that night . . . I thought you'd been with him. I did. But then I knew you'd never do that to me. That was just me being stupid. Jealous.

"Anyway, I thought you'd be there. I wanted to start again. I had this plan to wake you if you were asleep and I'd be down on one knee." He paused to see her reaction. "But you were gone. Nothing. No note. Nothing. All your clothes.

"I called Nina. She hadn't heard from you. Then I drove straight to the airport, convinced you'd gone to Ireland. I was going to follow you. I couldn't sleep afterwards, eat. I didn't go to work . . . and then Nina called me. You were with *him*."

Lucie felt the oxygen exit her lungs. She closed her eyes, releasing the tears that had been balancing there. Dropping her shoulders, she let her head roll back.

"I was so angry," she said through gritted teeth. "Not at you, but I thought I was. I was a mess. You were right. I *was* out of control." She turned to him. "The next day, I could hardly remember the night before, but I remembered meeting Hamish. I was so ashamed, Max. Nothing happened, but he made me feel lighter somehow than I'd been feeling with you.

"With you, I couldn't escape the grief – you knew me too well. But with him, I could put on an act. When I met him, I told him I was going to go to Ireland and he assumed we'd broken up. He told me if I ever needed anything . . ."

"Ah, I see," Max smiled sadly, now understanding her earlier reference.

"That night, I was so upset after you left, and Hamish was the freshest thing in my mind, so I called him, and he offered me a place to stay for a few weeks. I needed to be alone. I needed to think. I . . . then I . . ."

"Then you got together," he confirmed quietly.

"I never meant to, Max. Hamish was charming and it was different. I didn't want to feel like myself. I'd convinced myself that everyone I cared about left me. I thought you'd be next. It was like I was cutting you off at the pass. He was there . . ."

"I was, too. I had your past, I wanted your future." His voice broke, turning gravelly. "*I* knew you. *I* loved you . . ." He trailed off, and she met his eyes.

"I loved you, too."

"Then, why?"

"I don't know, Max. I really don't know."

"I know Hamish must love you. How could he not? But do you laugh with him like we did? Do you love him?"

"Please don't ask me that."

"Well, do you?" His voice was suddenly irritable.

Lucie didn't answer. "Max . . . I . . . I don't even know how to explain."

He was shaking his head. "You know what the funny thing is? Even without the ring, even without the wedding, I promised that I was going to love you until the day I died. It's never stopped. Not once, not since the day I spoke to you at that basin. Right there, I loved you, Lucie Maguire. And I still love you." He reached for her hand again. "Please, look at me."

"I can't."

"Please."

Her face crumpled as she met his eyes. "It was always you, Max," she whispered. "You know that."

He got up and kneeled in front of her, resting his head on her knees as she cradled it. Then he looked up and leaning forwards, he kissed her. He could taste her tears as she kissed him back – the years instantly slipping away, the gap closing immediately. Finally breaking apart, Max sat beside her and put his arm around her.

"Well, that was exhausting," he smiled down at her.

Lucie had let her body nestle into his, resting her head on his shoulder as she once had.

"Getting you to admit anything was always difficult, but I already knew," he teased.

"Knew what?"

"Well, you may have mentioned something about me being 'the one' in theatre before I put you under."

"Stop!" Her head shot up. "Oh my God. I thought I remembered something. Did anyone else hear?"

He shook his head. "Nope. At least I hope it was meant for me. It could have been for Professor Stone. You always had a thing for him."

They were laughing.

"Movie moment," she whispered, relishing his arm around her.

They sat that way for what seemed like an age, breathing together, feeling the closeness of the other.

"I can't help thinking there was a reason I came back to Sydney, Lulu. It was like something was drawing me back here – as if the past had caught up. Could we start again? With no more secrets . . ."

Lucie sat forwards suddenly, her face dropping, reality once again striking, and turned to face him.

"There's something I need to tell you . . ."

Afterwards, Max hadn't been sure what Lucie was going to say, or what he'd been hoping she might, but he hadn't expected her to say what she had.

"The thing is, this isn't a movie, Max. If it were, this would be the ending and we'd all sail off into the sunset. The truth is, I'm moving back to Ireland, *finally*." She had the grace to look abashed. "With the children . . . with Hamish."

Max sat forwards, too, shaking his head.

"Not now, not when I know you love me."

Once again, she couldn't meet his eyes.

"I know I might be asking a lot, but please, give us another chance, Lulu. I don't want to live without you. I know it won't be easy, but we can figure it out."

Lucie took a breath. "I can't, Max. I want to, more than anything. You have to believe me. But it's not just me any more. If it was, it would be different, but I have a family. I have to think of them.

"Hamish . . . he's not perfect, but he's a good father. And I can't deny Bella and Declan that." She closed her eyes, wrestling with her words. "What you told me today. I'm glad you did. I . . . I suppose I've always wondered, too, but I can't. I just can't. There are other things, too. I can't explain . . ."

"Try me, please. Let me help. Let me be here for you. What about you, Lucie? Don't you deserve to be happy?" he pleaded.

"I'm too old to think of myself."

"No, Lu, you're not. This is exactly when you should be thinking of yourself. This is you and me. This is us. Bella and Declan . . . I'll be whatever you want me to be to them, in time. A friend, an uncle, whatever you want. Just tell me. And Hamish? I don't believe you want to be with him. If you love me . . ."

But Max had already felt it splinter apart, the connection evaporating once again. The old Lucie whom he'd glimpsed for a moment had already retracted. Max had come to say what he had and now it was time to leave. It was still too late.

"Keep it," he said when she tried to hand back the box on the table. "I can't carry it around any more. It was meant for you. You alone."

"Max?"

He was almost at the door now.

"If I could go back . . . I need you to know, if I could go back . . ."

"But that's not how it works, Lulu. We can only go forwards. If you're not willing to, I can't make you."

"You don't understand."

"No." He shook his head and looked at the ground. "Unless you tell me, I'll never understand. He *always* wanted everything I had – Hamish. He always wanted to be better, was never content with himself, always wanting more. And it never bothered me, not really. Until he got you. *You* were the one thing I was supposed to have."

Then he walked away.

Chapter thirty-five

Lucie wasn't sure how long she sat there afterwards, staring ahead, holding that tiny somewhat insignificant box. If she closed her hand around it, she could almost make it vanish. Except for pain in her heart, the hollowness in her limbs, she might have tossed the box and pretended it had never happened.

Only it had. Lucie knew now, no matter what she did, or where she went, the contents of that box – the promise it contained – would always be with her. The words trapped inside it until now were free, drifting around her, embedding themselves in her skin. Those words, like Max, would always be a part of her.

For a second, she had almost given in. When she'd felt his arms around her, she'd wanted to stay in them forever. For one brief moment, she'd pictured herself telling him the truth. Brushing her lips against his had made her want to reach up and dig her nails into his flesh to anchor herself to him so that not even the revelation of her secret could break the bond.

The familiarity of him – his smell, his touch – had catapulted her back years. To before, to a time when she was his, and he hers. Being so close to him, listening to all he'd told her, hearing the regret in his words, something had stirred inside her, a feeling that she'd all but forgotten. Desire? Was that what it had been? Or was it security – the feeling of being wanted and needed? What had they done? Oh, God, what had they done?

They'd blown it. Wasted the gift they'd been granted, neither realising that what they'd shared *had* been a love to last a lifetime. Max had indeed been the great love story of her life – the one that Felicity had always told her would happen someday.

"Go back and marry that doctor."

She could hear Felicity's words again.

Why hadn't she listened?

Reaching up now, she covered her ears, allowing the injustice to rip through her. She didn't care who heard her wails as she rocked backwards and forwards. She didn't care about anything any more. Something had been smothered today – every hope she'd ever had, every dream of happiness, the life she was supposed to have had with Max and their daughter.

"No," Lucie blurted the word, righting herself and taking a breath. "No."

If she wished it all away, she'd be wishing Declan away, too – her precious boy.

Staring ahead again, she tried to calm herself, to remember what was important: Bella and Declan, that was all that mattered. They were the reason she was moving back to Ireland. All she had to do was keep her family together. Her own feelings weren't what mattered. She couldn't have both, not Max *and* the children.

Looking down at the box in her hand, she reached out to open it before her eyes filled once more, her head dropping slowly, her shoulders heaving. He'd remembered. They'd only spoken about it once. Stopping to stare through the window of a jewellery store in Sydney, he'd pointed out some enormous gaudy ring.

"Would that be your cup of tea?"

"Jesus, no. I'd lose it. I'd have to wear a cage or something over it. I'd need to have full-time security with me at all times. Could be awkward. And imagine if I was standing over someone having an appendectomy and I dropped it into them . . ."

"Okay. I get the picture." Max stopped her, knowing this could end up like the time he asked her what her perfect day would be and she was still talking about it at dinner, unable to decide.

"Do you not know me at all?" Lucie had asked. She'd squinted up at him, taken a sip from her can of Coke and looked back at the window, moving her head left to right along the rows of rings. "Ah! there."

"Which one?" He leaned over her shoulder to see where she was looking, and she'd immediately closed her eyes so he couldn't see.

"You tell me."

"Oh, a game. We know I always win these challenges," Max grinned.

It was something she was always doing. Pointing at several dresses in the window of a boutique and saying, "Which would I pick?"

He usually got it right. Except for the time he'd picked the hooker red, low-cut, spray-on spandex one.

"Max Woods! You dirty, filthy yoke. In your dreams, buddy. Shameful behaviour."

For a laugh, she'd gone back and bought it. Was wearing it one evening when he'd arrived home from work, teamed with a pair of runners and a woolly hat. His face had been worth it. Even more so the laugh they'd had trying to get it back off her.

"Best fifteen dollars I ever spent. Christ, don't put me near an open flame. I think it's made of clingfilm. Get it off me, Max. I'm panicking. Sweating!"

Max must have gone back to buy the ring he'd pointed at that day.

"That one," he'd said, gesturing over her shoulder at a delicate emerald, flanked by two diamonds on a gold band. "Green, white and gold. Irish, like you. Delicate, like you." He dipped one eyebrow as she got into the mock Irish dancing stance she always did when someone mentioned Ireland. "Am I right?"

He hadn't been right. Not by a long shot. But in hindsight, it was the perfect choice . . . it still was.

"Oh, Max," she whispered now.

His earlier words had been both music to her ears and a grenade to her heart. How was it possible for something so right to have gone so wrong? Hearing him tell her what he'd planned that night, how he'd wanted to propose and go to Ireland together to find Ann, it was too much to handle. All while Lucie had spoken those cruel words to him, she'd been pregnant with their future, their love fusing inside her at that very moment. Beautiful Bella had been there, newly made. Lucie wished more than anything that she could have kept her mouth shut that night, instead of gallivanting off with Hamish like some crazed lunatic.

Lucie pictured Bella and Declan again and shook her head. But if she hadn't, if she'd stayed with Max and ended up with him, there would be no Declan, and she couldn't regret that. Perhaps it had all worked out how it was supposed to. Besides, surely she didn't deserve Max. Max, who had shown her nothing but love, when she'd just destroyed it – and now she had to pay the price. And Max certainly didn't deserve the likes of her. No. Hamish was what she deserved.

She laughed bitterly. That was the punishment for her mistakes – sentenced to a loveless marriage built on lies. Well, she'd do her time, for the children's sake. Then again, perhaps she didn't deserve Hamish, either. She'd lied to him, too, all those years. The thought of him finding out had always frightened her, fearing that someday during a routine blood test someone would let slip that it was genetically impossible for Hamish to be Bella's father. There would be gasps and shocked faces.

"A mix-up at the hospital," Lucie often thought she might try. "Whose baby is this?" Cue dramatic music.

Or perhaps it would never come out.

Indeed, by moving to Ireland, she had more of a chance of keeping everything ticking along. Hamish had messed up, too – with the mortgage payments, the school fees, the cars . . . But she'd made more serious mistakes and now she had to live with them.

She'd been a fool to think she could come clean about the past. This was real life, not a fairy tale, and she'd become complacent. All the unfortunate events of late – getting fired from her job, the car being seized, needing surgery – must have been the universe nudging her, reminding her that she'd screwed up, again and again.

Lucie snapped the jewellery box shut. Max's words would stay with her forever. She'd carry them with her until the end of time, but she could *never* live them.

Tucking the box in her pocket, she looked at her watch. Max had been with her for almost two hours and since then, nearly two more had passed. Two hours of being without him again – and Lucie was still breathing. In and out. Life went on, no matter what happened, no matter who died, who you've hurt, what lies you've told – it just keeps going. All she had to do now was to keep moving.

Lucie stood uncertainly and, testing herself, took a step. She could still walk, one foot in front of the other. Back inside, she opened the fridge and closed it again. She wasn't hungry. She'd take a shower. Then she'd eat. Then she'd carry on with life. Hour by hour. Minute by minute – until she was back in a place that felt steady if nothing else.

Making for the hall, she stopped when she noticed the shadows at the front door. She hadn't heard the doorbell ring. Pulling it open to see the three figures standing there made her heart skip a beat.

"Bella . . . Declan . . . are they . . . ? What's happened?" The whispered question sounded like a foghorn in her own ears. Her legs turned to jelly and she reached for the wall to steady herself, all the while trying to comprehend the strange combination on her doorstep. "I'm sorry, I think I'm going to . . ."

It was Doug who reached out to steady her.

"Max," Doug signalled. "Lift her inside."

"Nina, get some water, a towel, something sweet," Max instructed and lifted Lucie just as her legs gave way.

"Copy that."

Lucie watched feebly over Max's shoulder as Nina disappeared into the kitchen while Max carried her into the living room, placing her on the sofa, propping cushions under her legs. Doug went to close the front door then followed Nina to the kitchen.

"Max?" Her head was spinning. "Just tell me, the kids . . . please."

He kneeled beside her. "They're fine. Everyone's fine."

"Oh, thank God." There were tears in her eyes. "I thought . . ."

"They're okay." He smoothed her suddenly sweat-drenched hair from her face.

"Hamish?"

"Fine," Max replied curtly.

"Here." Nina was back. "Drink this." She offered Lucie a sip of juice and placed a cold facecloth on her forehead. "You're okay. Kids are fine. Sorry. I was meant to say that. That was my job." Nina put her palms up. "I messed up. You okay down there, Lu?"

Lucie nodded.

"Just sit for a minute, okay?" Nina told her.

Lucie nodded again. She closed her eyes for a moment. Her mind still felt woozy. What was going on? Maybe Max had told them she was going to Ireland, but how could that have happened so fast? She couldn't think as panic began to set in.

"What's happening?" Lucie asked.

Max reached forwards and took her hands. "Lucie, there's no need to be afraid, okay?"

She frowned.

"I need you to do something. For once in your life, maybe for the first time in your life ever," he corrected. "We need you . . ." He shook his head. "But especially me, *I* need you to listen. *Please*. Be calm and listen. Can you do that?"

Robotically, she nodded, still confused.

Max went to sit on the sofa opposite her next to Doug, while Nina sat beside Lucie and took her hand.

"It's going to be okay, Lucie. Like Max said, just listen.

We're here, and we're not going anywhere," Nina added.

"You're scaring me. This feels like . . . what do you call it again? You know, when one family member is crazy, heading for destruction, but they can't see it because they've just had loads of fruit removed from their ovaries, and they're at risk of becoming Chairperson of the DVB."

Nina almost smiled at the private reference. "I'd never let you become Chairperson of the DVB. It's too big a title." She squeezed Lucie's hand.

"Am I the crazy one?" Lucie's voice was tiny.

"But that's mostly why we love you," Nina promised.

"It's called an intervention," Doug interrupted.

"That's the word." Nina nodded encouragingly.

"Am I dying? Did they find cancer, after all?" Lucie could hear her heart pounding in her ears.

"No. You're perfectly healthy. I promise," Max assured.

"I'm not an alcoholic."

"We know."

"I only did marijuana once."

"Twice," Max corrected.

"And I did steal a pack of Hubba Bubba from the corner shop when I was ten, but I got it stuck in my fringe and I ended up with a sticky-up bit . . ." She trailed off when she saw their faces.

"Lucie?" Doug interrupted the nervous babble again.

"Just tell me the truth," she begged. "What is it?"

Chapter thirty-six

Doug

If he seemed outwardly calm, Doug was feeling just as apprehensive as Lucie appeared to be with her huge eyes, blank face, hands clenched together on her lap. It wasn't precisely how Doug had envisioned the confrontation playing out. He'd planned to visit her alone and try to explain it all rationally, make her understand his actions. Lucie was a bright girl, after all. Surely she'd be able to see how it had come about, somewhat innocently. That the coincidence of their initial meeting had been just that – a serendipitous encounter.

That first day in the coffee shop on the beach where Lucie had told him about "the incident" at the school had been solely by chance. What came after, perhaps not so much.

Of course, after getting to know Lucie, Doug was nervous that her passionate heart might initially fill with rage before he could convince her of what he'd actually been trying to achieve. It was a risk he had to take. Recent developments had left him with no other choice.

Would Lucie believe him? Would she hate him for

what had been an honest betrayal, one where he'd had only her best interests at heart?

It concerned Doug, acknowledging how fond he'd grown of this rather complicated yet pure woman. This announcement would certainly, once more, knock her off her feet.

Driving towards Double Bay earlier, Doug had experienced a hollow feeling of in the pit of his stomach. Stopping the car near her house, he parked a little away from another vehicle and glanced across to spy Max making his way back down the driveway with his shoulders slumped, his head down. Astonished, Doug had almost driven away. What was *he* doing here?

Perhaps Lucie had decided to take the bull by the horns and tell Max the truth. It certainly looked as though he'd been privy to some form of adverse disclosure. In one way, Doug hoped Lucie had decided to come clean, but if she had, he wasn't sure if she'd now have the strength for one more momentous revelation. Regardless, today was the day – there was no more time.

Doug watched Max slowly walk towards his car, stop, then turn back towards the driveway. He walked up to it, stopped again, linked his hands behind his neck, then pivoted and made for the car again. This happened three more times before Max walked to the curb and hunkered down to sit on the path with his head in his hands.

The thought struck Doug then that perhaps Max hadn't even been to see Lucie yet and what Doug was witnessing was Max trying to pluck up the courage to ring the doorbell. Not likely. Judging by the look of despair on Max's face, he deduced that they'd spoken already. About what, though? Had Lucie told him that

Bella was really his daughter? Doug was getting impatient. This waltz could go on all day unless he interceded.

"I thought that was you." Doug got out of his car and walked towards him.

Max looked up sharply, his brow furrowed, before it dawned on him and he clambered to his feet.

"Sorry. I was miles away. Doug, isn't it? Lucie's . . ."

"Friend," Doug finished. "Were you visiting?"

Max nodded unsurely. "If you can call it that." Then he paused, shook his head. "Sorry. We go back a long way, Lucie and me. There was some unfinished business I needed to talk to her about."

"And did you finish it?"

"Excuse me?" Max jerked his head back.

"Did you finish your business?"

Max exhaled, stuffing his hands in the pockets of his shorts. "Direct, aren't you?"

Doug shrugged. "The best way to be. Cuts out a lot."

"Suppose you're right. I wish *she* was more direct." Max gestured with his head towards the house. "How do you know her again?" He looked puzzled.

"We met, by chance. Became friends."

"Hah. She's a complicated girl." Max sounded bitter before composing himself. "Sorry, again." He put his hand up. "It was a tough conversation."

"It's okay. Sometimes the important ones are."

"Wise, too." Max was smiling now. "Anyway, I'd better get on." He turned towards the car.

"You love her."

Max stopped and turned. "Is that a question?"

Doug shook his head. "No."

Max leaned back against his car and started kicking gravel at his feet. "That obvious, huh?"

"She speaks about you a lot."

"She does?" Max looked up to see Doug nodding.

It had suddenly dawned on Doug that this might be too big a situation to face alone and that Max, who clearly adored Lucie, might be able to help.

"Can I be frank?" Cutting to the chase, Doug began. "You're right, Max. I am a direct man. Most of the time. Can I ask you, did Lucie tell you anything today? Anything that might make you . . . concerned?" He was trying to choose his words wisely.

"Not really." Max's brow was furrowed again. "I'm sorry. I don't really know you . . ."

So, she hadn't told Max the truth.

"I know you don't, but if you care about her, can you listen to me for a few minutes? I have Lucie's back, Max. I'm ex NSW police department, I'm a widower, no kids—"

"What's this about?"

"Hamish."

Doug watched Max's face change.

"Hamish?"

Max glared at him, trying to sum him up. If there was one thing that was going to get Max's attention, it was the mention of his rival's name.

"There's a place down the road. Will you grab a coffee with me? I can explain," Doug suggested.

If Doug knew one thing for sure, Lucie was going to need everyone who cared about her, now more than ever.

"Lucie," Doug said now. "Max tells me you're planning to go to Ireland. For good."

Lucie frowned, glanced at Max quizzically and then back at Doug. "Yes. Hamish and I have just decided. How . . . how did you know?"

Lucie looked at Nina, waiting for an expression of surprise to materialise on her friend's face that never came.

"Yes," Lucie confirmed again. "As soon as we can. We want a break, a fresh start."

Doug nodded. "I'm afraid I can't let you do that."

It had been Max's idea to call Nina once Doug had divulged a quick version of the story to him, knowing that Nina would help to diffuse the situation if it got heated. Max had been shocked if not surprised on hearing Doug's version of events. The entire time, Max had sat cradling the cup of untouched coffee in his hands, shaking his head. Doug's delivery had been calm, as had Max's receipt – until Doug reached the final instalment, when Max's mouth had fallen open in disbelief.

"Jesus Christ. I'll kill him. I'll murder him. How could he? Are you sure?"

"I am. I thought by visiting Lucie I'd be able to make her see it herself. You know? Have it dawn on her. But she's been unwell and I suppose, being in the hospital, having time to think . . .

"Instead, Lucie ended up telling me all about herself, her family, losing them . . . you." Doug had looked up in earnest. "Perhaps it's not my place to say, but I'm an old man now, Max. It gives you certain liberties. One is that I don't care any more what I say, or how I say it. But that girl . . . she needs you. She always has.

"I have a feeling when I tell her what's happening, she's going to be very angry with me for keeping it from her. She's going to question if I had her best interests at heart and she's going to want to push me away." Doug paused then. "I need *you* to be there for her then, and Nina.

"I care for her, very much, maybe like the daughter I never had. I'm not proud of how it's all come to this, but you have to believe me. All I want is for Lucie to be all right."

"I believe you," Max had nodded. He could see it in the old man's eyes. There was nothing but genuine concern there. "I'll be there for her. I promise."

"What do you mean, you can't let me do that?" Lucie's promise to remain calm was about to be broken. "Max? What did you say? How are you all here, together? What the fuck is this?"

Max went to stand. "Lucie. Stay calm, remember. Just listen to Doug."

Doug took a breath and smiled at her. "Do you trust me, Lucie?"

"I think so. I mean, I did . . . You'd better hurry up with whatever this is."

"Okay. Before I do, I just want to say that meeting you, for me, has been a privilege. You've told me so much about yourself. You're a wonderful person, an incredible mother, friend, daughter – far too hard on yourself," he scolded. "But you've done so well – so very well."

Lucie was nodding, tears smarting. "Okay, I'm listening."

"Everything you've told me about your personal life." Doug nodded once and widened his eyes as a signal. "That's all confidential. That goes no further." Doug was trying to warn her, in case she thought that he'd told Max anything. "But I need you to tell me a few more things. Not about the past, but about what happened a few months ago."

"I don't understand." Her breathing was getting louder.

"When I first met you, you told me everything had started to go wrong for you a few months before. Do you remember?" Doug asked, and she nodded.

"I wasn't feeling well." She gestured towards her stomach. "Then there was the stabbing incident." Lucie rolled her eyes.

Max looked up abruptly and Nina covered her mouth to stop herself from laughing. Lucie shot her a look.

"Sorry," Nina mouthed. "Nervous giggles."

For a moment, the air felt lighter, and despite herself, Lucie smiled.

"I pretended I was going to stab a kid with a maths compass. You know, I never liked maths or arsehole children," she explained to Max, who looked baffled.

Nina snorted and even Doug sucked in his lips to stop himself from smiling.

"I didn't," Lucie assured. "You know, stab him. It was at the kids' school where I was working. Declan was being bullied by this prick. It was *him* who was holding a compass to Declan's neck. I caught him doing it, so I gave him a taste of his own medicine. I got fired."

"You did?" Max's eyes were wide.

"I did. So, I suppose that was when everything started to go wrong, to answer your question, Doug. That was *the* moment." Lucie had turned serious again.

"But it wasn't, Lucie, was it?" Doug asked.

Lucie looked confused. "How far back do you want me to go here?" She raised her eyebrows.

"What happened the day before?" Doug pressed.

"Oh, you mean "the shitstorm"? The house was burgled," she disclosed for Max's benefit.

This time, he didn't look as surprised. Doug had already told him this part.

"Tell us about that," Doug prodded.

Lucie looked unsure.

"Do it, Lu," Nina encouraged.

"I don't know what you want me to say."

"Try," Doug nodded encouragingly.

"But I don't see what this has to . . ."

They were all nodding.

"Okay, let me see . . . I'd been home all weekend. Declan was staying with his granny Vera in the city. I remember it was the weekend Bella told me that he was being bullied at school. I was angry. I was pissed off with Hamish because he insisted on playing golf. I wanted to collect Declan to talk to him, but Hamish said to wait until later. Until he was there, too.

"I was supposed to go to Sydney with Bella early that day to look around the shops, but she changed her mind, wanted to see her friends instead." She stopped for a moment, looking dubious. "Is this what you mean? I still can't understand what—"

"Go on, Lucie," Max prompted.

"Where was I? Hamish called from the golf course, which was strange, I suppose, as he never usually did. He made this big deal about Vera asking us for lunch and that I was to meet him there with Bella – to leave now. In the end, Bella never got to see her friends and I had to endure Vera for the whole day." She looked at Max again. "You know Vera. Small doses and all . . . But I wanted to see Declan, so I went.

"Hamish turned up later. In the end, Hamish got it wrong and Vera had actually meant dinner. So I was hanging around all day there waiting for Hamish to arrive. We got home late."

"Then what?" Doug asked.

Lucie was twisting her hands, fixing her hair repeatedly.

"Everything was gone. The house was ransacked." She pointed at the empty spaces on the walls dismissively. "I really don't want to talk about this." She was starting to shift about uncomfortably. "Okay, what the hell is going on?" She went to stand, but Nina stopped her.

"Did you speak to the police?" Doug enquired.

"Why?"

"Did you?"

Lucie tutted. "Yes, of course. I mean, Hamish dealt with most of it. I had other things going on."

"And how did they get into the house?"

"That window." She pointed over her shoulder.

Doug stood and walked towards it.

"Here?"

"Yes. Why?" She turned to look at Doug.

"There's a twelve-metre drop to the ground here."

Lucie shrugged. "They used a ladder, I suppose."

"Did the police fingerprint the house?"

"Yes, but they'd obviously worn gloves."

"So, there were no prints, the window wasn't forced and there were zero forensic clues?"

"No, they smashed it . . ." Lucie stopped. "Wait. How do you . . . I never told you."

Doug walked back towards her. "Was there glass inside on the ground?"

"I can't remember. I think so. I don't know."

"Did you sweep up the glass?"

"No. Hamish did."

"Did you see him sweep it up? If the window was smashed from outside, there would have been glass inside."

"What exactly are you saying?"

"And everything of value was taken?"

"Yes! I already told you. Doug, I know you're an ex copper, but what—"

"And how was Hamish after it all?"

Doug was asking her everything so fast that she didn't have time to think.

"He was upset. We both were. The kids, too. It's not a nice experience. We had to stay in the house that night. Then I lost my job. We were waiting on the insurance money to come through, which, might I add, never bloody did. He was between jobs. I told you all this."

Doug sat down in front of her on the ottoman. "You told me that Hamish started to act distantly towards you after it all?"

"He was under pressure."

"The paintings. Were they valuable?"

"Yes. I loved those paintings."

"You see, Lucie, normally when houses are burgled, it's mostly cash, jewellery, those sorts of things. Your jewellery was taken, is that right?"

Lucie looked up again from where she was staring at the floor. Her eyes met Doug's and she nodded slowly. "Yes."

"But the paintings. Is there anyone else, other than you, who might have known they were valuable? Anyone at all?"

This time she shook her head. "No, no one except . . ."

Chapter thirty-seven

Slow motion. Everything had slowed as if Lucie had exited her body and was now suspended above, gazing down on it. It had dawned on her as soon as she'd met Doug's eyes – and in them witnessed another truth. Doug was right. No one, certainly not the type who smashes a window twelve metres off the ground to gain access to a house, would ever have been after those obscure-looking paintings. Now, it all made sense.

The paintings must also have been a way for Hamish to bury money. Is that all they'd really been, the paintings? Those images, purchased for large sums of cash, had hung on her walls and now they were gone, taken by her own husband in a further act of fraud . . . He'd become so desperate for money, ducking and diving to avoid bills for months and months, that he'd obviously been forced to cheat himself. Pitiful.

Lucie sat staring at the wall, letting it wash over her. Doug stood and walked slowly into the hall before returning with a file in his hand – a thick brown ominous-looking dossier. Lucie's eyes followed it. Sitting in front of her, Doug opened it and rested his hands on the deep pile of paperwork. Lucie's eyes moved to his hands, to where they were only half covering the insurance company logo. Then she blinked as it hit her, as once again she became aware.

She could feel the anger begin to bubble, mixed with disappointment and absurdity. She'd been duped.

At first, Lucie had thought the reason they were all here was because something had happened to Bella and Declan. Then, she'd believed that somehow the hospital had discovered that she *did* have cancer. And then, naïvely, she'd thought that perhaps Max had summoned them all to help Lucie realise that she was meant to be with him and to dissuade her from going to Ireland.

When Doug started asking her about that day, she hadn't been able to understand why. The burglary had been the farthest thing from her mind through the weeks of delving into her past. Lucie opened her eyes then and glared at Doug.

He'd been expecting this.

"You were investigating me!" she spat. "All this time, you were investigating me! So what did you find, Doug – ex police officer clearly turned insurance investigator. I'm right, aren't I? I can see from your face I am. And you sat there and let me tell you all about my life. How could you?

"All the things I told you about. What a thorough job you've done!" She clapped sarcastically. "You got right down to the nitty-gritty, didn't you? Who else have you told? Well, clearly you told *them* . . ." She gestured at Nina and Max. "And now, you're all here to witness it. How stupid I've been. How stupid *I* am. Well, did I put on a good show? Did no one think to call Ann, so she could see it, too? Or let me think. What about Brent from the bank, or some of the mothers from the school? Shall I call the neighbours in, too?"

"Lucie, please." Doug reached out to put his hand on hers. "It wasn't like that."

She seized it away.

"Then tell me. What was it like, *Doug*? Now *you* tell me. I think I've told you enough. Now, it's *your* turn. So, it was Hamish? Is that what you've discovered? Or, hang on. Do you think *I* had something to do with it? Is that why you're all here?" She glanced at them in turn. "I trusted you all."

It was Nina who spoke next.

"Lu, I know this must come as a terrible surprise. But you're *right* to trust us. We're all here because we trust you. We know you had nothing to do with it. Don't we, Max?"

Max nodded in agreement. "Lucie, Doug needs to tell you more. Before this turns emotional, you need to hear the facts. Then you can rant and rave as much as you like, but first – facts. This is important."

Lucie scowled at him. "You must be loving this, Max. Is this what you wanted? Show Lucie what a shit she married? Show Lucie how much she messed up?"

Max shook his head. "No. This isn't what I want for you, but you promised me at the start that you'd listen. You need to hear this."

"You know what?" Lucie smirked. "People break promises every day. I want you all to leave. Go on, get out! All of you!"

Nobody moved.

"No." It was Doug. "Not until you know everything."

"I don't want to know. I want you to leave. Run back to the insurance company, Doug. Tell them to *keep* their fucking money. I don't want it. I'm going to Ireland. Away from all this crap. Away from Hamish now, too. That's the only favour you've done me. I'm going alone.

"You got me. I knew there was something weird about how he was acting and here it is. So thank you – and now fuck off." She exhaled loudly. "I should never have come to this fucking country." Lucie could feel herself losing control, but she didn't care. Not any more. She'd had enough.

Nina grabbed her hand then and Lucie tried to pull away, but Nina wouldn't let her.

"Lucie!" she shouted. "So help me God, if I have to sit on you, I will, but you need to shut up – now. If you ever want to see your children again, you need to bloody listen."

Lucie stopped suddenly, a ripple of fear rushing through her. "What?"

Nina looked at Doug sharply. "Tell her, *now*. Talk."

Of course, the mention of her children had been bound to stop Lucie in her tracks. Doug barely drew a breath as he began, eager to get to the end. The delivery was factual, backed up with evidence from the bulging file. He started in the middle, with Doug, lonely, in need of distraction, picking up a job as an insurance investigator. This was only his second case – that of Hamish and Lucie Woods, and getting to the bottom of an outlandish claim submitted following the burglary of their home in Double Bay.

"You were a name on a file, Lucie. You and Hamish. A burglary – the details of which didn't add up. So, I was sent to investigate. Plain and simple.

"From the start, it seemed odd. The police report, it's right here, showed no forensics – no forced entry except a broken window, with more glass found outside than inside. No traces of a ladder being there. The broken window – it was like an afterthought.

"The alarm had been set but didn't go off. The items taken, well, like I said before, they were unusual. Unless someone had known that you were amateur collectors, it seemed unlikely. The jewellery, too. Have you ever seen this piece before?" Doug produced a photograph of a sapphire and diamond ring with a matching necklace.

Lucie took the photo from him and stared at it. "What are these? I've never even seen them before."

"Yours, apparently," Doug answered. "These pieces alone are claimed to be worth fifteen thousand dollars."

"What? I don't understand. These weren't mine."

Doug produced more photos and put them in front of her. "A Ming vase?"

She shook her head again, flicking through the pictures.

"The total for the claim is more than a hundred and twenty thousand."

"What?" Lucie stared at him, trying to understand what was happening.

Doug continued. "It seems Hamish considerably bumped up what was *actually* taken, thinking that no one would ever check. He got sloppy. When I started to look into it all, it was unlikely that you'd ever had some of these items in your possession. The paintings?" Doug produced another file. "I take it they were yours."

Lucie nodded. "Yes, these are mine. At least, Hamish bought them for me over the years."

"And these?"

They were photos of Lucie, in which she was wearing her own jewellery.

"Yes, Hamish made me root through old photos to find pictures of me wearing my jewellery. He submitted them to the insurance company. But I . . . I . . . did he really fake the burglary?"

Doug nodded. "It certainly appears that way. Him making sure you were out of the house, acting strangely after it all, his need for money, the financial situation you were in . . ."

"Jesus Christ." It was a whisper. And then, "So, we retract the claim. I get him to retract the claim."

"I'm afraid it's not that simple. In fact, it gets worse."

Lucie listened, afraid to move. What else could there possibly be?

Doug went on to tell her that he'd started to look further into Hamish.

"There were other claims over the years. Hamish had been playing the system for a long time." Doug opened the file again, handing her various pieces of paper. "Whiplash, a fall on the golf course, stolen iPads."

From the blank look on Lucie's face as she looked at the papers, she'd never heard of any of it before.

"When you started telling me about your life, Lucie, I was able to check back over his claims. After each claim or pay-out, at least, you told me about a big holiday, a new car. It all added up. Hamish was putting in claims and then treating you all."

"Oh my God." She clutched her stomach suddenly. "I think I'm going to be sick." Then she looked up again. "And you used all that information? You were using it against me?"

"No," Doug promised. "No. You *have* to believe me. I'd already found the information and submitted it well before you told me anything. Whatever you told me, it went no further, I swear to you."

"I don't believe you."

"It's the truth, Lucie," Max interrupted. "Doug never meant you any harm."

"We can talk about that again." Doug looked at Max and nodded. "But there's something else more important. When I spoke with the bank, as much as they'd tell me without it being a formal police investigation, there was some concern about your original mortgage applications. I spoke to the insurance company yesterday and they confirmed it. They believe the application was fraudulent. There were forged employment and income references, which inflated his earnings."

"But he was with the bank then. How could he have—"

"Apparently, it was all well planned and quite sophisticated. Hamish knew what he was doing."

Nina reached over and put her arm around Lucie, whose face contorted.

"It was all a lie. Everything was a lie. Is that where he is? In hiding? Does he know?"

"I believe that someone tipped him off. Questions were being asked."

"Brent." Lucie said the name. "His friend from the bank. He was trying to get in contact with him. His wife told me." Lucie remembered thinking it was strange how panicked Brent was – enough to get in contact with Hamish. "Brent left him a message the day before Hamish left so suddenly for Singapore. When I rang Brent from the hospital to see how bad everything was with the mortgage, he just kept telling me to get Hamish home. Oh my God. I've been so stupid." The tears rolled from her eyes.

"Lucie." Doug leaned forwards again. "I swear I've never lied to you. I . . . I didn't know how to tell you. That day I met you in the café – that *was* a coincidence. I'd taken a drive to Double Bay to maybe have a look at where you lived. The address was in the file. I stopped for a coffee and you walked in," Doug smiled. "I only noticed you because you looked so like Rose. I showed you the picture – you saw it, too, the likeness."

Lucie watched him speak.

"Then those women were glaring at you and I felt sorry for you. It was only after you started talking, when you told me your name, that I realised who you were. Professionally, I should have walked away, but then you started telling me how everything had gone wrong for you.

"I wanted to listen. You're quite entertaining, you know," Doug laughed softly. "I wanted to hear your story. Not because of the case, but because I realised that you were lost, stuck in a situation.

"Afterwards, I kept telling myself that I wouldn't go near you again. I handed in my findings to the company and I told them, there and then, that I didn't want to work for them any more." Doug paused. "Then my bloody sister-in-law said something to me.

"It was that day I found you on the side of the road. It was something my wife used to say about helping people. I didn't even know where I was driving that day until I saw your car pulled in at the side of the road. Then I found you the way you were – so I helped.

"Visiting you in the hospital, I thought I could make you realise what Hamish had been up to, but instead, you told me all about yourself."

Lucie looked up through the tears. "I trusted you. I told you things I've never told anyone before."

"I know that. And you can *still* trust me. What you told me stays between us. All I wanted to do was help you out of this. You don't deserve any of it. You're a good person, Lucie."

This time, she let him take her hand.

"I didn't get the story that I thought I would. What I got was the real truth about you, Lucie. And the truth is that you're brave and honest. I think there's a reason I met you that first day. I believe we met so I *could* help you. And that's what I'm going to do, like it or not. But I need you to be brave one more time."

"Why?"

"Because this *is* now a police investigation. This is fraud. And your signature is on that claim. They take this sort of thing seriously. Hamish is in big trouble with everything else, too, but with Hamish not being here . . ."

"What?" Her face was white.

"Unless we can get Hamish back here fast, they're coming after you. And they will make an arrest. There's enough to prosecute."

Chapter thirty-eight

Afterwards, it was as if someone had died – the atmosphere permeated with an almost reverent lull. People walking aimlessly from room to room, cup after cup of soothing tea prepared and abandoned to counter the fragile ambience. Food offered, only to be pushed away with revulsion.

Aside from a handful of whispered exchanges, an eerie silence descended in the wake of the confession. As the others came and went from the room, all the while, Lucie sat frozen, her head tilted to one side, eyes narrowly staring at the empty spaces where the paintings had once hung.

If she blurred her eyes enough, she could still picture them. But then, through blurred eyes, Lucie could see everything more clearly: her past, her present, least of all this current nightmare she'd found herself in. What she couldn't now see was her future. Was this actually happening?

Attempting to evaluate it all, Lucie hovered in a coma-like state. She could feel her breath moving in and out, unaware of how she was making herself do it – yet here she was, breathing. Once or twice she'd stopped, to embrace total stillness, before her chest robotically filled once more. She was too exhausted to fight it. And the group of people who'd gathered to take over? Too broken to resist . . .

"And that's exactly what happens when there are lies." Her mother was talking to her again. "They build up and up until they—"

"Shatter." Lucie whispered the word aloud.

And shatter they had. Lie after lie. Nothing had been real. Indeed, not any of her life with Hamish. The rest of it, Lucie could hardly tell what was reality any more. All the stories she'd told Doug in the hospital about her family, about Max, her fears, her guilt, her life, were they even real? Had she made it all up? Had Max really told her that same day that he still loved her? It was all meshed together in her mind. All the talking she'd done, all the revelations she'd made, carefully ironing them all out, to once again throw them all together and watch them crease back up.

"Lucie?"

She moved her head slowly towards him. She hadn't even seen him walk in.

"Are you okay?" Max sat beside her.

She shrugged and stared ahead again. "I don't know. I really don't know. I'm breathing."

He took her hand. "You are. From my medical training, I can confirm that respiration is occurring." He smiled unsurely then squeezed her hand. "Look at me."

Seeing his eyes, she exhaled and her lip quivered.

"It's going to be okay," he reassured. "I don't know exactly how, but I swear to you, it will. I'm here – and I'm not going anywhere until this is sorted. And . . . I have money for legal fees, whatever. I don't want you to worry about that."

She nodded weakly. He tugged her hand again, so she looked at him.

"I meant everything I said earlier, when it was just us, here. I will be here for you, even if you don't want me," he grinned. "I'm *not* going anywhere. This time, I'm going to stay until I know you're safe."

There was little point trying to deter him when everything had changed so much in a matter of hours. Besides, Lucie didn't want him to leave. All she wanted to do was wrap herself in the safety of his arms once again. Earlier, the problem that had seemed insurmountable now paled into second place. There would be no escaping to Ireland, no making a new life and no more running from the truth. Lucie knew that for sure. She'd have to come clean about *everything* – as soon as this new issue was sorted.

"Max?"

"Yes."

"There's something more I need to tell you. Not right now. I don't think I could manage it at this very moment, but in time. I'm saying it now because when this is all over, I want you to come to me and ask me what it is. Can you do that for me?" Her voice was barely a whisper.

Max nodded. "I can. But right now, it's time to get *this* sorted. Okay? Doug knows what he's doing. He's a good man, Lulu. I know you must be angry with him, but try not to be. He didn't tell you who he was because he was trying to protect you. Sometimes people don't tell the full truth because they're scared it will damage everything further. Honesty isn't always the best policy."

She looked at him intently. "Do you really believe that?"

"With all my heart."

* * *

It was Doug who'd come up with the plan. After Max left, it was Doug who hesitantly popped his head round the corner of the living room arch.

"Come in." She lifted her head.

Sitting next to her, with his eyes on the floor, he waited for her to speak.

"You didn't tell Max, did you? About Bella?" she asked.

He looked up. "God, no. No, Lucie, I'd never do that."

"I thought that's why you were all here. Well, one of the reasons," she grimaced.

"Nothing you told me is in any of those files. All that you told me about yourself . . . well , it just cemented that I wanted to help you. I don't know Hamish, but I do know that you're not like him. I knew from the first moment I met you," he smiled. "I think there are two reasons why people steal: desperation and greed. I think Hamish was both desperate and greedy. You, on the other hand . . ." He shook his head. "What matters to you is people. Everything you've been through, I think you're fearless."

"I'm not brave," she cut across. "Your wife, she was brave. I still think of that story you told me about her diving. Now that's brave. She was faced with a difficult situation and she did what she should. Not like me. I've always made the wrong decisions."

"Rose didn't think she'd made the right decision, but we're all faced with hardships. It's how we choose to overcome them that matters. This is *not* your mess, Lucie. It's Hamish's. Did Max tell you the plan?"

She nodded. "Isn't there another way? Can't I just withdraw all the claims on his behalf, hand the house back?"

"I'm sorry, but no, you can't do that."

"But I didn't know what he was doing."

"I know that. But you signed the papers."

"And didn't read them," she sighed.

"Exactly."

"I'm an idiot."

"You're human. The only way to play this is how I've told you. Otherwise, you *are* involved. I know you're not at fault, but I can't guarantee a jury will see it that way."

She raised her eyes to him anxiously. She'd been about to tell him something more, but his words stopped her.

"I can't lose my kids."

"Then do as I say."

"I don't know about you, but if you weren't post-surgery, married to a criminal, about to be arrested, I'd say what we need is a large drink." Nina appeared round the door next. "But instead, I brought you tea. Here . . ." Nina handed her yet another cup. "How's your pain level?"

"On the scale of a happy face, sad face – I'd say very sad face."

"You've got to mind yourself, Lu. You're still recovering. I'm so sorry all this has happened. Did you have any idea?"

Lucie made a face. "That my husband is a criminal, faked a burglary and is now in hiding for fear of being arrested? No. Did I know that something was wrong? Yes." She put her hands to her face. "What a mess, Nina. All I want is the kids here, never to see Hamish again and to forget it's all happened." She took her hands away and looked at her friend. "Max was here earlier today before you all came."

"I heard." Nina placed her hand on Lucie's arm. "Did

something happen between you two? There are all these knowing glances. If it wasn't for Doug being here, I'd feel like the third wheel again."

"Nothing happened. We talked. Well, he kissed me."

Nina's eyes were round. "This gets more sordid by the minute. Did you kiss him back?"

"Maybe," Lucie half-smiled.

"Were you really going to go back to Ireland and meet Hamish there?"

Lucie said nothing. She'd never told Nina about the discovery that Max was Bella's father.

"I thought it would be a way to start again, save our marriage. I didn't want to break up the family, but I knew we were fucked financially. I just didn't know how much.

"Of course, when I suggested it to Hamish, he agreed straightaway. What a shit. He knew all along and he was willing to leave it all behind to save his own arse. Did he think I wouldn't find out?"

"I suppose so. He's obviously scared. Well, he will be when Max rings him."

Lucie exhaled. "Oh, God. Is it the right thing to do?"

"Yes," Nina assured. "We've been through this all day, Lucie. It's the only thing to do. Otherwise, you're going to be arrested or hauled in for questioning and you're not strong enough. You *have* to think of yourself and the kids now. That's it. Hamish wasn't thinking of you when he was fiddling the system, living the life on other people's money, was he? Trust Doug and Max. They'll fix it, okay?"

Lucie nodded weakly. "Okay. Nina?"

"Yeah."

"Whatever happens, if something happens, you'll be there for the kids, won't you? You'll make sure Ann looks out for them."

Nina shook her head. "I don't even want to hear it. You're going to be with your kids."

"They're so far away. I wish . . . I want to go to them right now."

"I know, but they're all right. Why don't you call them? Right now. It might help to hear their voices. Talk to Ann. Tell her what's going on." Nina patted her arm. "Talking of kids, I need to get home to mine, but I'm on the end of the phone. It's better that I'm not around for the next part. Too many cooks can spoil the broth, but Max and Doug are going to stay with you. A doctor *and* a cop! You *will* be safe."

"Thanks, Nina."

Nina hugged her quickly and then broke away to look Lucie in the eye. "While we're being so open and honest, I want to say something."

"Oh, Christ. You don't fancy me, do you?"

"With all your baggage? Are you mad?" Nina laughed. "But I do love you, Lucie. All those years here together. You're *my* family here, you always had me. I left behind my country, too, but I found you. And then my own little family.

"But you can't leave Australia. Okay? You're meant to be here." Nina's voice turned to a whisper. "With him . . ." Nina gestured towards the kitchen.

"Doug? He's far too old for me."

"With Max, you messer," she grinned. "It's never too late. We are but spring chickens, really. When all this is over, you'll see. I let you make mistakes before, that's all I'll say, but not again. This phase will pass and then it's time to set it right. Now, I'm going. Try to sleep."

Hearing Ann's voice after the day she'd had made Lucie crumble. She spoke to Bella and Declan first, reassuring them that everything here was great and that she was on the mend. They sounded so happy – missing her but delighted to tell her all of their news. It was only afterwards when Ann came on the line that Lucie choked.

"Lu? What's wrong? What's happened?"

"Everything."

There was silence as Lucie explained it all down the phone, telling Ann everything she'd discovered about Hamish from Doug.

"I knew we were in trouble, but not like this."

"Oh, Lu, I'm so sorry."

"Ann, I need you to promise, if anything happens to me, you'll look after them, please. Take the kids to Ireland for good. Do what I didn't do for you." Lucie was sobbing.

"Lucie, please. Nothing is going to happen. It sounds like Doug has your back. And Max. And you *were* there for me, Lucie. When I needed you, you were there. And you've nothing to be worried about."

"What if I do?" Lucie hadn't meant to say it aloud. It had been on her mind the entire day and the words had slipped out.

"What do you mean?"

"Nothing. Forget it. I just need you to promise."

"I promise. Do you want me to come? Will I bring Bella and Dec back?"

It was on the tip of Lucie's tongue to say yes. It was what she wanted more than anything. But deep down, she knew they were in the right place for now.

"Do you think they'll understand? Do you think they'll be able to be normal after this?"

Ann was silent for a moment. "Yes. They'll be normal. They'll have you, they'll have me and they'll be fine. We'll make sure they are. That's what we do, remember? We're here for each other. Never mind the past."

Lucie nodded silently.

"So, what now?" Ann asked. "What happens with Hamish?"

"Well, I suppose I'm about to find out just how slippery my husband actually is."

Chapter thirty-nine

In the end, Lucie had slept, eventually closing her eyes and succumbing to the exhaustion. All evening she'd pondered everything, trying to make sense of the new-found knowledge that had now been added to all of her other concerns. Perhaps Lucie had always known that this time would come, when it would weigh so heavily. Would she be able to weather it? Then again, there isn't a single person in the world who, at some point, doesn't encounter something that seems impossible to defeat. And here was *her* challenge.

It had happened to Felicity once, albeit when she was a teenager, then again when she lost Sammy and finally when she got sick. It had happened to Ann, too, after her marriage broke down, before finding peace with Nathan. Even Ann's story, though it now had a happy ending, had been filled with twists and turns, betrayals and secrets. And now it was Lucie's turn. Lucie had forged her path and now she had to travel it. She wondered if her story would eventually have a happy ending, or if she was only at the beginning of another series of arcs, where she might once again veer in the wrong direction.

Waking now, Lucie was too weakened to feel the fury she should at Hamish and his escapades. No. She was far angrier with herself for lacking the courage to do anything about her failing marriage. Well, there had been that one feeble action a few months before. At the time, it had seemed inconsequential. But in light of current developments, it now seemed enormous – and Lucie was afraid.

It had been yet another mistake – she knew that now. Would she never learn?

Lucie squeezed her eyes shut once more. She'd told no one about it, not even Doug. Hell, she'd barely admitted it to herself. Curiously, she'd convinced herself that perhaps by confessing to everything else, she'd be afforded this one small secret.

Opening her eyes, she once again held her hand up to count her tribe. Bella. Declan. Ann. Doug. Nina . . . and . . . Max? Like it or not, he was here now, at her side, at least until she told him the truth – until he asked her to tell him the something that she promised she would when this step was complete. Whatever happened now, though, Max was Bella's father. Lucie couldn't hide it for much longer. He'd be shocked, furious, hurt. But deep down, she knew Max would want to do the right thing. He'd want to be part of Bella's life, if not of Lucie's.

Lucie didn't want anything from him, other than the opportunity to set right what she'd done to him. And Bella would forgive Lucie, too, in time, wouldn't she? Lucie wouldn't rest until she did. It would be harder to explain it to Declan. He was still so young, but she'd keep trying until he understood. As for Hamish . . .

"Are you awake?"

"Yes." She looked up to see Max standing over her. She'd slept in the living room, too tired to climb the stairs.

"Did you sleep?" he asked, sitting down on the floor beside her and putting his hand to her face.

"A little."

"Doug's up already. I put him in the guest-room, like you said."

"Good. Is he okay?"

"Worried about you. We all are. I wanted to ask you something. It was on my mind all night."

Lucie sat up slowly. "Go on."

"Didn't you ever think to leave Hamish?" he looked at her unsurely.

She bit her lip, trying to answer honestly. "I don't know," she paused. "Maybe, yes. Things had felt unsure lately."

"Would you have contacted me?"

She didn't answer.

"Sorry." He shook his head. "I know, there's bigger fish to fry at the moment . . . Talking of which, I came to tell you I got a message. He's on his way."

"Already?"

Max nodded. "Doug is setting up."

"I don't know if I can do this."

Lucie looked suddenly petrified and without hesitating, Max leaned over and kissed her gently, then put his arms around her.

"You can. I'm here. We've got you. It'll be a few hours yet. Rest."

It had been Max who'd called Hamish the day before from Lucie's mobile to deliver the news. It had been the most believable choice. Hamish had been shocked to hear his cousin's voice, but even more so listening to what he had to say.

"But I only spoke to her earlier today. What the hell are you doing there, anyway?"

"I'm back at the hospital. I oversaw Lucie's surgery. Listen, Hamish, whatever beef there is between us, you need to get here as soon as possible. The kids are on their way back from Ireland. Ann's bringing them."

"What the fuck?"

"I know. I'm sorry, Hamish, but it's not looking good. There's an infection. It's not uncommon post-surgery. And when it hits, it's fast. They're doing everything they can for her at the hospital, but you need to get here. Soon. The children are going to need you. Unless you want me to call your mother?"

"I'm on my way."

Lucie had felt sick at the idea of telling such an enormous lie, but they'd convinced her that it was the only way. Anything else, Hamish would try to wiggle out of.

"Tell him the kids are on their way back. If he knows that, then he'll believe it's serious," Nina had added as an afterthought. "Oh, God. I'd almost feel sorry for him if he wasn't such a flaming galah."

Even Doug had smiled at Nina's Australianism.

"Am I going to be arrested, Doug?"

"No, love. We're going to make sure you're not. Nothing we're doing is illegal, just a little white lie. Try to stay calm."

"Easy for you to say, but I'll try."

Sitting here now, Lucie could feel a lump like a tennis ball lodged in her throat.

"I've told him to meet me here at the house. I said I came back here to get you some things. He's in a taxi now," Max had told her half an hour earlier. "Breathe."

Lucie closed her eyes, willing herself to remain calm for what lay ahead, trying to remember how Doug had told her to play it. She'd never been great at following instructions, but she'd try to be now.

Hearing a car door close outside, Lucie's eyes flashed open as she waited, hearing footsteps coming up the driveway, the door opening, talking in the hallway, a bag drop to the floor – three-two-one . . .

"What the—? What the fuck is going on?" Hamish looked from Max to Lucie, who was sitting calmly on the sofa, and then turned when he saw Doug materialise from the kitchen. "Who the hell are you?" Hamish looked the older man up and down, and then back at Lucie. "Where are the kids?"

Lucie attempted to swallow the tennis ball that seemed to have morphed to a melon. Why was it always bloody fruit?

"Ireland. They're in Ireland. They're safe," she managed over the knot.

Hamish threw his hands up and turned to Max. "You'd better have a good explanation for this, mate." Then to Lucie. "Well? Death's door? There's nothing bloody wrong with you, is there? What *is* this?"

Doug stepped forwards. "Hamish, my name is Doug Offer. I'm a friend of Lucie's. I'm here as a mediator. Some things have come to light that Lucie needs to discuss with you."

"Oh, yeah. Like what?" Hamish's face was red.

"Claims." Lucie's voice was a whisper. She coughed. "False claims. I've found some things out, Hamish, about the burglary. And other things." She coughed again.

"Is that right? And a mediator? You bitch! What the

hell are you doing, Lucie? Think very carefully before you do what I think you're about to. I think you know what I might be saying." Hamish gritted his teeth in a warning.

Max moved towards Hamish, but Lucie shook her head to stop him. No, Lucie had never been good at biting her tongue, and she wasn't going to start now. Seeing Hamish standing there, fierce and cornered, it was enough to unleash the anger that hadn't yet broken through the shock.

"Sit the fuck down, Hamish!" she spat. "And for once in your life, shut the fuck up. All along, I've wanted to live life my way, but you had other ideas. Now, it's time to listen. Doug is an ex police officer and he can have this street cornered in a matter of minutes." She nodded proudly towards Doug, who nodded back. "So, you listen to me now and listen good. If you ever want to see your children again, you'll listen. Do you hear?"

The three men were silent, taken aback by her outburst, by the venom that dripped through her voice. Hamish sat down meekly on the sofa opposite and closed his eyes. He looked grey, despite a noticeable tan – dishevelled from the journey.

Then Lucie spoke.

"I knew there was something, Hamish, but I never expected this. It's all there in that file, and that's just a copy. The insurance company have the original, along with the police. Guess what? Your dishonesty is now a criminal case. But I think you already know that, don't you?"

Hamish didn't respond, his jaw welded together, the vein pulsating at his temple.

"Which is the reason you suddenly fled. Isn't that right?"

Again, silence.

"You see, I think Brent told you that the insurance

company was sniffing around. That day before you left, you spoke to him, didn't you? And you realised that the money wasn't going to be paid by the insurance company like you thought. You decided they must have discovered more about you and your fraudulent claims. Unlawful claims that you'd planned to use to get you out of yet another hole of your making.

"And there were other claims, too, I now know. Whiplash? A fall? Really? Not enough to stop you from playing golf, going running . . . How could you do it to me?"

Hamish shrugged, his face like thunder. "I wanted to give you a better life."

"A better life? Please! A life of living on my nerves, more like. Wondering where the next bit of money was coming from, how I was going to feed the kids . . . Seriously?"

"Come on, Lucie. Don't be naïve. Everyone does it."

Lucie almost choked. "Really? Everyone does it! You know why I had to trick you into getting you back here? Because they're going to arrest *me*! And honestly, I don't even think *that* would have made you come back. With you gone, they wanted *anyone*, and that was going to be me.

"I trusted you. I signed those papers thinking it was a genuine claim – that the house had been robbed. Where is everything now? Where are the paintings?"

"Gone."

"Gone?"

"I sold them."

"You shit. You stole from *yourself* and sold them anyway? It wasn't enough, was it? And then you had to claim for them – double whammy! You arsehole." Lucie shook her head.

"Where are the kids?"

"I told you. Ireland."

Hamish barely flinched. "Then we go there. Just like we planned yesterday. We take off. Max isn't going to stop us and this guy, whoever the hell he is . . ." Hamish sneered at Doug. "Well, I bet he won't do anything, either. So, I made a mistake. Hands up. But I'm *not* going down for this. We can leave, Lucie. Remember what you said? Start again? That's what you wanted. We can still do it. Nothing has changed."

Lucie could barely believe her ears. "Hah. Except it has. What's changed is I wouldn't go anywhere with you now, ever, you spineless coward. The only option is for you to hand yourself in."

"She's right, Hamish," Max chimed in. "For the children, for Lucie. You can't implicate her in this. And you can't go to Ireland. Not now. What? And spend your life on the run?"

"Where the hell did you crawl back from, anyway, Max?" Hamish snarled as he turned to glare at him. "Couldn't stay away from her, could you? I wondered if you'd ever try one day. Well, you fucked that one up, mate. But let me tell you, if it puts your mind at rest, she wasn't all that great, once the party was over. You missed nothing."

"You're a despicable person, you know that?" Max stood over him, looking like he was about to thump him.

"Max, please," Lucie shouted.

"Yeah, talk your puppy down, Lucie. Still following you around. Pathetic."

Max scowled at him, then turned to leave the room before he did something he'd regret. Lucie watched Max march into the kitchen, then continued.

"You're the pathetic one, Hamish. Mortgage fraud, too? They know everything. You went a step too far. All this . . ." She threw her hands up. "All lies. The house, the marriage, everything. All a sham. I want you to hand yourself in. Admit what you've done, here and now."

"Go fuck yourself!" Hamish went to stand and then stopped, narrowing his eyes. "Actually, I think you should reconsider Ireland, Lucie. Especially after what you did that same day. Don't you? Would you like me to enlighten everyone?"

Lucie's stomach flipped as Hamish eyeballed her. So, he did know. All along, she'd been hoping that there was still a slim chance Hamish was clueless, that this smaller secret would remain buried with her others. No such luck. After Lucie had heard that it was Hamish who'd faked the burglary, pulled their house apart so horribly and taken all of their possessions, it had dawned on her that he might have guessed. She'd been right.

Lucie could feel Doug's eyes boring into her, desperately trying to signal something to her. She couldn't bring herself to look back, knowing Doug must have thought that Hamish had learned about Bella's real parentage and was about to out her. For once, Doug was wrong.

"Not so innocent yourself. Are you?" Hamish continued.

"Whatever you're referring to is a discussion for another time." Doug tried to interject on her behalf. "Let's stick to the current issue." He looked panicked, checking over his shoulder to see where Max was. "And keep your voices down."

Hamish ignored him. "You think you're so clever, don't you?" he laughed bitterly. "But it turns out Lucie here, in case you didn't know, has a habit of lying, too. Isn't that right, Lucie?"

Lucie could barely breathe.

"Always banging on about being honest, telling the truth. My mother used to say, blah-blah. I wonder did your mother know that you could spin a lie so well? Hell, we're perfect for each other, aren't we?" He laughed hysterically this time. "But you didn't think this one would ever come out, did you?"

"Hamish, please." Her voice was tiny.

"No. My turn. Let *me* talk." Hamish mimicked her earlier words. "You see, *if* it was me who took everything that day—"

"I think we've already established it was you, Hamish. You've already admitted it. Now, it's time to do the right thing."

"Let me finish, old man. Oh, and I hope this *is* being recorded. I assume it is, from the way you keep asking me to admit it. So, here's the next part." Hamish glanced around as if he were waiting for a microphone to appear, then raised his voice. "This is Hamish Woods talking. I repeat, it wasn't only me, was it, Lucie?" he paused, a satisfied smile on his face.

Hamish watched her face turn white, saw Lucie turn to Doug slowly, who stared back, confused.

"That's enough!" Doug attempted again, disgusted that Hamish would go so far. "Trying to implicate your wife in something like this – that's low, even for someone like you."

Lucie stared ahead again, sucked in her lips. Here it was. The moment of truth.

What was the point any more? This wasn't who she was. This wasn't the girl who'd arrived in this country almost twenty years before with her heart strapped to her sleeve, her mind open to finding a beautiful life. That Lucie *had* been honest, with a family who adored her, back in Ireland.

In time, she'd found a second family, with Max and

Nina. *That* was how it was supposed to have been, not like this. Now, she was middle-aged, broken and bitter, doing things she would never even have considered. *This* wasn't the mother Lucie wanted to be, or the friend, or the wife. Yes, life had been hard. Yes, it had thrown her obstacles that had seemed unmanageable. And she'd dealt with them, the best way she knew how. Not always in the right manner, admittedly, but this wasn't how it was supposed to be.

Lie after lie. And now this.

"Desperation and greed." She could hear Doug's words sounding in her ears. Hamish was right, she *was* a liar, *is* a liar. Just like him. Always hiding from the truth, scared of when it was going to emerge. And it had changed her, altering her so much that she no longer recognised herself. *A mother?* The children were better off without her if she was going to continue deceiving everyone, worst of all herself.

"Enough now," Lucie whispered. "Of *all* the lies. I can't do this any more." She put her head back, exhaled loudly. Then she looked from Hamish to Doug, her brow furrowed, her eyes sorrowful. "Any of it. I just can't. Enough now," she repeated, louder.

Chapter forty

"Lucie?" Doug was observing her curiously. What was she about to do? "Let's just stick to what we discussed." He raised his eyebrows at her. "To the burglary. Okay?"

"It's okay, Doug." Her voice was suddenly even, filled with resignation, her demeanour steady.

Max had come back in the room, having overheard the heated conversation from the kitchen, and now stood behind Hamish. All three faces stared at her expectantly. If she could, she would have stood, like the guilty person she was, but her legs no longer had the strength. Instead, she channelled every ounce of energy that remained into her voice to keep it steady. Then she took a breath and said the words.

"My name is Lucie Woods. I swear to tell the truth, the whole truth and nothing but the truth, so help me God."

"Lucie?" Doug said again, touching her arm to jolt her back to reality. "What are you doing?"

"What I should have done a long time ago, Doug. I'm telling the truth."

* * *

To this day, Lucie still wasn't entirely sure why she'd done what she had that evening following the discovery that the house had been ransacked. Her body had acted instinctively. It had taken her brain a few months longer to catch up, to come in line with how she'd reacted that day. In the face of panic and confusion, she'd carried out the act calmly. Looking back, Lucie could picture herself doing it, if not wholly remember the set of movements. She supposed now, perhaps it was the conversation in the car on the way home from her mother-in-law's house that had commenced the train of thought.

"In five years, I'll be eighteen." Bella had been chatting away, still upset that she hadn't been allowed to stay with her friends that day instead of being hauled off to have dinner with her eccentric grandmother. "Isn't that how old you were when you left home, Mum? When you went to do nursing. That's when I'll be gone, too. Free to do whatever I like."

"And then me after that," Declan had added innocently. "And then it'll be just you and Dad again when I'm gone."

Lucie had nodded and stared ahead. The thought of it being just Hamish and her made her chest tighten. *Five years?* Was that all the time Lucie had left with Bella? Then only a few years after that with her son . . .

Life had careered by so fast. In another sense, it felt like many lifetimes, watching her daughter and then her son change from baby to infant to toddler to child to teen to . . . *gone*? And then it would be just her again. Hamish and her?

No. They both knew, deep down, that once the children left, that part of their lives would most likely end, too. They'd never said it aloud, but the idea was silently present. And then Lucie would finally have to face all of her mistakes, all of her regrets. The fact that her marriage had stopped breathing almost as soon as it began – that she'd paused her beloved career to raise her children and may never be able to pick up where she left off . . . That she was still in love with someone else and always had been . . . That she'd lied.

"What the fuck? Kids, outside!" Hamish had shouted after Lucie had pushed open the front door to stare at the mess. "I'll check out the back."

Hamish rushed into the kitchen, clattering in a kitchen drawer for a knife as he went, before making sure that whoever had done this was no longer in the house.

"It's okay, kids. Get in the car. I'll be out in a minute," Lucie reassured their concerned faces.

Arriving back and seeing her home this way almost knocked Lucie off her feet. She'd left it another way that afternoon – organised, neat, safe – and had come back to find it in utter chaos. The thought entered Lucie's head right then how easy it was to tear something so seemingly perfect apart. Just like that. *Ta-dah*! Then again, hadn't that been the story of her life? Everything fine one day, the next ripped apart.

Lucie had experienced it with each loss of a family member. After this, Lucie would put the house back together, reassemble it as best she could, just as she'd tried to do to herself after her loved ones had died. But she knew, somehow, it would never be the same again. Something would always be different – changed.

Lucie walked to the living room archway and saw that the paintings had been taken, and immediately, she'd thought of Ann. Lucie had planned to give Ann one of the pictures as an upcoming wedding gift. Making her way back to the hall, Lucie had still been thinking of Ann as she stood at the bottom of the stairs looking around at her home that had been cruelly torn asunder. Lucie had also promised to lend Ann Tess's charm bracelet for her "something borrowed". *Was that gone, too?*

Lucie could picture the heavy gold rope on her mother's wrist, the charms knocking against each other, jingling as Tess moved. It had been Lucie's grandmother's before that, bought at a time when the price of gold was low – and treasured ever since.

"It's the only thing I have that's worth anything," her mother had told Lucie once, fingering the gold charms. "Actually, it's worth quite a bit. Solid gold. Imagine!

"I'll never sell it, but I like to think I've a bit of security here wrapped around my arm, just in case." She'd shaken her wrist and laughed. "This could get us all to America if we wanted. Or just me," she'd giggled. "Isn't that right, Paddy? You stop giving out, or I'll up and leave with my fortune." Then she'd leaned over to whisper in Lucie's ear. "It'll be yours someday, love.

"Keep it for my granddaughter. Tell her the same. Always have a bit of money tucked somewhere, just in case. You never know what's around the next corner."

Her mother had meant it as a joke, of course, hadn't she? Mam would often deliver a lesson wrapped up in everyday exchange.

Either way, it was what Lucie was thinking as she climbed the stairs, step after step, in a trance before pushing open the door to her bedroom to stare at the clothes strewn across the floor, the contents of the wardrobes everywhere. The horror that met her eyes forced a small squeak to escape her lips. She walked back into the hallway and glanced right to see that the hot press had also been emptied, all the towels and sheets scattered on the floor. Why? What had they possibly expected to find in there? Hours of pointless folding all dismantled in the sweep of an arm. Just like that. It would be just as easy to dismantle her own life. In the blink of an eye, Lucie could do it. It would only take one sentence, one utterance – *the* truth.

Lucie could hear Hamish calling her from downstairs. She should have waited for him. In her state of shock, she hadn't even thought about the danger, that someone might still be in the house. It jolted her and she moved back into her bedroom, over the clothes, towards the chest of drawers. Putting her hand in the top drawer, Lucie pawed around for what she was looking for. It was a trick her mam used to use, tucking all of her jewellery into a pair of socks and throwing it to the back of the drawer.

Lucie found the more-substantial-than-usual pair of socks and clutched them gratefully. Thank God. She hadn't worn any of her jewellery that day. It was all there, tucked inside – her engagement ring, her mam's bracelet, an eternity ring, diamond earrings, a diamond tennis bracelet – all of her treasures.

"Lucie?" Hamish called for her again.

That's when she'd done it.

Holding the parcel against her heart, Lucie had closed her eyes and remembered how easily everything can come apart. Right there, tucked in a pair of cotton socks, was the only bit of security Lucie had in the entire world. Their marriage was doomed. It *would* end, someday. *And* there was the burden of her secret about Bella. If it ever did come out, at least Lucie would have this – enough to run away with, with Bella and Declan, back to Ireland.

Maybe she'd do it anyway, stop waiting for the inevitable to happen – start again, now, before the years rolled by and the children left, when it would be just Hamish and her, alone, like Declan had said earlier. It had never been just Hamish and her, and it never would. From the very start of their relationship, Bella had been there, present, another man's child – not once had it ever been just Hamish and her.

Going to her wardrobe, Lucie had then reached to the very back and buried the socks inside the box of baby keepsakes. Treasure with treasure.

"There you are." Hamish appeared from nowhere. "You shouldn't have come up here without me. It's all clear. They've gone – bastards."

Lucie was back standing at the chest of drawers, still in shock.

"Everything's gone. It's all gone," Lucie whispered. "I wasn't wearing my rings. They were in there. I . . . I left them. I didn't think. It's all gone. My mam's bracelet, everything."

"What?"

Had Hamish sounded shocked?

Looking back, Lucie supposed he had.

He'd bent to paw at the upturned contents of the drawers on the floor. "No," he'd insisted. "Maybe they missed them. They must be in among this stuff."

They hadn't been.

Looking back now, it was almost amusing – both of them standing there bare-faced lying to the other, unable to admit the truth.

Hamish: that he'd got them into a situation that required desperate greedy measures, assuming no one would question someone like *him* for faking a robbery. Lucie: that she'd been so afraid that the truth of her deceitful life would come out that she'd carried out another deception, in case it ever did.

After that day, Lucie had tried to resume life, block out her curious actions. But within a matter of days, it began to materialise that life had other plans. As if she'd somehow altered her fate at that moment, creating a catalyst for change, commencing the process of her evolution. Or perhaps it had been karma . . .

Karma had acted fast, barely giving her a moment to breathe before delivering a string of gifts, starting with the dismissal from her job the very next day.

"Stick out your tongue. Is it black?" her father used to say, trying to catch them out in a lie as children.

No, her tongue hadn't been black, but her insides had been rotten with a fruit basket's worth of fibroids developing within her, probably being fed by all of her lies. Another gift, this time wrapped in a bloody red bow in the form of surgery, followed by a long period of rest, with nothing to do but ponder the past. It was something Lucie hadn't had in years – stillness, time to think.

Perhaps thinking was something Lucie had unknowingly avoided all those years, keeping busy, never allowing her mind to drift to the places she didn't want it to go. But even with all that unlimited time, she hadn't been able to force her mind to where it needed to go.

"Not until you came along, Doug." Lucie turned to him now after her confession. "Talking about my life with you, going all the way back to the start, well, I started to see things differently. I started to see that telling the truth, well, it's not the easiest, but it's the right thing."

She glanced over at Max, who nodded proudly, while Hamish scowled.

"So you admit it!" Hamish applauded slowly. "At first I thought you'd misplaced it, but when the jewellery didn't turn up after a few weeks, I knew it must have been you."

"And that's why you were acting strangely. It wasn't just that you'd faked the burglary. You knew I'd taken the jewellery."

"You were planning to leave me. Weren't you?"

"I'm not sure," Lucie admitted.

"Still, you were happy for me to claim for it, weren't you?"

"I wasn't, Hamish. I didn't know what I was thinking. I didn't fully understand what I'd done until everything started falling apart. Then it began to make sense."

"How so?" His arms were crossed defensively.

"I wanted some security, even a tiny bit. I took the jewellery because I knew that someday, *this* day would come."

Lucie smiled sadly at Max. Hamish caught it and looked from one to the other.

"Oh, please . . ." He threw his hands up and rolled his eyes.

"I never used to lie." She looked away wistfully. "I *was* honest. Too much so sometimes, but that was me. That was who I was. I want to be like that again. I want to be that way for Bella and Declan."

"Beautiful, Lucie. Really touching," Hamish spat sarcastically. "So, now we know that you're just as dishonest as me and you've admitted you're just as involved in this as I am. what happens now? Are you going to do the right thing and let's go to Ireland? Tick-tock, Lucie. In light of this new evidence," Hamish said loudly again, "I'd say you're just as fucked as I am. Wouldn't you agree?"

Lucie shook herself back to reality. "No, Hamish. I'm not going to Ireland. This is where I belong, here in Australia. I'm tired of lying. And yes, I made a huge mistake taking the jewellery. But I'll take my chances that by being honest, it'll see me right in the end. The insurance claim was a massive error, but I'm going to admit to it. The rest, that's all on you, Hamish."

"What about the kids?" Hamish asked suddenly. "Both of us will be arrested." His voice was getting higher.

"Then so be it," she issued. She was done lying.

"Lucie . . ." Max was staring at her. "You can't do this. Hamish will—"

"For fuck's sake, Lucie!" Hamish piped in. "Let's just go. While we have a chance."

"Lucie, you made a mistake," Doug interrupted. "It's understandable what you did, considering." He shot Hamish a disapproving look. "I'll vouch for you."

"Lucie, don't listen to that crap. They always say that." Hamish was getting nervous, rolling his eyes and tutting.

"Doug's right," she began. "I've been judging myself for my mistakes all of my life. I'd rather be judged by someone else now." The tears were rolling freely. "Please, Hamish," she was pleading now. "I'm so sick of being sad all the time. I don't want to argue any more. Bella and Declan are my whole life. All I want is for them to be proud of me. Someday, hopefully they'll realise that I made mistakes because I'm human. Maybe then they'll forgive me. But I can't spend the rest of my life wondering if I did it all differently . . .

"Hamish, you've been a good father. Not a great husband," she almost laughed. "But I know you tried, in a questionable way. And you're right. I have lied about more than stupid jewellery. You don't deserve what I'm about to say. Nor do you, Max. I'm so sorry. Please know that before I tell you. Oh, God . . ." She took a breath. "Max . . ."

"Wait." It was Hamish. He put his head back and exhaled, looking suddenly defeated. "I won't let you admit to anything about the robbery." Hamish held his hands up to stop Lucie from objecting. "I won't do that to Bells and Dec.

"I'm in a shitload of trouble as it is. You need to be here for them. Being in Singapore, I had time to think, too. Okay, I admit it. I've fucked up big time." He shook his head. "You're right. I knew it was all catching up on me, so I bolted.

"But I love my kids and I didn't want them finding out that I was some sort of crim. When you suggested Ireland . . . But it's not going to work, is it? Not now, anyway." He scowled at Doug.

"But you don't know what I'm going to say," Lucie cut across.

"But I do. I've always known."

Chapter forty-one

Hamish

It's a curious thing: reflection – meandering back over your life. It's even more bizarre when you realise that your life, as you knew it, is over, yet you're still very much alive. But it was precisely what Hamish had found himself doing for the past few weeks, holed up in a dingy hotel room in Singapore, searching for reasons as to why his life had transpired how it had.

Hearing Lucie's words, her anguish, telling him that she'd been doing exactly the same thing from her hospital bed – it was somewhat comforting, he supposed. For once, they were on the same page – both midway through their lives and glancing back with . . . regret?

It was the most united they'd been on any subject in a very long time, sharing thoughts of their disappointing lives. *Disappointing.* Wasn't that a piercing word? A word reserved for parents for the times when there's no other appropriate noun to describe their children's actions.

"I'm not angry. I'm . . . disappointed."

Disappointed. Nothing cut so deep as that seemingly

banal word. He'd used it a couple of times himself over the years with Bella and Declan, as a parenting device, before having to turn away so they couldn't see him smiling. Because in truth, Hamish had never felt disappointed in his children, not really, not like his own mother had in him.

Yes, there had been a time when Declan, being so different from his outgoing sister, had worried Hamish. Declan hadn't appeared to be equipped with the right skill set to navigate the hardships of life. But Declan would be okay, Hamish could see it now – different wasn't always bad. All that time, Lucie had thought Hamish was too hard on the boy, but he'd just wanted his son to know that life was tough. Because by God, it was tough!

"Life."

Hamish remembered one time sitting at his friend's father's funeral, listening intently to the eulogy, to words that had been written by the deceased himself, now being read in the shaky voice of his daughter. Hamish's ears had perked up when he'd heard the opening phrase.

"What is life? How can it be summed up?"

Go on, he'd urged the speaker to reveal the answer.

"It's for living. It's for experiencing both sides in equal measures. Happiness, sadness. Pleasure, pain. Gain and loss."

Hamish listened to the man's final thoughts.

"It's to feel everything, fully and without too much regret. To laugh until your sides split, to cry until you can't breathe. To love. To love someone in a way that you read about in books, with an all-consuming passion, within whom you find refuge."

Regret, yes. Laughter, yes. Tears, yes. Love . . . ?

"To adore your children."

Yes.

"To hold them to your chest and feel it bursting with pride, joy, animal protection. To know that everything before them was just a practice run."

Yes.

"To try to have faith that there is always something better to come. Stop fighting against what you can't control – it's exhausting. Focus on what you have. Love yourself with all of your faults and always make sure you know what those faults are . . ."

Hamish had tuned out, his mind focusing on the part about recognising your faults. "Stop fighting . . . it's exhausting." Yes. It was exhausting. There had been a lot to consider within those wise words, in a summary of what life *should* be. Then again, it must be simpler to write what life ought to be when it was about to cease.

Hamish had wondered if that man, whose words had touched all those listening, had lived in the way he'd described. Or had he, in fact, lived another way – and having lived that way, was able to see what was actually necessary, only now realising what was not? Had he, in fact, lived like Hamish – making constant mistakes? Had he loved someone the way he'd described, finding refuge with them?

Hamish hadn't. He'd wanted to – he'd even thought he might have found refuge once – but then life had veered along another path.

Lucie Maguire. Hamish had never encountered anyone like Lucie all those years ago. The few times he'd met her when she'd been together with Max, Hamish had felt inexplicably drawn to her. She hadn't looked like the type Hamish would usually go for. She'd been pretty, but more in a way that you had to search for her beauty. Then once you saw it, it was *all* you could see.

She'd been funny, hilariously so, reminding Hamish of how he might expect a man to joke. It hadn't been crass, it had been . . . uncomplicated. Was that the word? Or honest, perhaps that had been it. Much as it pained him to admit it now, Lucie had been honest.

But she'd also been in a relationship with Max. Drippy, boring Max. Max, the doctor.

They'd been close once – Max and him – a long time ago, almost like brothers. His aunt had been like a mother to Hamish when his own mother was off doing whatever she did, all day every day, at her stupid gallery, with her string of men, her put-on posh accent and eccentric hair. *No father.* His mother didn't even know who his father was.

"It was a different time," she used to tell him whenever he asked. "Free love."

Free love? Hamish had wished he'd lived in a time of "free love", because all of his life it had seemed he'd had to pay for the love he received.

No, Hamish wasn't going to do this. He wasn't going to blame everyone else for how he'd turned out. Hamish could be honest, too, if he chose to be. It's funny, though – even when you try to be brutally frank with yourself, you still try to make excuses.

It was my childhood.

I had no father.

My mother was never there.

I was lonely.

I was afraid.

I never felt good enough.

Bullshit. It was all bullshit. You are what you are.

Hamish had seen people go through far worse than he'd ever had to and not make such a balls of life. The truth is, he was a fool, nothing more – a bloody fool.

Meeting Lucie that night in the nightclub had felt like fate. She'd been drunk. If he'd wanted to, he could have kissed her there and then, but something had stopped him. He could see she was broken. Then she'd told him she'd been thinking of breaking up with Max. That's what Hamish had heard, anyway.

"If you ever need anything, and I mean anything, call me . . ."

It had been a line. If Hamish was honest, he'd thought it would be a great way to piss Max off. *Another truth.* Getting good at this . . .

For most of his life, Hamish had felt inadequate beside Max. Well, not at first. All through school, Hamish had been the good-looking one, who'd excelled at swimming and athletics. Hamish got the girls, was first to lose his virginity – and keep on losing it – had all the friends, went to all the parties. Hamish had liked it – the feeling of having the upper hand. *Another truth.* Back then, Hamish had something over Max – Max with the perfect family, the loving mother, the devoted father.

Then something had changed. Max had started excelling at rugby in their final year, where suddenly his enormous size was praised. Even the girls had begun to look at Max then, much as Hamish hadn't understood it. But stupid Max hadn't been able to see it, so lacking in confidence that he'd been blind to their advances.

Then Max had aced the exams and got into medicine. Game over. *Another truth* – now we're on them. After that, nothing Hamish could do would equate. A doctor – saviour of the Earth. Hah! Wealthy, respected, reliable Max.

Then Max had landed someone like Lucie Maguire and Hamish's seething jealousy had soared. *Another truth.*

Yes, it had just been a line – beautifully delivered with

plenty of knowing glances and sexual tension. "If you ever need anything . . ."

Hamish had watched Lucie wobble away, thinking he'd never hear from her again – until he had, the very next day. Lucie *had* needed something. She'd wanted Hamish, not Max – *him*.

Lucie had hidden away with him for weeks, telling him how she felt lost, afraid, unsure as to what life was all about. Everything she'd told him was how he'd always felt and never been able to articulate. Lucie had hardly mentioned Max at all and Hamish had taken it as a sign.

Those first few weeks had been crazy. They'd done everything together. Hamish took holidays from his job at the bank to spend time with her before she'd eventually return to Ireland. Like some sort of passionate holiday romance, they'd gone bungee jumping, swum naked.

Lucie had been wild – unconcerned about what tomorrow might bring. When they'd fallen into bed together after only a few days, it had felt right. Both of them had said it, not just him. But still, Lucie had talked about Ireland, about going home to her niece.

All Hamish had wanted to do was to beg her to stay. Before he'd had to, Lucie was pregnant – another sign. Lucie would stay. Had Hamish taken pleasure, knowing that he'd finally won something over Max? *Another truth?* Yes.

"She's perfect." Looking down at his daughter's face, Hamish had never felt so sure about anything.

There and then, he'd vowed to be there for Bella always, finally understanding what love really meant. Lucie was a natural mother with Bella and she'd seemed happy, any doubts about remaining in Australia long vanquished.

Besides, they were getting married. Lucie wanted to

wait until the baby was born, but Hamish had asked her almost as soon as she'd discovered she was pregnant. His mother had tried to stop him.

"Just wait. She's not that long out of a relationship with Max. Apparently, he's devastated. How could you do that to your cousin? He's such a lovely man. Lucie mustn't be thinking. She'll see sense and then where will you be?"

She'll see *sense*? Her words were like a knife.

"It's *my* baby. It's the right thing."

"Is it?"

Is it?

It was only months after Bella was born, and after the wedding, that Hamish finally understood what his mother had been suggesting that day. She hadn't been asking if getting married was the right thing, she'd been asking if Bella was his. But by then, Bella Woods had already stolen Hamish's heart. No one – not Lucie, not his mother, not Max – was going to take that away.

It was Hamish who made Bella's chubby wrists twirl with delight when he came home from work. It was Hamish who'd make her gurgle with glee – regardless of what his own mother had tried to suggest.

"How's Lucie?"

Taking Bella each week to visit her grandmother was always met with the same question, coupled with raised eyebrows.

"Distant."

For once, Hamish had answered honestly. By then, Bella was almost seven months old and Lucie wasn't herself.

"For the past few months. I wonder if it's post-natal depression."

Lucie had gone from being happy, or what had seemed like happiness, to becoming instantly flat. One day, he'd come home from work to find her acting strange, as if someone had grasped her smile, pushing it downwards, so her mouth was permanently set in a straight line.

"Regrets," his mother exhaled behind him, and Max had to stop himself from punching her.

"Having a baby is hard, Mother. Surely *you* remember. Or was it your sister who did all that for you? Aunty May used to say having Max and I had been like having twins. Except, *I* wasn't hers."

Vera ignored the jibe.

"Look." His mother placed the photo album in front of him at the table, pointing repeatedly at the picture. "Tell me what you see."

"A fat head," Hamish replied impatiently, averting his eyes from the baby picture of Max and him. "I see a fat head." Hamish pushed the book away and stood up. "What are you trying to do?"

"I know you can see it, too, Hamish. Look at Bella. I just don't want you to get hurt."

"From where I'm standing, the only one trying to hurt me is you."

After that, it was *all* Hamish could see. Did Lucie suspect the same? Did she know? From the way his wife was acting, it certainly seemed as though she'd discovered something. Was it this? Or was it, like his mother had warned, that Hamish wasn't who Lucie wanted to be with? There was only one way to find out.

A few weeks later, he'd known. *Another truth.*

"You were wrong," he told his mother on another visit. "Whatever you were suggesting, you were wrong. I did a paternity test."

"And?" His mother observed him.

"Bella *is* mine. How could you even think it?"

"I was only saying what I saw. Well, that is good news. Looks like for the first time in your life, you've done something right. Don't mess it up, now. Give that girl everything she wants – make sure she stays."

So he had. Hamish had given Lucie everything he could and all that he couldn't, in the hope she'd stay.

At times, Lucie had seemed happy. At others, she'd stare so intently at the blank wall in the living room that it frightened him. It was the reason he'd starting buying paintings for her, in the hope that she might see something other than regret, or the truth.

Bella was a joy and Hamish loved her more than anything.

"You two make me feel left out. I'm like the outsider," Lucie would often say.

"Let's have another. One for you, one for me," he'd suggested.

When Declan was born, things were better again. But then, Declan was so different from Bella. It took Hamish a few years to clock it – oh, the irony. His son, Declan, was more like Max – quiet, studious, steady. Regardless, Hamish loved his son. Of course he did. But there was a special bond between Hamish and Bella. It happened, he supposed. It was normal. *Wasn't it?* It was *all* normal – his marriage, the debts he'd created to give them all a good life. All perfectly normal.

Until it all got out of control.

That's when Hamish had disappeared off to Singapore, to mull it all over, to remove himself from the heat that he'd created that was closing in fast. When he thought about it, all Hamish could come up with was that he'd fucked up. Over and over. He'd wanted a big life – too darn big – and he'd lied to achieve it. Had it all been for Lucie?

No. *Another truth.*

It hadn't all been to hold on to a wife he knew didn't really love him. Perhaps some people, people like him, were simply born feeling inadequate, like an internal glitch. Maybe if he hadn't always felt less, he might have had more – and he wouldn't be sitting here now trying to explain himself.

"I was trying to give you all a better life, but I was also trying to prove something – to myself. The deeper I got myself into the situation, the more I couldn't get out." His shoulders drooped and he closed his eyes. "I just kept digging. When I got that call from Brent, he told me the insurance company was snooping around. I just had to get the hell out of here. I was due in Singapore, believe it or not, but I left a few weeks early. I'd pushed too far this time. You're right, I am a fraud."

He looked up at Lucie. "I tried to stop. I did. But every business deal went wrong. I kept promising you the next one would be better and . . ." He smiled sadly. "It was the way you were looking at me ... *disappointed*. But I'd already disappointed myself.

"I thought it would be easier if I headed off, never came back. Then, well, you offered me the chance to go to Ireland. But it would still *all* be a lie. Wouldn't it? I always wondered if you knew, Lucie. At times I wasn't sure, but you did, didn't you?"

Hamish turned to Max.

"I never hated you, mate. We're family. I . . . I took what should have been yours and I'm sorry. From the bottom of my heart, I'm sorry. But I want you to know, I love her with every inch of myself. I'll always love her. She's the one thing I'll *never* regret."

Max stared at him, confused, then at Lucie, whose face crumpled like paper.

"I don't mean Lucie, Max. She should have been yours, too, though. I suspect she always has been," Hamish said. And then, "Bella. She's yours. You're Bella's father."

Chapter forty-two

Max

From the moment Hamish had walked through the front door, his hackles had been up. Max hadn't been sure what to anticipate from his wayward cousin, but he hadn't expected it to unfold how it had. As soon as Hamish opened his mouth, Max had detected sheer inadequacy dripping through his words – with his pathetic pleas to Lucie to move forwards with their plans to go to Ireland, regardless of his actions.

Hamish hadn't even tried to deny any of it. Like a tennis match, Max had bounced from Hamish to Lucie as he'd listened to Lucie's accusations, Hamish's mistakes, him trying to fight back, how he'd lied, her disappointments. Bearing witness to Hamish's hard truths – betrayals, lies, deceits – the whole time, Max had thought what an absolute deadbeat Hamish was, and that was being generous.

At one point, Max had had to escape to the safety of the kitchen while Hamish tried to claw his way out of the sticky mess, at first trying to blame Lucie. There, Max had rested both of his hands on the worktop, willing himself to breathe, to count to ten, so he didn't pick the bastard up and hurl him out of the same window Hamish had smashed in the fictitious burglary.

From what Max could glean, his cousin had certainly given Lucie some twisted rollercoaster of a life, filled with uncertainties, while he fecklessly conned whoever he could. And for what? To save face?

Max hadn't been able to comprehend how brazenly Hamish had admitted to fabricating the burglary, hissing angrily like a cornered rat but with no rebuttal. "Everyone does it." Those had been his actual words. Do they, really?

Max had wanted to grab him by the throat and pummel him. What could possibly drive someone to behave in the way Hamish had? It certainly hadn't been for Lucie, nor the children. No, to begin with, all Max had heard was the tribulations of a selfish, greedy little man – one who was clearly averse to hard work. Hamish had dug himself into a massive pit of lies and debt, trying to cover whatever latest escapade had failed with another deceit. And now he'd been caught.

Max had to hand it to Hamish, though, his forthrightness was almost admirable.

Then again, Max was hardly surprised. Even as children, Hamish had always been the same. Whatever hare-brained scheme he'd invented, eventually Hamish had invariably owned up – shrugging his shoulders, half-smiling, clearly lacking whatever gene makes you culpable for your actions.

"Easier to ask for forgiveness than permission," Hamish would always say proudly. "Do the crime, pay the time." His motto obviously hadn't been modified over the years.

What a strange existence!

Hamish had been happy to take his chances with the lies, now making little effort to disguise his choices. Hearing it all, Max's heart had been breaking for Lucie and the life in which she'd ended up captured. Imagine, it was Max who was the one feeling responsible – guilty for not having come sooner, for walking away from her back then without putting up a fight. Not that she'd have listened, but he should have tried.

"Not so innocent yourself."

Max had re-entered the room on hearing Hamish's anger-fuelled words and watched as Lucie's face turned white. Doug had tried to interject, to stop Hamish from trying to condemn Lucie. Then Max had seen Lucie close her eyes, roll her head back.

"Enough." She'd taken a deep breath and uttered the words as if she were on trial. "My name is Lucie Woods. I swear to tell the truth . . ."

Lucie had told Max earlier that there was something she needed to say to him – that when all this was over, he was to ask her. Was this it?

Doug had tried to stop her, putting his hand out on her arm, but she'd ignored him. It was as though she were in the room on her own and was going to say whatever she needed to, no matter what.

It had been dramatic, so much so that for one fleeting moment, Max had thought Lucie might admit to having murdered someone and buried them beneath the patio. He'd felt giddy with relief when she'd revealed that it had been her who'd taken the jewellery and how she was going to take command of her actions. What he'd heard in *her* words, unlike his cousin's, was desperation. He'd even smiled proudly at her when she'd finished.

Lucie disclosing the truth hadn't shocked Max – not in the slightest. In fact, inside, he'd silently been applauding her.

"Bravo, Lucie," he'd wanted to shout, "you married a fucking idiot. It's not your fault – you were driven to it."

Lucie had looked so ashamed, shaking her head, gulping back the tears. Right then, Max had wanted to pick her up and carry her away, far from Hamish and the lies. Hamish had listened smugly to her confession, thrilled with the possibility of implicating Lucie in his sordid crime.

Max had understood why Lucie had looked so terrified, afraid of hurting her children or hindering her chances of being with them. But neither Doug nor Max were going to let that become a possibility. There and then, Max had vowed to do everything he could to help her, particularly if Hamish intended to try to take Lucie down with him. Max would lie if he had to, anything to protect her, to make her happy again.

Then, just as the situation had reached a crescendo, Hamish had backed down, immediately surrendering and admitting defeat. It would almost be gallant – if it wasn't Hamish – but nonetheless, the undulating drama began to level. No. Hamish wasn't going to allow Lucie to admit to anything.

Max supposed it had been the mention of Bella and Declan. The idea of them being without both parents that must have made Hamish reconsider, making him sit bolt upright, remembering that by hurting Lucie, he'd also be damaging them. It was the same way Hamish had been as a child – initial denial, fight, followed just as quickly with, "Okay. I did it. Let's get this over with."

It was a game, one Max should have recognised

earlier. Hamish had been trying to make Lucie suffer before setting her free. Like the time Max had tried to stop Hamish from taking his mother's car up the road without permission when they were fifteen.

"It was his idea, too." Hamish had pointed instantly at Max before conceding that it had, in fact, all been Hamish's idea.

And here he was now, doing it again.

At that moment, considering the shift in the atmosphere, Max had felt sure that everything would be fine. Lucie was going to be okay, Hamish was going to do the right thing.

Max could hardly remember now how it had come about, but suddenly Hamish was talking non-stop about the past, about how he'd met Lucie, how he'd felt when she got pregnant – like some form of epiphany, a memoir of his life. Then the story had started to reverse, far from his recent actions, to years back, even to before Lucie. Max could barely keep up. Mind you, by now he'd begun to tune out, not wishing to endure the sob story as to why Hamish had turned out to be such a loser.

Then all of a sudden, the story had veered again. Max had tried to focus. Word after word, Hamish had kept talking, on and on, until the meaning began to blend. Until all Max could hear was white noise, coming in and out, blood rushing in his ears. Max still hadn't understood, finding it impossible to combine it all to form a conclusion.

Paternity test. Daughter. Always known. Love. Protect. Yours. Yours. Yours.

And then Max had heard his name.

"I took what was yours."

"Max." This time it had been Lucie calling his name.

That's when Max had stopped breathing. Who was his? Lucie?

Then the name . . . Bella. Only then had it made sense.

The tears were rolling freely down Lucie's face in streams, right off the end of her chin like a tap, landing on her clasped hands. And bloody Hamish kept on talking, while all Max could do was stare at those tears.

"Max . . ." Her voice was a whisper. "Max," she repeated over Hamish's drone.

Max blinked, shook his head and stood, hands limp by his side. He watched Lucie put her hand on the arm of the sofa to hoist herself up. Doug rose to help her until they were all standing – the situation far too grave to remain seated.

Lucie took a step.

"Don't."

"Max, I . . . I don't know what to say. Please, let me explain."

He walked into the hall and she followed him, clutching her stomach, hobbling from where her legs had turned numb.

"Please, wait."

"When did you know?" He whipped round to face her.

This time she reached for him, but he stepped back again and her eyes settled on the floor.

"I didn't, not fully. I assumed. I never did any test and I had no idea Hamish knew. It's as much a shock to me." She paused when he didn't respond.

"Really?" His tone was bone dry. "*When* did you know the truth?" he asked again.

"It was after I got that box from Nina that you gave

her to give me. My diary. There was a note."

Max nodded sarcastically. "Ah! the note. You never saw it until then . . . You didn't even remember we'd slept together."

Lucie nodded. "I was such a mess. I had no idea that losing Felicity would do that to me."

"So when did you know, Lucie?" This time he spoke through gritted teeth.

"Bella was nearly six months old. Nina was moving house. She'd had the box in the garage." Lucie stared at her feet.

"So what's that? Thirteen years?"

Lucie swallowed, not knowing how to answer, afraid to lift her eyes.

"So, for thirteen years, you've lied?" His voice changed, now saturated with more than shock.

Lucie looked up.

"For thirteen years, both of you have robbed me of the life I was supposed to have."

Lucie let out an anguished whimper, but this time Max didn't seem to care.

"I was married. We were a family – and Hamish adores her. She adores him. I . . . I was in too deep. You *have* to understand. I was so alone."

Max snorted. "Alone! Alone?! You were never alone, Lucie. You just couldn't see it. I used to think you were the most honest person in the world, but *him*?" Max gestured back towards the archway. "He's right. You *are* a liar. A bare-faced liar. Just like him. He stole money, you stole my life. All these years, I've pined for you like a fool, and today, earlier, you tell me you've always loved me . . ."

"I do. Max, I . . . I want to make it right."

"Would you *ever* have told me?"

"I was going to. I swear. After this business with Hamish. I told you there was something I needed to tell you . . ."

Max reached for the door handle and swung it open.

"I don't believe you. I don't believe anything you say." Then he paused. "*I* would have loved her, too – and you, if you gave me the chance. Without lies or deceit. *I* would have loved both of you. But you and Hamish are perfect for each other, I see that now."

"Max . . ."

But he was already gone, once more walking towards his car, only this time, there would be no going back.

Chapter forty-three

Doug

Creeping back into the room, Doug peered at where Lucie was asleep on the sofa, at last. He watched her for a moment, lying with the truth now laid bare. It was all out there now. No stone left unturned, no further revelations to be made. Did she look at peace? Or was she now more troubled than she'd ever been?

Doug reached out as if to shake her awake, then stopped himself. Instead, he sat on the sofa opposite and rested his head back. More than anything, he wanted to assure Lucie that everything was going to be all right and that she'd done the right thing earlier, but all of a sudden, he wasn't so sure.

"Don't disturb the past." Rose had always been adamant about that.

Oh, Christ, what had he done?

Doug hadn't disturbed *his* past, he'd violated someone else's. That said, how was he to have known that in doing so, he'd destroy Lucie's future? Watching it all play out had been harrowing. In the end, it had become less about the crime committed and more about life – mistakes, an error of judgment, but perhaps worst of all, missed opportunities. That was what he'd heard over and over – a million missed opportunities. For Lucie – to be with the person she loved. For Max – to have had the chance to be a father to his daughter and a husband to Lucie. For Hamish – to have done the right thing and come clean about the discovery that he wasn't Bella's father.

Then again, Lucie had lied about that, too.

Perhaps Doug was biased, but he could appreciate why Lucie had kept Bella's parentage a secret from both Hamish and Max. Lucie had genuinely believed she'd been doing the right thing, acting with the best intentions. After marrying Hamish and realising her error, she'd stuck it out – done her time, so to speak. Of course, *that* admission hadn't come as news to Doug. She'd already told him. No. It was Lucie's other disclosure that had momentarily shaken Doug – that it was her who'd taken and hidden the jewellery.

Had Doug been shocked? Not really. Who could blame her? He'd been able to hear the hopelessness in her voice. Doug *knew* Lucie. She hadn't been acting out of hunger. Lucie had been afraid.

As soon as she'd admitted it, he'd wanted to rush over to the sofa and pull out the recording device concealed there to grab Hamish's confession. Again, biased, Doug could understand why she'd taken her jewellery. It had been to keep a small sense of security, in case the truth about Bella ever came out and she'd find herself having to start over. She hadn't even known when she took the jewellery what actually lay ahead, nor that it was Hamish who'd ransacked the house – that she was now possibly facing arrest. It had all been for nothing.

* * *

"I should have taken that jewellery, sold it and left for Ireland. I should have gone long ago. I'm an idiot. What happens now?"

Doug had returned from delivering Hamish to the police station to find Lucie in a state, eyes wild, frantically clawing at her hair.

Doug sat beside her. "Hamish has been arrested," he revealed calmly. "I assume he'll be let out on bail in a few days – if there's money to pay it, that is – then it's a case of awaiting trial, which is usually about three months later."

Lucie stared at him, trying to take it all in. "He's in jail! Is he okay?"

Doug smiled – after everything, Lucie was still concerned for him. "In custody. Hamish was surprisingly calm. And you've been cleared, Lucie."

"Just like that?"

"Yes. Hamish has admitted to everything. They have their confession."

"Oh my God. Thank God." She was breathing heavily.

Doug had to admit that Hamish had surprised him. After an initial temper earlier that day, he'd calmed quickly, resigning himself to his fate. In the end, they hadn't even needed the recording, which, by the by, now implicated Lucie. Doug had already destroyed it. Hamish's side of the story was almost moving, if it hadn't been so deplorable.

"Will you do me a favour, mate?" He'd turned to Doug outside the police station. "Look out for her, will you? If you can. Make sure she and Max get their shit together." Hamish had shaken his head in surprise. "I thought Max would step in immediately . . . wonders never cease. He was always a bit emotionally inept. Didn't think he'd storm off that way. I basically handed him my wife, on a plate . . ."

Doug hadn't bothered telling Hamish that he'd missed the point and that the only emotionally stunted person in the room that day had been him, Hamish. It was almost amusing, in a dark comedy sort of way. Hamish's eccentricity and non-plussed attitude were somewhat commendable.

"What do you reckon we're looking at here, Doug? How long inside?"

"Hard to say. Handing yourself in will help. Being honest, regretful."

Hamish nodded along.

"You might struggle with the regretful," Doug added.

"I *am* sorry. I didn't mean to hurt to Lucie, or the kids. I regret that – does that count?"

"It does. I suppose. Could be five to eight years, probably in low security."

"Summer camp prison, right? I can do that. Could be worse."

Could be worse? Not for Lucie. For Lucie, it couldn't possibly be worse.

Was it all Doug's fault? Should he have turned a blind eye? Pretended that it had been a legitimate burglary? No. Hamish had gone too far. The bank was after him also. Sooner or later, it would all have come out.

Doug wondered then, even without his intervention, would Lucie have ended up meeting Max again. He presumed that might have happened, too. Perhaps she may never have admitted that Max was Bella's father. But Doug had a feeling that that, too, someday, would have found its way to the surface.

Help her.

That's all Doug had wanted to do.

Had he helped? Well, he'd prevented her from getting arrested. He'd revealed the truth about Hamish. He supposed he'd achieved what he'd set out to do. Doug could leave now, allow Lucie to move on with her life.

"Have you not learned anything?"

The words were so vivid that Doug jerked forwards, expecting to see Rose standing there with her arms folded, tapping her foot. Instead, his eyes settled on Lucie. Yes, Doug could leave now. Lucie had told him as much earlier.

"Thanks," Lucie had said after the tears had dried up, replaced by a mottled face and dead eyes.

"For what?"

"It could have turned out far worse if it wasn't for you."

"Could it?" Doug raised his eyebrows and laughed.

For the first time, she smiled.

"I had no idea you were going to confess *everything*, Lucie. It was quite the day. Why did you decide to do it? Tell Max that way."

She shrugged. "It seemed right, with everyone there. Anyway, it was Hamish who told him in the end. I still can't believe he knew. I don't know whether I admire him or hate him for not telling me before."

"Hmm. Tough one. He's some man." Doug opened his eyes wide. "I think he, too, was trying to do the right thing, bizarrely."

"I'm sorry I didn't tell you what I'd done."

Doug patted her hand. "That's our secret now, okay? One little one can't hurt. But please don't sell any of the jewellery. All right?"

She nodded weakly. The people who mattered knew the truth. This little secret was for the good of Bella and Declan. Lucie could swallow that.

"Although, I might have to sell it all after this. I'm stone broke." She rolled her eyes. "I can't even think past today."

"You'll be okay. We won't see you starve."

Lucie nodded gratefully, then smiled. "You know what it was like . . . ? It was like shaving my legs, then waxing them immediately after, then getting laser hair removal and then climbing into a bath filled with acid."

Doug grinned. "I could only identify with the acid bath. I've never been big on hair removal!" He turned serious. "I'm sorry for all this. I'm sorry I lied to you about who I was."

Lucie nodded again. "I can hardly be annoyed with you, can I? After what I've done!"

"I suppose not. But I *am* sorry. Max . . . he'll come round."

"You know what, Doug, I don't think he will," she exhaled. "Some cuts are too deep. All I can do now is what I should have done a long time ago. Stand on my own two feet.

"I'm going to explain it to Bella, and Declan somehow, beg them to forgive me, and then I'm going to start again. With no baggage and no more lies . . ." she'd paused. "You can go now, Doug, if you want. Your job is done. Thank you. You . . . well, in a way you did save me."

Watching her now, Doug wondered if Lucie had got it wrong and if it was, in fact, her who'd saved him. Yes, Doug could go, he pondered as he continued to sit. Off he could go, back to his lonely house, talking to his dead wife's ashes on the shelf, back to watching the ocean every day, at the waves coming in and rolling out, wishing he could go with them. Doug could go now. He'd done his job.

"You're still here?" Lucie was leaning on one elbow, watching him in the half-light.

"I am."

"Nowhere to go, either?"

"No. I wanted to ask you a favour."

"Anything."

Chapter forty-four

Lucie

"You see, one action leads to another and another. I've always said. It's how I met Rose. It was how I came to meet you."

Lucie tried to smile at the tale she'd already heard at least a hundred times. She knew Doug was trying to distract her – take her mind off the fact that she was about to face the final hurdle, perhaps the most terrifying one of all. It was three weeks now since it had all happened, since that day – the day of reckoning, when her world had ultimately imploded.

Then again, it had already fallen apart long before that, Lucie could see that now. All it had taken was that final nudge for it to disintegrate fully into dust before her eyes. Even since then, a lot had changed. Lucie was still trying to get her head around it all and settle in her new surroundings. Physically, she was feeling much better – her body almost fully mended after being torn apart during the removal of the fruity fibroids. She supposed her soul was healing, too – more slowly, but it was a start.

There was an absolute comfort in knowing that everything that could possibly come out, now had. All of the dirty laundry now loose from the cupboards, the skeletons walking freely once more. It had been Ann's idea to give Lucie an extra couple of weeks before bringing Bella and Declan home to Australia.

"It'll give you time to catch your breath. A lot has happened."

That was an understatement.

Ann had listened with disbelief over the phone when Lucie told her everything from Hamish coming home, to the truth about Max being Bella's father, to the "stolen" jewellery.

"Mother of Jesus. And I thought my life was exciting. Christ, Lu. Are you okay?"

"I think so. Are you shocked?"

"Not really. There's very little that astounds me nowadays. Aren't we some bonkers family."

"I'm sorry I didn't tell you before. I wasn't well after Felicity died. I was really suffering, then I fell pregnant. It was why I didn't come to get you in Ireland after Felicity died."

"Yeah, I can see that now. You don't need to explain it to me. People do strange things when they're hurting."

"I wanted you to know, though."

"It doesn't matter. It really doesn't. All that matters now is the future."

"I thought I'd be able to carry it with me my entire life, but I couldn't. I just couldn't any more."

"You've done the right thing. I know it's hard to see now, but it will work out. Maybe even with—"

"No. Not with Max. That bridge is burned."

"Maybe in time . . ."

"Do you think Bella will ever forgive me?"

"Yeah. I think she will in time. Eventually, she'll understand. She's still so young. I suspect she'll make you pay first, though," Ann laughed.

"Do the crime, pay the time." It had become Lucie's latest catchphrase.

Lucie deserved both Bella's anger and to be punished. But she was going to take her punishment on the chin, Hamish-style.

"I'm going for a walk," Lucie called to Doug now.

"Want me to come?" He popped his head in the conservatory.

"No, thanks. I'm just going to get my thoughts in order before—"

"Fair enough. See you in a while."

Heading out of the back door, Lucie made her way to the beach. It really was beautiful here. The beachside cottage was precisely where she'd always imagined she might live someday. Of course, minus the seventy-year-old widower. The favour Doug had asked was for Lucie to stay with him a while. It had been typical of Doug, wrapping it up with bows as if she'd be doing him a service.

"It's not good for me being on my own in the cottage. You'd be the one helping me out if you think about it."

Lucie had agreed straightaway. She didn't want to be on her own, either. Besides, what choice did she have? Her own house would be gone soon enough and there was a spare room for the children here. Bella would love that! Lucie could almost picture the face of disgust when her daughter realised she'd be sharing a room with Declan. It would probably hit her harder than any of the other news.

It was a temporary situation, of course, but it felt like a peaceful place to heal – and Lucie was sure Doug would act as a useful buffer to ensure Bella couldn't completely lose it at her mother. Despite everything, Lucie was dying to see them both. The longing for Bella and Declan had changed to a physical pain in the pit of her stomach.

Sitting down on the sand, Lucie pulled her knees in tight, cradling them, and rested her head down. It was hard not to think of Max, although she was trying not to. Undoubtedly, the agony would eventually pass whenever he shot into her thoughts. Which would be quite a lot as soon as Bella arrived back. Perhaps in time, it would morph to a dull ache, then a niggling presence. *Wouldn't it?*

Lucie would be lying if she didn't admit that once or twice, she'd taken out the small red box from the drawer beside her bed to slip the emerald ring on her finger. Closing her eyes, she could almost imagine the life she might have had with Max by her side. But yes, Lucie would be lying to herself – and that was something she'd never do again. Instead, she'd keep the ring as a reminder of what she'd done. Not only failing to be honest with Max, but most of all with herself.

Max hadn't contacted her since that day. Although Hamish had seen him, just once. Max had turned up to pay Hamish's bail before telling him he was on his own now and that he never wanted to see him again. He'd said that he'd like to meet Bella if she wanted to and that maybe when the dust settled, he could build a relationship with her.

"But with regard you, Lu," Hamish told her. "I'm afraid that ship has sailed. He was pretty clear on that. He asked me to give you this."

It was a note with an email address and phone number. Nothing else. No words, no instructions, just clearly written digits.

"He said it's for Bella. If we decide to tell her about him, she can contact him directly."

Hamish watched her face fall.

"I'm sorry, Lu. I really am. For everything. I thought for once, coming clean about the truth, that it would all work out for you. I thought—"

"It's okay, Hamish." She took a sharp breath in and swallowed her tears. "We both screwed up. We built a life on lies. I should never have married you, nor you me. Can I ask you something?"

"Yep."

They'd been sitting on Doug's decking outside.

"Were you ever unfaithful to me?"

Hamish regarded her for a moment, leaned back in his chair, his arm slung over the back.

"Would you believe me if I said I never was?" he grinned.

"Probably not," Lucie smirked.

"Well, for the record, I wasn't, not once."

Lucie raised an eyebrow. "But we weren't exactly swinging from the bedposts, were we?" The side of her face was twitching in amusement.

"You can say that again. What a let-down." Hamish was laughing before his smile faded. "I suppose I didn't realise how much pressure I was under with all the lies. I know I can play the cool exterior to a T, but I was shitting it, Lu, deep down. *All* the time. It wasn't exactly a great aphrodisiac! Not that I'd have any problem in that department now I'm free from the burden. If you fancied a quickie for old time's sake?"

"You're grand, thanks," she giggled then frowned. "Really? Never?"

He shook his head. "You sound *so* surprised."

"Do you blame me?" She was laughing now.

"Nah."

"I almost wish you had been. It would give me more of a reason to hate you."

"Have I not given you enough?"

"But that face . . ." Lucie reached over to squeeze his cheek. "Hard to hate that face."

"The face of an angel, that is."

"With the morals of a complete scumbag."

"So, what now?" he'd asked.

They'd agreed to face the children together. There was a lot of explaining to do and reassurances to be made. For once, Hamish was agreeable to everything. Truth be told? Lucie would have been lost without him. Even Hamish and Doug seemed to have found common ground, able to converse politely whenever Hamish popped over to see Lucie. The house was gone. It would be sold by the bank and while Hamish awaited trial, he was staying with his mother, Vera.

"Vera has a *new* word," Hamish revealed. "Despicable. It's a little heavier than disappointing. I'm almost looking forward to prison. Anything to get the hell away from her."

"Will it really come to that?"

But Doug had already told Lucie that it would. The law was only too happy to make an example out of those who tried to diddle the system – and Hamish had certainly diddled.

Lucie lifted her head to look at the sea, then closed her eyes against the wind.

"It *is* going to be okay." Lucie could hear Felicity clearly.

"It will, you know. Jesus, little sis, you made a pig's ear out of all that." Sammy.

"But in the end . . ." Her mother's voice.

"Yes, Mam." Lucie opened her eyes again to stare ahead. "In the end, the truth always comes out."

"I'm proud of you, girl." Her father.

"We all are, aren't we?" Mam.

"We are. Just be yourself. Just be Lu." Felicity.

Lucie could barely see through the tears. For so long she'd wanted nothing more than to be with them all again. She still did, in one way. She always would, but she now had a second chance at life. Lucie had come to realise that over the weeks.

So, she wasn't the young girl she'd once been, arriving in Australia all those years ago. She was now middle-aged, with saggy skin and a slight turkey neck if she held a mirror under her chin and looked down. She had varicose veins and greying hair, lines and wrinkles, all of life's bruises. She'd been chewed up and spat out. Lucie was now less an entire body organ. She had a failed marriage, a broken relationship. Her parents were dead. Her brother was gone, her best friend, too. The father of one of her children was about to go to jail. The father of the other never wanted to see her again. She was going through the menopause. She had no job, no home – *that* was the truth.

But Lucie had lived – enough for several lifetimes – and she was going to keep on living until she got it right.

"We all get two lives," Doug had told her again the night before. "That's what my Rose used to say. And the second one starts as soon as you realise you only have one."

So, this was it – her second life.

Lucie had made a lot of mistakes, but she'd admitted them. She'd told the truth, and now she was free. She had people – friends, family. Not *everyone* she wanted in her life, but enough with which to rebuild one.

"It's going to be okay. In the end, it always is," Ann had told her over the phone. "It's what you said to me once."

"I know. I believe me."

Lucie looked out one last time before standing up and walking back towards the house. She could see Hamish standing on the decking with Doug, waiting for her. Ann and the children were on their way. The final hurdle. It *would* be okay. And Lucie would smile again, just not yet – but in time she was sure she would. She stopped briefly. Then she turned back towards the ocean and felt the corners of her face lifting ever so slightly.

"I have to go now," Lucie whispered as the wind picked up, whipping her curls around her face. "Wish me luck."

Epilogue

Six months later . . .

Ann raised her eyebrows as Bella came and sat beside her mother and briefly rested her head on Lucie's shoulder. Lucie tried not to react but gently reached up and patted her daughter's face.

"Can I go and meet my friends? There's a few of them up on the green for a game of rounders."

"That should be okay. Don't be too late. It's a big day tomorrow."

"I won't. Text when me when you want me to walk back up." Bella stood, made to leave and then stopped. "Dec," she called to her brother. "You wanna come?"

Declan shot up from where he was lying on the grass beside them.

"Really?"

Bella nodded and rolled her eyes.

"Do you want money? Do I have to pay you?" He narrowed his eyes at his sister's unusually generous offer.

"Always. Ten euro," Bella whispered, then clocked her mother's frown. "Okay. Okay. This one is free. Are you coming or not?" Bella went to walk away.

"I'm coming, I'm coming."

"Mind him," Lucie called over her shoulder before turning back to Ann, who was beaming.

"I told you she'd come round."

"Took long enough," Lucie groaned. "But we're getting there. It hasn't been easy on her – on either of them, really. But we're slowly getting there. Having this to look forward to has helped. Are you all set?"

Ann nodded with a huge grin. "I think so. Weddings *are* my business, after all, so I should be able to pull off my own one. I can't believe I'm getting married tomorrow," she squealed nervously. "For the second time!"

They both laughed.

"I'm sorry you had to postpone the wedding because of us," Lucie said.

"It was nothing. You had to be here. I wouldn't do it without you."

Having Ann's wedding to look forward to had kept them all focused during the painful months of awaiting Hamish's trial. They'd gone to visit Hamish once again in his new home before leaving for Ireland. He seemed happy enough, as well as could be expected for someone in prison. It certainly wasn't like the usual prisons in Ireland, or the ones you see on TV. It actually was like some form of grown-up male summer camp. Hamish's positivity and sense of humour about it all had kept the kids buoyed. Doug had been right. Hamish had been handed down five years for fraud.

"The old white-collar crime. I'll be out in three with good behaviour, wait and see. Let it be a lesson to you, kids!" He'd wagged his finger at them after receiving the sentence two months before.

Lucie was still shocked by how unfazed Hamish was by everything, but since then, Hamish had admitted several times that for many years he'd been living on his nerves. He now seemed relieved, content with the idea of a more relaxed life ahead when he came out the other side.

"I think I'll be a chef, or something uncomplicated," he'd mused. "I work in the kitchens here and I'm not bad."

"Wow, Dad. This is cool," Declan had said, sitting down on the picnic table in the visitors' section of the low-security prison and looking around.

"Definitely not cool, kiddo, but not too bad. Don't go getting any ideas. You hear me?" Then he'd looked at Bella. "How are you doing, girl?"

Bella had smiled. "I'm okay, Dad." Then, "Obviously so embarrassed by all of this . . ." She'd shot Lucie a glare.

"Hey, be nice to your mother. This isn't *all* her fault."

Bella had been anything but pleasant to Lucie, screaming at her, calling her every name under the sun.

"I never want to meet *him*. *Never.* Who the hell is he, anyway? *Dad* is my dad."

Of course, Lucie had known that Bella would remain loyal to Hamish. Even with all of his mistakes, Bella still adored him. No, it was Lucie with whom she was furious.

"How could you? You've ruined everything and now look where we are! Living with some weird old man, in the middle of nowhere. I have zero friends and my father's a crim. My mother's a . . . *prossie* and a liar."

Lucie had calmly reminded Bella that being with only two men in her entire life did *not* make her a prostitute. She'd admitted her mistakes and was now trying to make everything right. There was so much more Lucie could have said – blamed Hamish more, told Bella that it was because of him and not Lucie that saw them living with the *weird* old man. But she'd held her tongue, as it was to be expected. Their lives had been turned upside down.

Funnily enough, it was the *weird* old man who'd eventually got through to Bella. Telling her all about life, people, the mistakes they make, the odd, inexplicable things ordinary people do sometimes – the strange secrets they carry. Lucie would sit on the decking and watch them walk along the beach together in the evenings after Bella and Declan returned from their new "terrible" public school.

"Bella loves it really, Mum," Declan assured. "I do, too. It's much better than Woodfield."

Declan was perhaps more like Hamish than they'd initially thought – taking everything in his stride. Bella, it turned out, was Lucie – frantically trying to work through it, figure it all out. But bit by bit, Bella started to come round, thanks to Doug.

In the end, Bella fell for Doug in the same way Lucie had, adoring his calming presence. He was a distraction from her anger, and she loved hearing Doug's stories about Rose and their life together. Doug was going to teach Bella to dive and in return, Bella agreed to help Doug find Rose's family in Ireland. Doug had watched in fascination as Bella scoured social media and the internet with the small snippets of information Doug was able to give her.

"A detective in the making." He'd ruffled Bella's hair proudly when she showed him what she'd found.

Rose's sister, Iris, was still alive, or at least she had been a month before at what looked like her granddaughter's communion. A face familiar to Rose's stared out at Doug from the laptop. An email was sent and they awaited a response.

Then the phone call came.

Iris was a widow, still living in Wexford, in the same town Rose had left behind all that time ago.

"She sounds nice," Doug told Lucie after the call. "Regretful. She was happy to hear that Rose had had a nice life here, after everything."

"Everything?"

Doug had shaken his head. "You were right, Lucie. There was a reason she never went back."

"It was a long time ago," Iris had told him down the phone. Her accent was so like Rose's. "I don't want to go dragging up the past. I'm just happy to know she was loved. I made my mistakes, too. But there hasn't been a day that goes by that I haven't wondered, what if . . ."

Doug could hear her tears.

"Can you tell me about it?" he asked. "It sounds silly. I know she's already gone, but I think she wanted me to know, if that makes sense."

"I can," Iris began. "Do you know what happened to Rose on that dive?"

"Yes, she told me."

"Well, afterwards, she wasn't the same. Then Mam died. My husband, he was . . . I'd love to say he was a good man, but he was a shit, actually," Iris chuckled. "I didn't know until years later, but he'd had Mam sign over the house to us, leaving Rose with nothing. When Rose found out about it, it hurt her to her core, thinking Mam would leave her destitute. We were on bad terms already. Let's just say, I didn't agree with her life choices.

"Ah! it was a different time, you see, and I was her older sister. I suppose I was disapproving of her. Anyway, she called over to confront us. She didn't want anything that wasn't rightfully hers. Himself was having none of it.

I did what I was told back then," she paused. "If I could have my time over, I'd do it differently, believe me. Anyway, Rose took what was hers and she left."

Doug had listened, wondering what she meant.

"Took what that was hers?"

"She stole the chequebook. She must have known I kept it in the kitchen dresser. Our mam used to keep it in the same place in her house. Then she forged my signature on a cheque and went to the bank. Sure, we all knew each other in the town, so they cashed it for her. Again, it was a different time, more informal.

"She had to request the amount and they had it in for her the next day, then she bolted. Rose could be very persuasive," Iris chuckled. "It was only that afternoon that the poor young fella called me from the bank. 'We cashed the cheque for Rose,' he says. 'Your signature was enough, but when you get a minute, can you ask your husband to pop over and put his name to it, too. For the records,' he said. Well, all hell broke loose."

"What happened?"

"Rose called me from the airport. She wouldn't tell me where she was going. She said she needed to get away, to start again, and that she was sorry, but Rose was only taking what she was owed. I tried to get her to come back, but then himself grabbed the phone. 'The guards have been called. You need to come back,' he was shouting at her.

"I don't know to this day what she said to him, but I'll never forget what he told her. He said if she ever set foot in this country again that she'd be arrested and she'd never see the light of day again. 'If it's the last thing I do,' he said." Iris stopped. "I never heard from her again. My husband died two years later. Good enough for him. But my sister was gone."

* * *

"Another missed opportunity," Doug told Lucie afterwards. "My poor Rose."

Yes, all along there had been a reason she'd never returned to her beloved Ireland.

"I'm glad I know the truth now, thanks to Bella. I wish Rose had told me. I could have fixed it for her."

"Like you fixed me." Lucie had patted his arm. "You said Rose sent you a sign to help me, and you did, Doug. More than you'll ever know."

Doug had left for Ireland shortly after that to reunite Rose and her sister, Iris, after thirty years apart. Together, Doug and Iris had released Rose's ashes from the urn, to watch them circle in the wind before floating out to sea. She was finally home – free.

"As soon as you're sorted," Doug told Lucie when he came back from his trip, "I'm going to sell the house. I won't see you out on your ear, though. What I need is a little apartment, no upkeep. I'm going to buy a little boat for myself. There's a nice social life with fishing. It'll do me good."

Doug was moving on and Lucie was happy for him. It was time she did the same.

Sitting here now in the garden of Knockmore House, Lucie smiled at Ann.

"What are you grinning at?" Ann asked.

"Nothing, just thinking."

"Oh yeah?"

"Yeah, about life and what the hell it all means."

"Now that's very deep altogether," Ann giggled.

Lucie said nothing.

"Are you sure about the house?" Ann asked. "Is it what you really want?"

"It is. Besides, I've no other choice, do I? Are you okay with it?"

"This is my home now . . ." Ann gestured towards Knockmore House.

"Fierce posh, so you are," Lucie laughed. "A far cry from the little house in the Estates."

Earlier that day, they'd walked around the rooms of the house in the Estates where Lucie had been born, where she'd grown up and been a part of the Maguire household. It was like looking back at a movie reel.

"You did a great job doing it up, Ann. It'll make a lovely home."

"It will. For the right person." Ann had smiled at her aunt. "Are you ready?"

Together, they'd walked outside before lifting the For Sale sign and hammering it into the grass at the front. It was time to let it go. To start a new phase. They both agreed. Lucie needed the money and Ann wanted to help her.

The sale of the house would be enough for Lucie to pay off some debts and start life again in Australia, where she was meant to be. She'd secured a job at the hospital in Sydney, back nursing, back to her roots and her passion. She and Nina would have the chance to work together again, just like old times. Lucie was starting as soon as they returned from Ireland. She was going to buy Doug's house after falling in love with the little cottage, filled with lovely memories.

"It's what I was hoping," Doug assured when she phoned to tell him her plan. "As soon as you get back, we'll sort out the details."

"You'll still come and visit?"

"All the time. Declan and I have big plans for doing up my new boat and don't forget, I'll be teaching Bella to dive."

Doug was relishing spending time with the children, acting like the grandfather they'd never had, and he was such a positive influence on them all. Back in Australia, the kids would be able to visit Hamish and Lucie would be near work.

Lucie had been left with nothing, but in a short space of time, she'd begun to rebuild, just like Ann had once done. Since it all happened, Lucie and Ann had talked a lot about the past – Lucie admitting how she'd felt all those years ago about Felicity moving in on her life in Knockmore.

"It's understandable," Ann had said. "Sibling rivalry, I suppose. You were like sisters."

"We were," Lucie admitted. "Jesus, I wanted to kill her after she died. Kill her!"

Ann had giggled at her choice of words. "That would have been hard."

"Ah, you know what I mean. When I was back here for the funeral, I was so pissed off with Fliss for dying that I stuck my fingers up at the coffin when no one was looking."

The pair had burst out laughing.

"Ah, Lu, that's why I love you. Mam would have loved that story. It's good to hear you laugh again."

Yes, Lucie had started laughing, once again able to see the funny side of life. In fact, once she'd started, she was barely able to stop. Albeit at times it was hysterical, wondering if everything would work out, at others it was genuine heartfelt laughter, the type that would see tears of joy, in place of despair, rolling down her face. Nothing was perfect, but she was getting there.

* * *

"What?" Ann asked again. "The face on you."

"I think I have it. The meaning of it all."

"Go on."

"Well, life is like a kitchen," Lucie began.

Ann was giggling already, rolling her eyes. "Here we go! A kitchen? After everything that's happened, you liken it to a kitchen!"

"Yeah, a kitchen. Hear me out. So, every day you tidy it and it gets messy again, but you just keep tidying. Again and again. On and on it goes. It never stops, but it's just what you do."

"Okay, I think I get you."

"Yeah, and remember, in a kitchen, that's where life takes place. The best of times. And the worst," Lucie smiled before continuing. "And every so often you might get the kitchen painted because it looks a bit stale. Shake life up a bit! And someday it might need a total remodel. Like, get rid of everything and start again," Lucie shrugged. "And who knows, you might end up with a better kitchen than you ever had before."

Ann was laughing out loud now. "Get rid of the husband, you mean! We've both done that now. I'm not sure I'll ever remodel again!"

"No, you won't need to. Not if you keep your spice drawer in order." Lucie was giggling, too. "Don't go leaving any old spice jars in there for years. Free the musty old saffron that you only used once to make a soggy paella. Otherwise, the saffron will grow legs, climb out of the cupboard and walk across the kitchen for all to see."

"So the saffron is the secrets, tucked inside the drawer, waiting to leap out?"

Lucie's shoulders were shaking. "And boy when it's ready, will that saffron leap! Now you have it, Ann! Keep your condiments straight. And don't forget to mind your appliances," Lucie finished smugly.

Ann gestured towards the upstairs window, where a figure appeared and waved down at them. Lucie turned and waved back, smiling broadly, and then winked at Ann.

"Is he like a new appliance, then?" Ann raised her eyebrows.

"I suppose you could say that's my new fridge," Lucie laughed. "And a fine big fridge *he* is. He's like one of those ones with the double doors and the thing inside that makes the ice. Real fancy."

"And is it going to be an integrated fridge, do you think?" Ann asked.

"Maybe someday," Lucie grinned. "But for now we're going to leave it free-standing. Just in case ..."

"I heard you were having trouble sleeping?"

Lucie had opened the front door of the cottage three months before to see Max standing there.

"I am," she answered, the tears already welling in her eyes. "How did you know?"

"I had an interesting conversation last week with someone about missed opportunities. Not letting life pass you by because you just never know what's around the next corner. He went on and on about one small action leading to—"

"Another and another," Lucie grinned through the tears. "It's how he met—"

"His wife." Max finished her sentence this time. "Lucie, I . . ."

"Please, Max. I'm so sorry for everything. Doug's

right. Not having a life with you *was* . . . is, a missed opportunity. I'll live to regret it for the rest of mine."

"We can't have that now, can we?"

He was smiling and she couldn't help grinning back.

"I also had a call from my darling cousin, Hamish, in prison, who gave me his blessing to 'Screw his wife,' was how he put it."

"Charming."

"I told him I'm not ready for that, but that I'd keep him posted," Max paused. "If you were willing to . . . I don't know . . . go on a date with me? I still have a lot of questions and I don't know what the future holds, but I'm hoping you'll be in it somewhere and . . ." He looked coy.

"Bella?" Lucie offered.

Max nodded. "And Declan, of course. And I suppose I could learn to tolerate Hamish."

"Can you hug me, Max, please? Just hug me."

"You're not fooling me, Lucie Woods," Ann said now. "Playing it all coy. You and Max are perfect together. And Bella seems really comfortable with him."

"I just don't want to rush things. Bella's getting on really well with Max and he's great with her – not too pushy. He talks about Hamish with her, too, which must be hard for him. I don't want to mess that up for her. God, Ann, he's even great with Declan. He's just great," Lucie smiled contently.

They *had* tried to take it slow, but it was hard not to slot back in where they'd left off.

"You won't mess it up. Go with it, enjoy it. Does it feel right?"

"It feels like truth."

"So, there's your answer."

Lucie stood and walked over to sit down beside Ann and put her arm around her. "Are you going to keep your name?"

Ann shook her head. "No, I'm going to be Ann O'Keefe. You? Will you change back to Maguire?"

"No, I'll stay Lucie Woods. It would feel weird to have a different name from Bella and Dec."

"Understandable. So that's it, then. From tomorrow, there'll be no more Maguires."

Lucie put her head back to look up at the sky. "Except up there somewhere." Then she turned to Ann. "You know, I always thought it was *their* story – Felicity and Sammy's big love story, and that I was just a bit player in it. Then all of a sudden, it was bloody *all* about me. Do you know what I mean?"

"I do," Ann nodded. "But it was always about you, too, Lu, and me. It's all of our stories. And someday it'll be all about Bella and Declan – and maybe even my own children. Life will just keep going. On and on."

Lucie rested her head on Ann's shoulder and smiled. On and on it would go, evolving and changing forever, and that was the truth.

The End.

Now that you're hooked why not try Judith Cuffe's new book

Unexpected Events

Coming spring 2021

Here's a sneak preview of Chapter One

Unexpected Events

Seren:
Look for something, find something else and realise that what you've found is more suited to you than what you thought you were looking for.

Gigi:
Greed, in the end, fails even the greedy.

Marie Helene:
Before you embark on a journey of revenge, dig two graves.

Nicole:
You see a person's true colours when you're no longer beneficial to their life.

Now

The air is heavy, so dense that she's finding it difficult to breathe. Her diaphragm is pressing against her lungs no matter how hard she tries to relax, to breathe through whatever emotion she's feeling. The colours in the sky are beginning to descend, altering before her eyes, morphing from purple to orange to yellow . . . to black. She reaches her hand out as if to touch it one last time, this dusky light – the end of one day and the start of another.

When she'd first arrived here, she'd gaze at the setting sun, in awe of the tones, the natural sounds, inhaling the exotic fragrances, the sense of longed-for freedom. She'd never been part of anything like it before, so opposite to where she came from, where the air is thinner, the sky so often grey, the breeze fresh, the sounds somewhat manufactured. Here, she'd felt nestled in warmth, peace, headiness, light – as if transported to the place where all life began.

For the first time in a long time, she'd felt home, part of the grand design. Undoubtedly, she'd been led here by some higher power. To this place with its lush green fields, vineyards heavy with fruit, rows and rows of grapes ripening, their tones slowly taking form. Deepening to almost black, until they were ready to be picked – lovingly and gently removed from the vine and transported to the winery to be converted into rich red wines. The types of wines that had so often sat breathing at her kitchen table, to be savoured over dinner with friends all those years, when life was simpler. It made sense now that those wines tasted how they had: firm, earthy, tannic, with traces of blackberry, vanilla, cherry – strong and dark. She understood the process now, what it takes to work the land, to make something extraordinary out of something so natural.

It takes blood.

Should she have known?

Should she have anticipated that the journey into the unknown would open up parts of the past that should have remained as she'd considered them – perfect? But then, how could anything in this place be anything less than it seemed, where life is so vibrant. Where the rustic beauty of the earth contrasts against sprawling structures of grandeur – the likes of which she'd only seen in books and on postcards delivered to her back home in Ireland, from those who journeyed to reach out and touch it for themselves. They still hang there, vision after vision, pinned to large corkboards, running the length of the little wine shop in Ballycross, next to the home they'd made – together.

How strange it now seemed that all those years, they'd never made the time to come here, to the place of which they'd spoken so knowledgeably, to land over which she'd felt some sort of right. In many ways, she'd felt as though she'd already seen it – or could imagine it, at least, from stories told. Or perhaps she hadn't wanted to shatter the illusion of those majestic stone buildings rich with history, contrasted by living fields, and *that* setting sun.

Perhaps she was naïve. Maybe she was a fool. But when it came to it, she'd decided *she did* need to see it for herself, to uncover the reasons as to why she'd never known that this slice of life had even existed, to understand why it had been kept secret. How different her memories would be if she hadn't endeavoured to decipher the mystery.

Now, she was connected to these people. And yet, still she couldn't comprehend it, no matter what way she looked at it. But then, wasn't that the point? Accept that we aren't always meant to understand life's twists and turns, the unexpected patterns that can lead us along curious paths. Despite what had happened lately, in many ways, the universe had delivered. She'd been lucky for much of her life, despite the unanticipated sorrows, the hollowness that still took her by surprise at how life could be so inexplicably cruel. But then, there had always been a balance – parts of her life had been as beautiful as they had devastating.

"Good with the bad," her mother often told her. "No one gets everything. That's not how it works, but be open. Accept everything as part of the journey. Eventually, the universe see you right."

From where she stood observing now, masked in the shadows, trying to control her ragged breath, it was impossible to consider that *this* could have been part of the plan, that *this* was where she was meant to end up. Perhaps she'd unwittingly invited recent events, beckoned to them, opened herself up to them. It was, after all, how she'd been governed to exist from birth – guided by the law of her name – watching the universe bend in her direction, presenting her with seemingly accidental and unexpected fortuitous circumstances.

Throughout the years, even when she'd momentarily lost faith, serendipity would once again reveal itself and her trust in the universe would be restored. That is until her confidence was shattered and she was delivered the ultimate blow – the type of heartache from which you never truly recover.

There had been no sense to that time. No saying powerful enough, no devout belief, no words of wisdom, no explanation to wipe the pain away. For a time, she'd laid to rest what she'd come to consider whimsical beliefs. For a while, she'd seized back control, taken back her power. It was she alone who decided what happened from now on.

But she'd slipped up. It's quickly done when deep down, you still believe in truth, in the power of destiny, in love, fortune and luck.

Did she still believe? How could she? Not any more.

From where she's positioned, near the gate, she can barely make them out. As she's stood wondering what to do next, whether to walk away or finish this out, the light has faded further, so now there's only a suggestion of orange in the distance behind the darkened house. For a moment, it appears as though it's ablaze.

They are barely shadows, the three darkened figures gathered on the balcony, set above the imposing front door that no one ever uses. It's rarely opened, aside from when the rare busload of tourists descend, twice a year, for brief access to the ground-floor rooms inside one of the finest establishments on the left bank of Bordeaux in the Médoc region.

She can picture their faces upon seeing it. They'd mirror her own expression of wonder, the first time she'd set foot inside, when suddenly it had all made sense. She wonders if two of the figures standing there now had been admitted through the main entrance. Perhaps they'd instinctively walked towards the back of the house, to the courtyard with the sandstone fountain, the imposing wall with the arch separating the house from the vineyards, the winery, the outhouses – their purposeful feet crunching against the gravel.

She advances slowly along the driveway, nestled by the oak trees flanking the path. Coming closer, she can see the figures moving, gesticulating expressively in typical French fashion. Raised voices travel across the deserted grounds. She's too far back to understand, her French too rusty to decipher the sounds. Are they discussing her sudden departure? Are there accusations?

In one way, she wishes she was among them. In another, she feels safer spectating from a distance. What's come to light over the weeks is certainly not what she was expecting. It's thwarted and tarnished her past, everything she held dear. Her connection to these people feels like some sort of sick joke, regardless of what they have in common – *him*.

Earlier, she'd almost got as far as the airport before pulling the car in to the side, resting her head back and closing her red-rimmed eyes. All she could picture was his face, the man who'd brought them all together, the man who's still everything to her, despite the revelation that she never truly knew him at all.

Now, there's only one person on that balcony, of whose life she was supposed to be a part. She's come to care for them in a way she never imagined possible. They're the reason she turned the car around earlier, why she's come back. But what if she's wrong? What if they're not as innocent as they seem?

Pausing, she tries to muster the earlier feeling of dread that enveloped her as she roughly shoved her belongings into her bag, glancing over her shoulder as she did so. For the first time in her life, she'd been petrified.

Once again, she glances up at the balcony, following the ornate black iron railings surrounding it, twisting and turning around each other, spiralling. Her head starts to spin. *No.* Turning, she creeps back towards the gate. That's when she hears it.

A scream. A shout. A name.

Her head whips back in time to see a single shadow falling to the ground. It's too slow – its limbs flail pathetically, attempting to latch on to the thick air.

Then a thud – silence.

At that moment, Serendipity Temple is confident of two things: she should never have come here in the first place and worst of all, she's sure that the body splayed on the gravel below the entrance to the chateau was meant to be hers. This time, there's nothing in the atmosphere left to breathe. Her legs falter momentarily, then she runs.

Chapter one

I get the same feeling I often get lately as I drive the final stretch of road from Carrigbyrne to Ballycross – a sudden tightness in my chest, an unexpected lump in my throat. I reach for my bag on the passenger seat, pat it, feeling for the hard plastic shape of my inhaler tucked inside. It's there, just in case I need it. My asthma hasn't been bad in years, but I've become reliant on the presence of the small blue-and-navy device to loosen my lungs when I feel I can't catch my breath. It's on the checklist whenever I leave the house now. Nothing to chance, not any more.

It's a far cry from how I used to be, living openly in the knowledge that anything can happen. Anything used to happen to me all the time. Little positive twists and gifts landing from nowhere, making me feel like the luckiest person alive. Now, it's what I live in fear of – anything could happen. I've learned that "anything" isn't always good.

The road weaves its way along the river, where the

river will open its wide mouth into the harbour, in a never-ending yawn. Sporadically, I acknowledge oncoming cars as I go with the turns. It's a village thing – a full wave for friends, a hand lifted from the steering wheel for acquaintances. For strangers, two fingers, but in a polite way – a curt nod for someone who's got on the wrong side of you but you can't bring yourself to ignore. Luckily, I know the road well. Driving in Ballycross is as much about recognising the car, giving the appropriate salute, than it is about the destination.

"Sure, I only recognised you when you were past me!"

"I still don't know the new car! Hope you didn't think I was ignoring you."

You get to know the licence plate numbers, so you can decipher who's approaching, be ready with your salute. It can be tricky, since so many drive very similar "mammy mobiles" in black or grey. Or white – lately, there's a lot of white, I've noticed that – a mix of five- or indeed seven-seaters, depending on their needs, or perhaps their fortune.

There's no hiding in my own ancient little white van with the name of the shop, "*Quelle Surprise*" – images of bottles of wine proudly emblazoned down the side. We added a coffee cup and a picture of a croissant several years ago when we morphed into a patisserie shop to make use of the morning trade. Even in Ballycross, coffee has become a big thing. People stopping on the way to work for a takeaway blast of caffeine. Mothers meeting after the school drop-off. Tourists. The summer trade is always significant. Everyone wants coffee. "Bigger than wine," I'd enthused when I first had the idea. They go hand in hand, I suppose – coffee in the morning, until lunchtime, then everything tidied up, reverted to what we started off as: wine merchants.

Over the years, we've built up quite a name for being experts in the field, helping to plan the wine list to accompany the menus of many restaurants in Cork. It's so far from what I thought I'd end up doing in life. Wine was never *my* passion – not really. But you might say it became so over the years: that and the coffee.

At the time, adding coffee and pastries to our offering had seemed like the right thing to do. We'd had space in the shop, not to mention the time, and it took off quickly, making us busier than we'd ever been before. At first, I'd loved it. I've always been a morning person. There's subtle energy to the start of each day. Faster than those who come in later in the day to peruse the rustic-looking wooden shelves to find the perfect bottle of wine – usually French. It's our speciality, you might have guessed from the name of the shop.

Lately, though, I find the persistent morning chatter exhausting – an act. I can feel them all watching me as they sit there, sipping from their white mugs, picking up the last bits of flaked pastry from their plates and sucking it from their forefinger – wanting to ask how I am, but not knowing how. It's something else I need to make a decision on – whether or not to continue with the coffee or go back to just wine. I still haven't fully decided what to do. Choices have never been my forte. Until recently, I'd have looked for a sign.

Then again, perhaps there was one. A few months ago, someone picked away parts of the picture of croissant on the side of my van and coloured it in brown with a Sharpie pen. It was a good job – realistic-looking. Now, the van bears the image of what a dog might produce along the river walk leading away from the harbour, over which the local councillors have a field day.

There was an entire debate last year at the council meeting as to whether it sufficed to "stick and flick" canine excrement into the undergrowth. As head of the Traders' Association – a position that had "fallen" upon me – I'd had to go along to the meeting. It got almost as heated as the contents of one of those peach-coloured nappy bags that most people use to pick up their dogs' excrement, only to hang it from a tree to retrieve on the way back home. They'd usually forget, often leaving the "decoration" dangling for weeks before someone got irate enough to dispose of it on their behalf.

The bins they canvassed for were a welcome addition. After all, who wants to walk the river path, looking out at the boats moored uniformly to orange buoys – the wind turbines spinning in the distance, cows grazing the green fields on the other side – swinging the still-warm contents of that bag in their hand? The use of plastic, of course, is a problem in itself, but Rome, nor Ballycross, wasn't built in a day.

It's much cleaner now. It's only Marian Cummins from the dry cleaners who still refuses to remove Tiny's offerings and is allowed to continue to "stick and flick". She has an extreme gag reflex, as she argued herself at the meeting, putting across her point seamlessly, retching and gripping the back of the chair at the very mention of the act.

You might have thought it an excuse, but I'm not the only one who's witnessed Marian's attempts at removing her pet chihuahua's tiny deposit. Sean Cooper from Centra, the local convenience store, spoke up for

Marian, reiterating her point. He's good like that. Marian's watery eyes, profusely sweating brow and violent retches was enough to make her exempt from a possible fine or prosecution.

I've often offered to do it for her if I pass her on Tiny's toilet run. The last time, both Marian and I had tears in our eyes. Her: from the kind gesture. Me: because contrary to his name, that dog can deliver.

"I've always said you're the nicest girl in Ballycross, Seren. I only wish you had more luck, but I'm praying for you." Marian had given me that sad smile – the type with which you exhale, tilt your head and squeeze your lips tightly together.

Marian had been a close friend of my mother's. Under normal circumstances, I'd have loved to stay and chat longer, but I'd had to change the subject when I felt the familiar tightness travel across my chest.

"You should really get that picture on your van fixed, love," she'd waved as I'd scuttled towards it. "Not good for business."

"It's on the list, Marian."

It *is* on the list of things to get done. Marian's right. Who wants the thought of a steaming French coffee accompanied by a plate of dog shit? I just haven't decided whether to remove the coffee and dog shit from the side of the van altogether, or get it fixed. Mind you, I haven't quite got round to ticking much off my list lately. You might say I've been otherwise disposed.

That would be an understatement, of course, and I've always hated understatements. I'm far too honest to waste my time trying to play things down.

"Serendipity Temple, you're an absolute scream! Talk about saying it like it is."

I've heard it a thousand times, matched it with my typical response.

"Well, I'm an open book. Sure, I'm named to be that way. Open to life and all its surprises."

It probably doesn't quite match their point, but I'm proud of my name, always liking to slip it in wherever I can. Although most people, especially the older generation like Marian, call me Seren, or Sheren, sometimes Sharon. I get all sorts. But Seren is less of a mouthful than Serendipity, more comfortable to manage with a thick Cork twang, where all five syllables blend together. It always sounded far nicer accompanied with a smooth French lilt. It's something I hang on to, though – my name – even if I no longer believe in its meaning. I cling to it like the old van, I suppose – the one I can't seem to bring myself to part with. Besides, I've never gone very far in it. Until recently, it's always been enough to make the bi-weekly trip to the cash and carry in Carrigbyrne. And I get to park right outside the shop, also my home, right in the loading bay.

Not that anyone would ever stop me. I've been in that house since the day I was born. Everyone knows me here, in Ballycross, where I've always lived in the grey house opposite the harbour, looking directly out at the yacht club. Waking each morning to the grounding whispers of the sea or shouts, depending on the weather. The boat masts clink and ding reassuringly like a ticking clock in this place where the wind always breathes.

Coming through the village, over the bridge, past the B&B – more a hotel – I try to swallow the lump, remembering a time when this road felt as though I were edging towards safety. Up until recently, that's what Ballycross was to me: home – a little kingdom, right at the edge of the world. My world – small yet big enough in which to lead a full life, one that over my almost forty years here has developed wholly, despite the ten-mile radius.

It's where my parents had been born, theirs before that, where they'd died. It was where I'd been born and in many ways, where someday I'd always expected to finish my journey. It happens a lot – more than you might imagine. Those born here rarely leave and if they do, sometimes by choice, at times forced, they usually come back. "Ballycrossers" like to think it's testament to the type of place Ballycross is. Nothing outside rarely matches up to the beautiful seaside village, with its choice of beaches, its proximity to Cork city, while still making you feel as if you're miles from anywhere.

"You'll never find a sense of community akin to Ballycross," those who'd returned with growing families would often claim. "It's the people who make it."

I'd always felt the same. Strangely, though, it's the people, lately, who make me feel like I'm suffocating. Those who once provided me with great comfort now make me feel like I'm drowning.

After pulling into the loading bay next to the shop, I grab my bag from the passenger seat and get out of the car. It's not yet midday. It's bright but not sunny. The wind is up, making my hair blow across my face, reminding me of another appointment I need to keep – another item on the list. It's been months since I've had my hair done. The telltale signs of age are beginning to bleed from my roots down the front sections of my brown hair.

"Afternoon, S-heren."

I look up to see Bobby Cronin standing in his usual

position facing the harbour, cigarette hanging from his mouth, one foot poised on the wall, watching the sea. "Choppy, today."

"Will you get out later?" I ask.

"Looks like it's blowing across. I'll wait it out."

Bobby's one of the local fishermen – unmarried, no children. I have no idea how old Bobby actually is. He's looked the same for as long as I can remember. He had white hair even when I was a child, but his face is youthful, lined by the sea but still fresh. Bobby would often be invited to share Christmas dinner with my parents and me. He'd eat hungrily, say very little and be off just as fast. I once asked my father if he thought Bobby was lonely or sad.

"Bobby! Sad! There isn't a man more content. Sure, as Bobby says himself, he has the life. Him and the sea. That's all he needs."

It's how I once felt. That I, too, had "the life". But it wasn't the sea that kept me afloat, it was something else. Now, what I have is "a life". There's a gaping expanse created by those two words – "the" and "a".

Bobby's a real presence in Ballycross, if that's what you could call it. Always there to help. Whenever anything needs to be done, Bobby's your man. Tree fallen – Bobby. Boat adrift – Bobby. Car stuck in a ditch – Bobby. Life torn asunder – Bobby? He's a man of few words, which are chosen wisely.

He turns to look at me, tilts his head, frowns.

"Are you doing all right?"

I smile.

"I am, Bob. I'm okay."

"You know where I am if you need me. I . . . " Bobby thinks for a moment. "I still think about—"

Please don't say it. Please don't say it.

"Anyway, I'll be off. Mind yourself, S-heren."

"I will, Bob. Take care out there."

Relieved, I lock the car, glance over at the activity beyond. Ballycross is shaped like a horseshoe. All the shops gathered together at the end – nothing beyond but the Atlantic.

"Our house is on the horse's leg. See . . ." my mother used to point from our front door. "But we're close enough to absorb all the luck from that horseshoe. Sure, isn't that how I have you?"

My favourite story. How I came to be. I suppose the surprise of discovering she was pregnant at the age of forty-eight after she'd lost all hope was the reason my mother named me Serendipity. Then, of course, there was the added bonus that in the end, I'd turned out just fine, despite her age and the concerns that the entire residents of Ballycross had had, that I'd be born another way.

"You were all I ever wanted. Then as soon as I decided I'd settle on a camper van instead, travel around Ireland with your father, along you came. Hope for one thing, get another."

I wish she was here now – more than anything, I wish she was here to tell me everything was going to be all right. Mind you, I knew from a young age that I wouldn't have her forever, nor my father, who was older again. In exchange, they'd spent every possible moment with me until it was their time to leave, giving me a magical childhood, nurturing me right into my late twenties, equipping me for my journey ahead. They gave me more because they had less time. It's only lately that I feel their loss more profoundly than ever before.

You see, I've done something. Something that I should be more sure of than anything before in my life. But I'm not. I've done something and so help me God, now I wish I hadn't.

Printed in Great Britain
by Amazon

56497376R00267